Word Fest, Celebrating Ideas

Mississauga Writers Group

Word Fest, Celebrating Ideas

Layout and Formatting Copyright © 2014 Mississauga Writers Group
Cover Design Copyright © 2014 Shutterstock, Inc.
Individual Pieces in this Collection © 2014 Individual Authors
Book Editing by Nicholas Boving
Copy Editing by Elizabeth Banfalvi

First published in Mississauga in 2014 by Mississauga Writers Group

***

All rights reserved. No part of this book may be used or reproduced by any means, graphic, electronic, or mechanical, including photocopying, recording, taping or by any information storage retrieval system without prior written permission from the copyright holders, except in the case of brief quotations embodied in critical articles and reviews. The rights of individual works collected in this publication remain the property of their respective authors.

These are works of fiction. All of the characters, names, incidents, organizations, and dialogue in this anthology are either the products of the author's imagination or are used fictitiously. The views expressed in this work are solely those of the individual authors. Any existing characters and people that may have been mentioned in individual works have been duly acknowledged to the original creator/author.

ISBN 13: 978-1-50069883-6
ISBN 10: 1-50069883-0

Mississauga Writers Group,
Mississauga, Ontario, Canada

http://mississaugawritersgroup.webs.com/

http://www.facebook.com/MississaugaWritersGroup

All enquiries: mississaugawritersgroup@gmail.com

OFFICE OF THE MAYOR

August 2014

Anais Nin once said, "*The role of a writer is not to say what we all can say, but what we are unable to say,*" which speaks to the dedication and passion of the Mississauga Writers Group members and their unique ability to reflect the world around them through words. I commend the organization on its first anthology, "*Word Fest,*" which will provide members with an opportunity for creative self expression, a forum from which to share their literary gifts and will help to promote Mississauga's burgeoning arts and culture community.

Sincerely,

HAZEL McCALLION, C.M., LL.D.
MAYOR

In Appreciation

Mississauga Writers Group officially began in January 2013. In such a short time, we have gathered a wonderful group of writers of all genres. With the help of everyone in our group, this anthology has been born. I would like to thank all the writers who donated their wonderful works to make this book a success.

Elizabeth Banfalvi

Contributing Writers

Cheryl Antao-Xavier

Chitra Ayyar

Bev Bachmann

Elizabeth Banfalvi

Nicholas Boving

Evelyn

Angela Ford

Samna Ghani

John Henderson

Veronica Lerner

Joseph A. Monachino

Maria Cecilia Nicu

Rashmi Pluscec

Jasmine Sawant

Henry Shel

G. Ian Stout

Table of Contents

1. Making A Difference 1
   Dealing with Stress....*Cheryl Antao-Xavier* 2
   Between Two Worlds....*Veronica Lerner* 3
   The Scruffy Boy.... *Elizabeth Banfalvi* 4
   Style and Essence....*Maria Cecilia Nicu* 6
   Laughing therapy....*Veronica Lerner* 9
   Sanctum Sanctorum....*Rashmi Pluscec* 12
   My Wish Granted.... *Elizabeth Banfalvi* 13
   A Different Kind of Friendship ....*Veronica Lerner* 15

2. The Challenge of Life 19
   Drowning....*Maria Cecilia Nicu* 20
   In Search of Normality....*Veronica Lerner* 21
   Haiku Inspired by Artwork....*Cheryl Antao-Xavier* 24
   Spotlight....*Rashmi Pluscec* 25
   Fantaisie Impromptu....*Maria Cecilia Nicu* 26
   The Table....*Elizabeth Banfalvi* 30
   Lessons from Nature....*Cheryl Antao-Xavier* 33
   Habit – Impetus or Burden? ....*Veronica Lerner* 34
   The Anatomy of Fear....*Maria Cecilia Nicu* 37
   Second Chance....*Bev Bachmann* 39
   Rebate.... *Maria Cecilia Nicu* 47
   The Other One....*Elizabeth Banfalvi* 50

3. In The Neighbourhood 55
   Murder....*Rashmi Pluscec* 56
   A Dark and Stormy Night.... *Nicholas Boving* 57
   Church Lets Out.... *Bev Bachmann* 60
   My Neighbour....*Veronica Lerner* 72
   The Kallus Next Door.... *Jasmine Sawant* 73

The Old Man....*Elizabeth Banfalvi* 109
Salma....*Chitra Ayyar* 110
4. Matters of the Heart **125**
Rewind.... *Rashmi Pluscec*... 126
Putting Loving Sex Back Into Your Relationship!....*John Henderson* 127
Felt by the Heart....*Angela Ford* 131
Turn Back The Clock....*Samna Ghani*................................ 135
5. Loss and Hope **155**
Mother's End .... *John Henderson* 156
When he is Gone.... *Elizabeth Banfalvi* 157
Elegy for the Creative Soul....*Cheryl Antao-Xavier*............. 158
Aniruddh Remembered.... *Jasmine Sawant* 159
Do not scold me....*Veronica Lerner*.................................. 160
The Phone Call....*Elizabeth Banfalvi*................................. 161
Let Him Go.... *Jasmine Sawant* 165
Ruins.... *Rashmi Pluscec*.. 168
6. Creating Success **169**
Today.... *John Henderson* 170
The Role Model.... *Bev Bachmann* 172
A Woman's Way.... *Elizabeth Banfalvi*............................... 178
Golden Age Sonnet....*Veronica Lerner*.............................. 180
Where is YOUR ATTITUDE AT?.... *John Henderson* 181
Failure leads to Success.... *Elizabeth Banfalvi*................... 186
7. Discerning Thoughts and Beliefs **189**
Epitaph....*Rashmi Pluscec*.. 190
CBC gossip....*Veronica Lerner*.. 191
Cowboy.... *Maria Cecilia Nicu*.. 194
What is it but just a Game....*Joseph A. Monachino* 197
With – or Without – Entitlements....*Veronica Lerner*......... 198
A Photograph.... *Elizabeth Banfalvi*................................... 201

Aha....*Maria Cecilia Nicu* 203

8. Family, Friends, Lovers **205**

Historia....*Maria Cecilia Nicu* 206
The Fruity Pen....*Elizabeth Banfalvi* 207
Soul Mates....*Rashmi Pluscec* 210
Willie's Last Ride.... *Nicholas Boving* 212
My Grandparents....*Elizabeth Banfalvi* 243

9. Reaching For The Stars **247**

There's So Much Winter....*Veronica Lerner* 248
Operation: *Dreamgirl*.... *Henry Shel* 249
The Transporting Device....*Joseph A. Monachino* 261

10. Thrills and Chills **271**

Curtain.... *Rashmi Pluscec* 272
Murder Unedited.... *G. Ian Stout* 273
Crickets.... *Evelyn* 282
Still...*Angela Ford* 285
For the Love of God.... *Nicholas Boving* 300

Contributors 324
Copyright Acknowledgements 327

Making A Difference

Dealing with Stress
by Cheryl Antao-Xavier

This too I learned from my neighbour's cat.

Stressors are only that which directly affect
One's physical wellbeing and food supply
Treat persistent stressors with a one-time show of claws and fangs
Pick your battles carefully
Others' problems are…others' problems.

Cultivate an aloofness
A liberal outlook on life…
In the face of chaos
Manifest serenity
From a place of safety.

Between Two Worlds
by Veronica Lerner

every so often
the time clings to me
like a wet garment
I shiver hidden deep in a swing-clock
it rings around toll or peal
louder and louder
faster and faster
while beating quicker and quicker

on the field over there
it smells like rain
haystacks and cowbells
fade into the stained glass
some white pebbles
smudge the silence

on the field over there
the vesper bell is muffled
the time caresses me
I no longer shiver
I came out of the swinging-clock
listen to the stillness
and regain my breath
between the two worlds
I dream of
as a pair of twins

The Scruffy Boy
by Elizabeth Banfalvi

He was in my older son's kindergarten class. I volunteered as a teacher's assistant and came in once a week to help. I noticed him not long after I started. He was small and very slight. He was unkempt with messy hair and clothes that didn't fit right. He was very quiet and didn't interact with the rest of the children. Nobody played with him including my son. They all avoided him and other than his appearance, he seemed fine. I kept an eye on him in case I had missed something but nothing happened and he was just quiet. Eventually I found out he didn't have a mother and he was being raised by a single father who worked in a bakery.

I used to read stories to the children to keep them occupied or just watched over them as they had an activity. One time I was reading a story and they were sitting on the floor at my feet all of them looking up at me. There he sat with his hair hanging over his eyes and there was a slight odor to him of not quite clean hair and body. I read the story and he just sat there looking up at me. His hair almost covered his eyes. I asked the teacher for 2 bobby pins. I took them and pinned his hair aside so I could see his eyes. I told him that his eyes were too nice to hide. He was embarrassed because here was someone who was paying attention to him. I was pinning his hair back like a little girl would do. He did seem embarrassed but I kept reassuring him that I liked to see his eyes and that is why I was doing it. He didn't remove the bobby pins.

The next week I came in and his bangs were cut to just above his eyebrows. His hair was a little neater because of the cut. Of course, I noticed and commented on how much better he looked and that I could clearly see his eyes. I read them a story and did whatever else I had to do with the little group he was part of it. I always paid a little more attention to him to know how happy I was with his bangs.

The next week I went back and there was a new little boy in the class. Here was this beautiful little boy with fresh clothes and a short haircut. I asked the teacher who it was and she told me it was the same boy. I didn't even recognize him because he had changed so much. Now he got my attention. I walked up to him and made him model his new haircut. He was so proud. I just went on and on how good he looked and how nice his eyes were. I even asked him out for a date which he refused and he lowered his head with his shyness. He had a smile on his face for the rest of the class.

Weeks later it was my son's birthday and he, of course, wasn't invited. All the children were there and there was a knock on the door. Here he stood with a pie in his hand that his father had baked in the bakery. He didn't have anything else to give. I had to talk my son into letting him stay and he did.

I often wonder what happened to this little boy. I can't remember his name but I hope my teasing gave him something because he surely made a difference in me.

Style and Essence
Ortansa Moraru's art.
by Maria Cecilia Nicu

Brancusi said once: "I give you pure joy", emphasizing the idea that art has the "mission" to enhance and enrich our life. "A true form ought to suggest infinity. The surfaces ought to look as though they went on forever, as though they proceeded out from the mass into some perfect and complete existence".

What he's saying is that we should accept art as a road of discovery, that every step taken is controlled by the desire to find something good enough to keep on searching, good enough to want to go further and find that remote way into that turbulent universe of emotions, thinking and living. How far the artist hankers for it is expressed in his inner capability to find that ephemeral originality of transforming earthy materials into a hieratic bouquet of fillings.

Talking about art is never easy.

In November 2008, Varley Art Gallery of Markham hosted a remarkable Collection of art work, "Aligning with Beauty" and one of the artists included in the exhibit was Ortansa Moraru, whose contribution was black and white ink woodblock prints on Japanese paper.

I've written that time: Black & white can impose a very dramatic interpretation of life and produce a string of emotions which will invade your mind with inquisitive questions.

Named Nest (II IV V), they give you an idea of primordial life, but the clarity of an answer is far from the images Ortansa puts in front of you. Black and white color dance around one another into a frantic twist, each color fighting to keep its purity, sometimes successfully, other times losing. The dye is tinted; purity of life, right from the beginning, being an illusion.

Born in Romania, in 1968, and moving to Canada in 2002, Ortansa Moraru earned her MFA and B Ed. in 1997 from Western University of Timisoara where she studied Lithography,

Drawing, Painting, Compositions and the hand pulled Woodcut technique.

Awarded with scholarships from Holland, Italy and Canada with exhibitions across Europe, Asia and North America, confirms that Ortansa is a remarkable artist with an outstanding talent.

On March 5 of 2011, Ortansa had an Open House exhibit, her work displayed - as a shocking experience - a chromatic universe that will provoke our visual perception and reveal the complexity of her personality. The artist is willing to travel from integrity of drawing to the intensity of woodblock cut printing, from the precision of graphic lines to the colourful palette of paintings using unexpected shapes and styles, giving the impression of passionate strive to discover what Brancusi called, "pure joy".

The "Nest" motif is still there, but is sometimes amplified by a splash of colour, bright intervention in a dramatic display of black she calls "Passing By". This is a new series of woodblock print projecting a light interpretation of the protective sense of a nest which surround and insure the growing life that it's supposed to embrace.

"The Fences" become a very special surrounding, a jump over them seems to be a necessity, a chance to achieve what we desire. In charcoal decisive lines, fences spell out the thought of that open road we dream about and dare to look for.

Searching for her own style, Ortansa plays between realistic, easy translatable images and some confusing or intriguing tangled layers of lines or colours.

With this, she's giving herself the liberty of an imagistic originality and the chance to go inward and discover a world of ideas, passions, regrets and melancholic reveries, all of those secrets and rich human fillings.

Two of her new series of woodcut print, "My Way" and "Roots", unveil once more Ortansa's technical capabilities as well as her intense exploration of life.

With almost egg shaped images, "My Way" exploits the dramatic power of black fighting, as we know from "Nest", to suppress white's sense of serenity or to entangle in a highly emotional scuffle.

Series of "Roots", having an ample format, the woodcut prints give new meaning to the word root. Going deep under the surface of the earth, the artist unveils a new world, a mirror reflection from above. Colours, hues of brown and red mangled with pale dies of green implying a sense of déjà vu, nothing is new nothing is unknown.

And yet "Alphabet Tree", a series of paintings on Egg Tempera on Somerset Paper is a revelation, a different approach of the subject somewhere between the traditional (Romanian, Canadian, who can say?) view of nature and the borderline symbolism, even abstract interpretation of it.

A chromatic palette moves leaves from green of summer to the golden touch of fall charging a sentimental mood or perhaps a joyful way of looking around.
A new alphabet emerges from Ortansa's paintings, an alphabet of nature, the trees could offer a hint and we can begin to follow it.

To tell the truth, I wish I had the theoretical schooling that is required to discuss art so that I can use a proper translation of my feelings "vis-à-vis de" Ortansa's art.

What I can say for sure, is that I left her Open House exhibit convinced that she has a bright future ahead and that her art will offer – as Brancusi said -"pure joy"!

Laughing Therapy
by Veronica Lerner

Nowadays there is a widespread belief going around that any emotional discharge is to be seen as a "therapy" of sorts. In this respect, no one will venture to deny that laughing, in particular, indeed has a therapeutic effect. Moreover, following some studies that concluded that laughing has a beneficial effect on people, a number of centres have been opened in our Toronto the Good with the sole purpose of actually teaching people how to laugh. The basic tenet of this "laugh therapy" is that the human body and psyche make no distinction between laughter that comes naturally – as the result of people having fun - and the one that is artificially induced; hence, we have to learn how to laugh several minutes a day, in a mechanical way just to benefit from the therapeutic effect thereof. More specifically, this unnatural – or, shall we say, weird - kind of laughing is supposed to enable a better blood oxygenation as well as a better general mood of the person who laughs this way.

As I am neither a trained medical doctor nor a professional psychologist, I surely cannot offer a professional opinion on the issue, although I do believe that the tenet holds rather for the 'natural' laughing as defined above. I, however, also believe that crying – which could be largely perceived as an opposite emotion - might also have, at times, positive effects. When I worked as a Research Assistant at the Technical Institute for Oil & Gas, back in Romania, we had a lab technician who used to watch only movies that made her cry. In her mind – I assume - the movies rated based on the length and intensity of the crying sessions they induced. I must say I've met a significant number of such individuals ever since. However, as I do not pertain to this category, I won't dwell further on this topic.

So let's go back to the "laughing centers" I mentioned in the beginning, centres which I dare qualify as just another sort of support group; and, if anonymity is also guaranteed, "Laughing Anonymous" would be an apt name. I once watched on TV such a "class" whereby a moderator – or, shall we say, "teacher" – laughed at her "students" (well, "laughed at" is not exactly the right way to put it; "laughed towards" better describes the action.

The students, in turn, were mimetically laughing back at – or "towards" - her, again, for no reason. (To make a parenthesis here, I'd say that, by the same token, we might as well hold some "yawning classes" as yawning was also proved to be beneficial (not to mention, contagious as well).

On interviewing that teacher, some journalist inquired about the technique employed in this particular sort of laughing. The "teacher" solemnly asserted that the necessary technique – like any other technique – could be learned. She also stated confidently that people at work should take breaks in order to laugh hardly, for any reason whatsoever but just as an exercise. While watching that interview, I noticed that the teacher – who was highly adept at that "technical" kind of laughing - was in fact a very serious person; moreover, a person who took herself seriously. The interview then continued without any mention or reference to the "normal" laughing, the one induced by a good joke, a funny life situation or a hilarious movie. This kind of laughing was – at no time – considered as a worthy alternative. Was this exclusion deliberate - since offering alternatives to the "technical" laughing could have led to a loss of business for the said teacher? This, I don't know. What I do know, however is that the "students" were sitting in front of some monitors that displayed detailed instructions on how to "perform" laughing. I, for myself, thought that having a movie with Laurel & Hardy running on those very monitors could have produced a far better result.

I also asked myself what kind of credentials that teacher had in her field of choice. I don't think she'd studied acting by no means did she come out as an actor. Neither did she seem to have had any training in respiration techniques, for her laughing involved a strenuous physical component, an effort not unlikely the one requested from a weightlifter in action. What kind of exams a person, in her position, had to pass; what essays she had to write; and who were *her* teachers/professors/examiners/graders? I imagined her diploma - hanging on the wall but never zoomed on – might have read something like "Professional Trainer for Therapeutic Laughing".

Finally, I questioned whether the kind of resources brought about to support teaching "artificial" laughing could not have been better redirected towards engendering the natural, normal laughing. Anyway, the image of dutiful employees rising from their chairs every two hours or so for a "session" of therapeutic laughing would certainly induce "natural" laughing in any person who comes from either our past or our future.

Sanctum Sanctorum
by Rashmi Pluscec

The hungry horde of the media pressed forward as
the visiting dignitary slid the tiny panel across the
tiny window. Through the rusted bars he saw a
crouching figure: a rough sketch of frail bones,

old scabs and faded rags. Loose flaps of eyelids
tried to fight off the sudden invasion of bright
lights. whaddya want? it croaked. HEY Watch it.
Don't you know who this is? Someone has taken

time off their busy schedule to do something nice
for you. (Flash! Flash! This way, Smile please, Just
one more, An autograph for my son, please!) Now
be nice and, shit, try to look nice ... away from the harsh

realities of life love friendships and revenge there is
a niche i have carved there is a home i have created in
this grey ceiling is the colour of compassion between
its brown walls there is the warmth of comfort on its

decaying floors there is strength and security now this
is my pretty place this is my safe place i don't bother
you don't bother me with your Ribbons and Bows and
Hair and Make Up LEAVE ME ALONE STOP IT
STOP

PRETENDING TH-- the faded figure became comical
in a rising animation of tragic indignation. The stench
of stale urine was too much to bear anyway. Fucking
psycho, the celebrity muttered and hurried on. Someone

quickly slid the panel shut. The brilliant flash of teeth
and
cameras moved on, leaving behind the heart of darkness.

My Wish Granted
by Elizabeth Banfalvi

I taught meditation classes for the local school board for many years and through the years there were so many impactful moments for me. In one of the classes I would always ask them "what do they want to be remembered for?" I listened to their answers and their acknowledgments about what they wanted and one time one student asked me what I wanted. I told them that I wanted to change lives and I already had my wish granted. They asked me about it, of course, and I told them but it was difficult to hold back my emotions as I told them. I still get emotional when I speak of it – not of sadness but of a loving choice that was greater than most of us will ever know.

Years before I had had a woman in my class who was in remission from breast cancer. It had been at least a couple of years. She had a husband and two young girls. They owned a city house but also a small cottage in the country. She came with a friend and both were great students. I used to bring in alternative therapists to talk and be questioned in the series and this time, Molly, an acupuncturist, came and talked to the class. The series of classes ended and I always invited them back to another series to relate how their lives had changed and talk to the new students.

A couple of years went by and I got a phone call. It was this woman and the sad news was that the cancer had returned in her other breast but she had chosen not to go through the treatment again because the cancer was more aggressive and the chances were slim. She wanted to live the rest of her life in peace rather than living with the side effects from the treatments she would have gotten. They were in the process of selling their city house and moving to the cottage with their daughters. She asked if she could come to my next class and I said I would love to have her. She asked permission if she could bring some friends with her including her original friend and of course, I said yes.

As the class wore on, I noticed one of her friends almost being angered by her. I asked her what was wrong and she said she wasn't taking her condition seriously. She actually was making fun about things that were happening to her. I looked at the angry friend and said "this isn't about you". I told her to look at my woman and see how beautiful she was with what she was going through and the acceptance. I looked at her angry friend and told her that she should be supporting her not wanting her to hold her hand. My woman and her family were making choices for the best and the angry friend should be supporting her not expecting the other way around. Finally the angry friend settled down and didn't say any more. The other friends were teary eyed but they all seemed to agree with me and not the angry friend.

The class ended and all of my students hugged my woman and stood quietly with her giving her special wishes for herself and family without assuming she would pull through. I gave her a gentle loving hug and wished her all she wanted. It was the last time I saw her.

More than a year later, Molly called and told me she was with her at the time she took her last breath. She had spent the last few months with her daughters and husband living quietly. She had sent a message to me through Molly. The message was that I had changed her life. In truth, she had changed mine.

A Different Kind of Friendship
Dedicated to Dr. Gapsky and his assistant, Debbie.
by Veronica Lerner

Quite often, as we meet old or new friends, we ask ourselves whether the relationship we have with them is a "true friendship". A lot has been written about friendship and the topic was examined from many points of view. As we well know, friendship usually develops among people who share common interests or goals. That explains the friendships among school or work place colleagues. Those friendships are based on camaraderie and, in a way, on the relative equal status of the people involved.

There are also other types of friendships, less talked about, such as, the friendship between a doctor and a patient that he or she is taking care of. In the case of the doctor–patient friendship, even as the two share the same goal, the relationship between them is different from what happens between colleagues. Although I would not use the word "subordination", this is not exactly a relationship built on equal terms, because the doctor has a certain responsibility to the patient.

It is interesting how in my case, being treated by several doctors, the relationship I had with them was always one of "friendship". I "worked" with my doctors and I always wanted, as a child, to be their "success". I will never forget, the time when, being only 5 years old, I could not move my left hand because of polio. The doctor at the hospital was coming every day to see me and ask me to raise my left hand. I was using my right hand to lift the left the best I could. One day the doctor said: "My little girl, make an effort and raise your left hand, do it for me!" I remember how I tried as hard as I could to do this just for him. Later, my parents told me, on that day the doctor declared to them: "This child will be cured, for sure". And indeed this is what happened.

The notion of friendship between doctor and patient came back into my mind recently during my annual visit to a specialist I have regularly seen for the last ten years. At the beginning I went four times a year, then twice a year, and finally only once a year. In Ontario, when the disease has not come back after ten years, a patient is not required to see the specialist anymore; his condition can be monitored from then on by the family doctor.

As I mentioned above, I recently visited my specialist for the annual checkup. At the end of the conversation the doctor said: "After 10 years of seeing you regularly I can say that you are free of disease now. The moment has come for me to transfer your care to the family doctor." After a pause, he continued: "It is, however, hard for me to do it; during all these years, as I watched you fighting the disease, we became friends. Through your will power and determination you helped not only yourself but you also helped me. Through you I achieved a new "medical success". In addition, as those ten years have passed, we learned many things together and…" He stopped talking but I believe that he wanted to say "we grew older together". I did not say anything. I thought he was right; the doctor and his assistant, who has been working with him for 30 years, have become very "familiar" people to me. We lived together through moments in which important decisions had to be taken. They were, all those years, the witnesses to my anxieties.
Every time I was coming for the checkup I could see on the assistant's desks new pictures showing her grandchildren, a little more grown up at each visit.

Normally, parting ways in this mode with a specialist ought to be an occasion to rejoice as it signify the liberation from the status of "sick person". I remember that, over the years, in the waiting room of this doctor I witnessed quite a few patients coming out of the office and declaring: " I do not need to come for checkups anymore" to the applause of everybody in the waiting room. The assistant, at her desk in the waiting room, enjoyed those scenes too, and I was wondering about the day when it will be my turn to come out of the office, tell everybody that "I am free as a bird" and receive my share of applause. I was waiting for that day, I was dreaming about it. Now, when the day had come, the joy was diminished somehow. There was a new element to consider, that "friendship" that people form when they share, as I said, common preoccupations and goals.

At the end of the visit the doctor made a decision: "You will come next year for a last consult and then you will see only the family doctor." I got out of the office with tears in my eyes. Joy? Sadness? A mixture of the two? The assistant made a note in her book about the date when I would come next year. She was fully aware that this was supposed to be the last time and indeed she wished that it could have been the last time

I believe that this type of "different friendship" where friends wish from their hearts not to see each other again is a very beautiful friendship. Of course, people can renew their relationship outside the medical context, but then that will become a friendship like those others about which so much has been written.

The Challenge of Life

Drowning
by Maria Cecilia Nicu

this ocean
is a boat fully loaded with rambling ideas
saved from drowning
after…
no matter how much I stir my hands and feet
I wake up in a large wasted space to throw my knick-
knacks
or to preserve them

you step right on your heart if you looked around.

In Search of Normality
by Veronica Lerner

I asked myself many times if anybody in this world can precisely define what is normal and what is not at all times. My own view is that in-between normal and abnormal lays a vast gray area. Also I believe that the perception of something being normal or not is highly dependent on one's personal experience, background and that all these factors are determined to a great extent by the environment we lived or grew up.

Personally, I was born and spent half of my adult life in Romania and the way I evaluate the normality of something is always influenced significantly by that important detail of my biography. I will provide below a couple of examples.

When I arrived in Canada and started working in Montreal I had as supervisor a French Canadian lady. I confessed to her that her rolling "r"s sounded not quite normal to me. In turn, she told me that my "straight" "r" sounded equally strange to her. I guess I should not have expected anything else from a true Quebecoise like her.

At about the same time, I rented a safe deposit box at the bank to store some important documents among which was my birth certificate. Needing the certificate a few months later I went to the bank and asked the clerk to let me open my safety box. Following the rules, the clerk asked me for a government issued piece of ID which, unfortunately, I did not have on me on that day. To me, that looked very strange since she was the one who rented the box to me in the first place. My natural East-European reaction was to think that she was looking for a bribe and I offered her some money. Her reaction was very negative and, in the end, I had to go home and bring my passport. This example illustrates very well how strict adherence to the rule can seem pretty natural to a Canadian person and totally abnormal to someone from Romania.

I was reminded of how different perceptions of normality can be when I recently read a book written by a European traveler to Japan. Apparently in Japan, due to almost daily rain, people carry umbrellas with them all the time. The peculiar fact, for us the non-Japanese, is that they carry the closed umbrellas holding them by a ring attached to the spiky top. This is very abnormal for someone like me used to hold umbrellas by their handle.

From the same book I also learned that the principles of bargaining in Japan are quite different than ours. For example a European lady sees a nice vase in an antique shop and is told that the vase costs ten yen. The woman tries to bargain a bit by suggesting that perhaps the vase is not so valuable as to justify such a high price. Offended, the shopkeeper takes the vase away and refuses to negotiate any further. A friend of the lady, well versed Japanese customs volunteers to show her the right approach for getting a good deal. He goes to the same shop, looks at the same vase and starts praising the object in the most effusing and flattering words. The merchant is very pleased, invites the gentleman to tea and asks him if he truly wants to buy the vase. When answered in affirmative he offers the buyer the vase for only five yen. Well done! The writer invites us to observe the rather "abnormal" fact that in Japan, the customer sings the praises of the merchandise and not the seller.

Another area where there are big differences among things that people consider normal or not is the way we dress for our day to day activities. From my balcony, in a high-rise building, I watched sometimes a couple of old ladies enjoying breakfast on the patio of a nearby house.
Those ladies are normally dressed in loose t-shirts and tight shorts. This is very comfortable attire for the summer. Unfortunately it highlights in a very unflattering way their overweight and out of shape bodies. Strangely for me, this does not happen to bother them at all. Where I am coming from people looking the way they do won't be caught dead wearing such clothes. Go figure!

Watching children playing around the pool reveals another different idea about what is considered normal. Back home, children frolic naked in and out of the water until they are bout five. Here in Canada you can see girls as young as six months wearing elegant bikinis.

Going back to the book about Japan, it is worth mentioning that Japanese people do not believe that we should hide our bodies but rather that we should hide our thoughts. That may sound to us like an invitation to hypocrisy. To the Japanese however, this is the key to politeness and respect to others. Reading about this I understood, twenty years later, the "abnormal" behaviour of a Japanese person that I worked with at one time.

I think we can safely say that achieving "normality" is probably an overly ambitious goal. Here in North America we have more modest goals. There is a reason we call the most popular variation of coffee "regular" and not "normal".

In the famous novel "Foucault Pendulum" by Umberto Eco, one of the main characters says: "Each of us is sometimes a cretin, a fool, a moron, or a lunatic. A normal person is just a reasonable mix of these four ideal types". We should always remember that every time when we struggle to find out what "normal" means.

Haiku Inspired by Artwork
by Cheryl Antao-Xavier

Silent falls the stream
Forest echoes feel the loss
Change comes quietly

Bud bursts into bloom
Behold its time of glory
The first petal falls

Spotlight
by Rashmi Pluscec

Huh? where am I? what is this place?
I'm on a dais. In a dark auditorium.
from the belly of the monster emerge curious whispers.
In this endless darkness I see only one light,
a brilliant white light. On me.
I guess I am supposed to perform. but what?
neither song nor soliloquy comes to mind.

Somewhere a cue card reads:
wear that pretty mask, say the proper things.
I offer to present 'me', my ideas, my feelings
from the shadows i sense puzzled resentment.
nervous, i rush to comply;
i smile and skip and i clap my hands.

i pray that i am accepted. or at least not ridiculed
instead the whispers get louder.
and tiny darts of comments break through my skin.
i wonder if i should feign insanity.
"Loser" cries one. "Weirdo" shouts another,

and they all chant "Go Away"
of course! why didn't i think of that?
i take a small bow and turn to leave…
Only, what is this??

why are my feet stuck to the ground?
i am shuffling, struggling, twisting, writhing
and i still don't know what is expected of me.

Who am I?
and why am i here?

(*can someone drop the curtain please?*)

Fantaisie Impromptu
by Maria Cecilia Nicu

"The blue pelican, grandfather used to say, had been floating along with those swans that you've seen after your father told you to listen to Tchaikovsky, do you remember? He'd been drifting around with Ismana's ducks - nobody knew how many on the smallest pond you've ever seen in your life.

Your grandmother had only one, one duck I wanted to say, and I'm still thinking why she had to have a duck when nobody else had one but Ismana. He had a pond, that's right but water is not at all a commodity around here.

The duck followed her everywhere. Sundays, as you know, Granny's going to church with a boiled wheat cake for alms, all the time she could find to honour somebody's memory. The duck - why grandmother didn't name her I don't know - totters along the way, too fat and too lazy to keep the pace of walking, but going anyway. People knew they were coming together and even understood why the duck followed Chiva everywhere.

As long as people worshipped, her duck's toying with the grass, picking the flowers blooming on the graves. He is waiting patiently until the priest finished the service, the sermon and reading names from the list of eternal memory, and I'm telling you, it is always a long list with all the families' relatives dead either in the wars or from sickness. Your granny found the duck dead beside the cat, that hairy cat we had for a while.

Ismana had the idea that he has to have some unusual birds, some nobody else had, and if he had his own pond why not take advantage?

I guess the blue pelican felt like a rooster among those swans but to me it would've been much better to see him alone, spinning the water around him, swimming majestically and undisturbed by anything.

But, you see it is my idea, not his!"

"The old man, your grandpa said grandma, had some foolish thinking, I could say, and he let it out unexpectedly; always sitting on the porch on that wooden bed he made and I am telling you, I don't know why, for I don't like to sleep outside and he was not around more than one or two days before he had been gone to drive the cattle herd to the fair. It is a long way to Craiova, but he preferred that one than others, and sometimes he didn't come back for a month, anyway, it felt like forever. Your uncle, Ionel – being the oldest - would've liked to sleep there, but you think I let him?

'What did I say? Oh, yes, Costandin used to light his pipe and starts his crazy stories, one more unusual then another, but the blue pelican had never been missed.

Now, Father- the priest I mean - told me to come to church and have a service to ask God to protect him, for you never know where he's going all the time he's not home. But to tell you the truth I didn't have the courage to do it. How can you have a religious service for your husband's soul when he is alive and is much older then you and has more knowledge than you have?

What can I say, I liked his wayward stories. I can even see the blue pelican drifting on Galbenu's water, even if he'd been talking about a lake, Ismana's pond I presume, but he kept saying lake covered by white water lilies and soaring white swans. And you know how strange it is to see him become furious because Ismana's ducks disturb the purity of his images? "The blue pelican got tired of this crowd," I remember him saying, "and opened his wings and flew away." and all that miraculous lake he's been seeing all the time disappears ... the swans and even Ismana's ducks wandering on a dry and dusty earth, "where even the grass couldn't grow".

Trust me, it is true!"

*   *   *   *

It is not easy to open the tall gates. We did it though.

Such rich estates are not very common for us; "fer forge", arabesque ornaments, some French frivolous interpretation of iron's beauty, may be baroque, may be rococo, symbolic images of an old world, "dead and gone" as we were taught.

"It is going to be some time until we get to the end of the alley - dad said, and he guides me inside - we'll have to walk around the pond- and he names "pond" that insignificant spot of water artificially put in the middle of the road; classical strategy to give you time to look around and enjoy the view."

"I like that."

"Of course you do, Water and earth are complementary. Flexibility and rigidity create this harmonic surrounding we need to connect and discover it is an axiomatic necessity to know - to know we are alive!

And, son, your grandfather should've been around a bit longer, I still have a lot of questions standing by and I cannot chat with an image I have in my mind. A photo' would've helped all these years, but we have a disembody spectrum as foggy as the cold autumn mornings.
And we call it dad and granddad!

No matter how much I try to tell you that I know what I intend to tell you, you know I don't know!"

In my mind the blue pelican reign over the pond, I think, I would like to see the swans around him and even the Ismana's ducks, but who cares of my dreams?

In the morning sun hits my eyes and some time I like it sometime I don't but always I feel that I lose all the questions nights spell for me only to give or to take the understanding I need.

Eh! It's quite elusive this time of understanding isn't it?

I'm trying to preserve images and words, I'm trying to recall nostalgic things I heard about and sometime forage my memory to discover things I thought I deserve to hold or perhaps I only want to find who I am and where I'm coming from.

Am I naïve?

Maybe, but what I think I am is a personal history with a spectral grandfather and stories about him some fabled some real almost the same as all those moments life offers and we dream to be true and they are "ombres"!

Oh, stupid me, I forgot to ask my father, how did grandfather knew about Tchaikovsky?

The Table
by Elizabeth Banfalvi

It was a beautiful oak table and her parents had bought it for her when she married. It had three leaves and it came with 12 chairs. She was looking forward to entertaining the whole family on holidays and special occasions. She was so happy the first Christmas with her new husband. They invited both families over and she had set the table with her new wedding silverware, glasses and dishes. She put her fancy candlesticks with the tall candles in the centre and lit them when everyone was there. The tablecloth was fine white linen again another wedding gift. The linen serviettes were folded neatly by each place setting. Everything looked beautiful. She was the perfect hostess that day and she was proud of the meal she had made. She smiled the whole day and when everyone left, she cleaned up the dining room and then went to change for bed. He stayed in the living room and just drank silently. He worked hard and deserved to relax. He was still there in the morning but he had fallen asleep and hadn't gotten to bed. Several years later, she left with her young child and took the table with her.

Many years later, a young couple found the table in a used furniture store. They loved the look of the table and bought it for their little apartment. It had two leaves and 10 chairs and they invited their friends over and had many parties. They would put lace tablecloths, chunky dishes and glasses on it. Their parties had many finger foods and take-out menus. The young couple worked very hard and soon they bought a beautiful new home and the table was put in the basement. They played many a card game on it.

More years passed and a young mother bought the table from a local bargain store. It was the perfect size for her young family. It had one leaf and 6 chairs. She put a big tablecloth on it and her children would play hide and seek under it. The table was just the right size when the children ate. They had plenty of space for their cereal and juice glasses. They coloured many a picture on it and did their homework. Eventually when they grew, they moved and left the table behind.

The next people who moved in were an older couple. Every night she would make dinner and serve it on the faded tablecloth laid on the table. They ate and talked about their day. The table served them well and they loved the old fashioned workmanship in it. She didn't have any children but the ones from the neighbourhood would come and have something to eat at her table. Her husband would come home and find the little ones there. It made her happy. He died the next year. She moved in with some relatives and the table was left behind.

The neighbourhood went downhill afterwards and there were many people who lived there. They broke the chairs and the leaf was thrown out. The table top got scratched and burned and it started to wobble. Eventually someone threw it in the yard.

An older man walked by not sure of where he was or the address. He saw the table and it was the right size for what he wanted. He remembered a table just like that when he was younger. He asked around if he could have it and nobody cared so he put it in his car. He cleaned and fixed it so it no longer wobbled. He put it by the window and ate his meal that night looking out the window. He would take the time to redo the top and remove the scratches but for now it would do. He sipped coffee from his mug and read his newspaper while the evening grew darker outside.

He couldn't remember where he had seen such a lovely table. His mother had one and he would play under it and hide when his father was drunk. His mother would tell him to stay there until she called him out. Sometimes it took a long time but he was safe there. He never saw what happened to her. He remembered his mother had carved their initials underneath the table so he could look at it when he was under there. He sighed and then he thought why not check if it could possibly be the table.

He got down on his hands and knees and looked under the table but he couldn't see. He got his flashlight and lay on the floor and carefully checked under it. He couldn't believe it but there were their initials carved into the wood. It was his mother's table and it had been a wedding present. He remembered how she had protected him and then finally left his father. He was so young and they moved many times but eventually they had found a home. A wonderful man came into his mother's life, married her and took care of both of them.

His mother had died several years ago but she had lived happily and had more children. He had married; had several children and now many grandchildren. His wife was away arranging his younger daughter's wedding. He definitely wanted to redo the table now and would keep it for his own. It had returned home.

Lessons from Nature
by Cheryl Antao-Xavier

storms pass
gloomy skies lighten up
earth thrives refreshed

an analogy for life

burdens of yesterday lighten with time
new doors open
probability yearns to be possibility
and possibility, reality
refresh, renew
see the old world
in a new light…

rivers flow to the sea
from streams to oceans
coursing through dams
around hindering rocks
same water, changed forever
by life along the way

youth to old age
what a journey!
same soul, changed forever
by life along the way…

Habit – Impetus or Burden?
by Veronica Lerner

I've always been intrigued by the various meanings associated with the concept of habit, which Cicero, the Roman orator defines as, "Consuetudo quasi altera natura" ("Habit is second nature"). In my humble opinion, depending on the context, habit could sometimes be an impetus; some other times, a burden.

I profess that Cicero's dictum should serve as a guide for both parents and educators. The saying maintains that a certain action, when repeated many times over, develops into a reflex. To greet people when entering a room or to say, "thank you" when receiving a service is a habit that has become a reflex by way of upbringing and/or education. Yet, there are still people who have developed one or any of these reflexes.

Another Greek philosopher of old, Democrit, sees habit as a result of constant exercising: "Persistent labouring becomes easier when turns into habit". This very principle is applicable when learning foreign languages, as well as attaining a certain level of virtuosity in sports, arts or performing arts. Years of exercising makes one more familiar with the action, the performance therefore becomes routine.

To go back to Cicero, he expands on his dictum by stating: "More people become skilled via exercising than owing it to being just talented". This means that talent with no hard work does not bear results; and neither does simple exercise when talent is lacking. Sometimes, quite often though, a pianist that became a virtuoso via relentless exercising could reach stardom easier than a gifted one, which is to say, that a pure technical performance can often trump an artistic one.

Life itself, through its repetitive cycles of lightness-darkness, coolness/warmth or the carrousel of seasons, engenders habits related to those states. Physicians also recommend a regular approach with respect to the eating and sleeping regimen of the patient. In turn, our biological "clock" demands this as well. To add to the list, Aristotle was also preoccupied with the phenomenon and noticed that habit becomes inherent in human psyche because it is intrinsically natural. In fact, Aristotle states when discerning between *habit* and *nature*, habit is *most of the time*, while nature is *always*.

The notion of habit has some other connotations as well. So far, we've seen habit as an impetus or a stimulus; however, habit could also represent a burden on the individual. Immanuel Kant, the German philosopher, comes to add a corollary to Democrit's tenet. Thus, he says: "Simple routine allows actions to become easier to undertake; entrenched routine makes them necessary". In other words, and also quoting the Romanian philosopher Tudor Vianu, "it is healthy and useful to employ routines in our daily activities; however, it is unhealthy to become dependent on these routines". Kant also warns about being dependent on a routine, thus causing our often-noted, sometimes fierce resistance to change.

Oftentimes, habit is associated with rigor; however, there is a notable distinction between the two. Thus, rigor is mainly a disciplined effort imposed from the *outside*; while habit is a natural product of a human being adapting to his predicament with no outside imposition. A disabled person will become accustomed to his condition; a psychological trauma will heal itself overtime, unless it is a very severe one. In his book "Diary of a country priest", French writer Georges Bernanos notes that "There are many people who, while pretending to protect order, are in fact defending hard-entrenched habits or routines." The idea Bernanos advances is that our clinging to *order* masks our resistance to, or fear of, change.

All these facets of habit as daily exercise or repetition, being these physical or mental, are by no means covering the topic thoroughly. Thus, I am going to give you another interpretation, this time a poetic one (though very real as well). In his celebrated play" "Waiting for Godot", Samuel Beckett asserts that "Habit is a *mute*", in this case *mute* refers to a device used to significantly dampen the sound of a string or brass instrument; therefore, by extension, one could also see it as a gun silencer. By asserting this, Beckett maintains that life breathes color and character; and that applying a muffler/silencer/mute will necessarily blunt these traits. Isn't he right? Don't we look at a new thing with interest and, sometimes, even enthusiasm while losing interest over time and when the "novelty" has aged? Aren't we becoming accustomed and slipping into "habit"? The child is the typical example of this phenomenon as they quickly become bored with two-day old toys. In this respect, parents have been fully aware that toys are not to be presented to the child "in bulk", but gradually, in small "installments". Same applies to adults for whom "novelty" is a vital necessity. A mere change in our physical surroundings – by either moving or "re-painting" – brings new, rejuvenating, energies. By the same token, holidays – however expensive - are most necessary breaks of routine.

But if novelty/newness/freshness is a necessity, what does this mean for the old, established, entrenched, habit? When is one to promote and encourage change; and when to stick to habit? It is hard to say as there is no universally applicable recipe in this respect. In our technology-driven time, the pace of change is such that one can hardly get accustomed to it. Is it that these gushing-forth changes satisfy our need for novelty; or are these rather pushing the envelope by forcing us into a most strenuous effort at adapting?

When not finding answers to all these questions, I rather turn to poetry...

The Anatomy of Fear
by Maria Cecilia Nicu

What a stupid dream is this drowning... you're floating unconscious waving your dress like a lousy boat dancing the water waltz, and it's the one they bought yesterday...you are going to get a nasty spanking...it costs a lot of money, you should know that it always costs a lot of money...and the sandal dropped down to the dam' bottom and you won't have time to take it out...you can't walk with only one sandal, one skate... yes...it was possible...on ice... but this is another story and anyhow, what kind of chance can you have trying to get out of this dark eddies ?

"Enfin", I have to accept I'm a little confused, well maybe a lot, but I trust it's quite the same to be overwhelmed by this water vortex or to chock myself fighting with my dried- crippled lungs.

There's no end to confusion in this story, something like existential Red Wire keeps everything and everyone under the spell of absurdity, every step of life hangs on it and it's gently rocked or moved convulsively...teeter- totter I'd say, nothing defined, only an undecided aggression towards unknown.

The result? Nothing good only a deadly impact as you were hit by the train... but only "as if"!

So...at ten you drown, not really, they shake you up-side-down, water is coming out, dress you up in dry clothes and as it's expected you get some smacks - deserved or not ...how could they know about great explorations: Mississippi running his water right here between Lespedea's banks and Winetou playing hide-and seek with everybody coming to grandfather's mill ...

They don't!
At fourteen you start to see the mirrors, scratched knees could be eventually covered but climbing up forbidden apricot tree could still be an attraction, soccer play loses some of its marvel, novels, stories, poetries get in line to conquer your imagination

and time surrounds you with cryptic discontent...Val loses his privileged as the interdictions partner and forget to send you his secret notes for Lilia, school simplifies somehow the whole family life, but it sends you alarming signs of mental unrest... "cohorts" of questions knock at the gates of answers and nothing seems to be at the normal distance, to see, to hear, to touch and mostly to fill exist only around yet.

After?

Not much.

You mimic understanding and even entertain some pleasure on it and when you get the guts to accept that you know what you don't know you chock yourself with a spoon of soup for good and inconceivable.

Damn Red Wire!

Second Chance
by Bev Bachmann

Michael's attention was focused on the small metal object he was clutching in his right hand. He told himself it was nothing but a cordless phone, still he wondered if he shouldn't hurl the thing across the room and watch it smash to smithereens against the far wall. That might be fun.

On the other hand, some part of him tried to access that source of reason and logic that had seen him through eight years of university. Hanging up a phone could hardly qualify as a monumental achievement.

Decisions. His world was full of them.

A few minutes earlier he had been sitting up in bed cramming for the upcoming bar exam, his notebook computer on his lap, his wife Marcia by his side.

Then the phone rang. Reluctantly Michael picked it up.

After what seemed like hours, the call was completed. That was when Michael started staring stupidly at an inanimate object. He managed to get a grip and replace the phone on the night stand by his side of the bed. Then he put away his computer as well. Concentration was a thing of the past.

Too agitated to keep still, he donned slippers and began pacing the narrow confines of the bedroom floor. Marcia watched him out of the corner of her eye but kept reading her novel. Michael would talk when he was ready.

"That bastard! That damn, damn bastard!"

"Gordon?" she asked, keeping her voice level.

"Who else?" Michael spit the words out bitterly. "Just another one of his crummy guilt trips!" Michael stopped pacing for a moment and stood at the foot of the bed, facing his wife.

"Can you believe it? He wants me to forget about the bar exam, put my future on hold, and fly to Vancouver on the next plane. He even had the nerve to say, and I quote, 'Mom would be so hurt if you didn't come home for Dad's retirement party.'"

Marcia carefully inserted a book marker in her novel and composed herself to listen. She had a pretty good idea of what was coming. In the three plus years she had been married to Michael, she had heard many stories about her husband's family. She even met them once, when they flew out to Toronto for the wedding. She had been impressed. Michael's parents were great—warm, friendly, affectionate. And they loved her too.

"Regrettably," Gordon couldn't make it, but he did send the newlyweds a card of well wishes. When Michael heard the news that his only brother was going to miss his wedding, he had one response. Unqualified relief. That was Marcia's clue that whatever was going on between these two grown men, it was no ordinary sibling rivalry.

* * * *

Michael's birth had been something of an upset—showing up as he did 14 years after Gordon's arrival. His parents had resigned themselves to having an 'only child,' but then, miraculously, Michael appeared on the scene. The child's unexpected entrance into their lives was an answer to prayer, and they were delighted. Michael was their "second chance."

Throughout his childhood, Michael's parents lavished love on the little boy who never let them down—not at home, and not at school. When it came time for Michael to graduate, they made sure he had the means to continue his education at U.B.C. When he told them he wanted to study law at Osgoode Hall in Toronto, they didn't balk. Whatever Michael wanted, his parents were ready to supply. They were happy to do it. A second chance doesn't come along every day.

Gordon's mindset about Michael's existence, however, was another story. He saw the little boy as the one who got all the breaks—the one who was privileged. It galled him to stand by and watch while his parents doted on the child, but what Gordon really resented was the thousands of dollars they poured into Michael's education, thereby guaranteeing him a ticket to life on easy street while he, Gordon, never even got a foothold on the ladder of success.

* * * *

When Gordon was young, he was a rough and tumble kid, always looking for a fight. He was big for his age and he liked to throw his weight around, especially on the school playground. When his parents asked him why he behaved like a bully, he said it made him "feel good."

More than once Gordon's parents were driven to the point of despair by having to deal with their difficult child. They tried every form of discipline they could think of, but it only hardened the boy's resolve to rebel. He proved it in grade eight when he was suspended from school over an incident where he had been caught, literally, with his pants down.

Apparently he had enticed a girl into a lavatory cubicle where the two of them did god-knows-what until a hall monitor heard suspicious sounds coming from the boys' washroom. A teacher was summoned, and soon thereafter Gordon and the young lady in question found themselves sitting in front of an irate vice-principal. When confronted about the episode, Gordon merely shrugged while the girl giggled nervously. When coaxed to confess what exactly they were doing in the washroom, she said it was "all Gordon's idea," although she "really didn't mind." Her parents, on the other hand, did.

This occasion was serious enough to involve the authorities, and it looked like Gordon would have to pay the piper, but out of a sense of remorse or responsibility—or whatever it is that parents feel when their kid becomes a source of social embarrassment—they stepped in to rectify the situation. They met with all the parties involved and hammered out a "deal." After that, Gordon was off the hook.

* * * *

When the boy was fifteen, he entered high school. It looked like Gordon was about to start over with a clean slate, but then he decided that school was "boring" and began skipping classes—a lot. His parents insisted he stick with it until he got his diploma, and, for a time, he did make an effort. But then, somewhere around his sixteenth birthday, he got his girlfriend pregnant. He saw it as an opportunity. Ignoring his parents' pleas to "think it through," he packed a bag, opted for a shot-gun marriage, and dropped out of school for good.

The next twenty-five years saw Gordon drifting from one dead end job to another. For a while he and his wife lived hand to mouth, but then the cheques started arriving from his folks, motivated by their concern for the grandchildren.

Michael knew all about Gordon's troubled past, and he often felt badly for the guy, but what could he do? He wasn't responsible for the way his brother's life turned out. That was Gordon's choice, and yet the man never stopped resenting Michael for it.

* * * *

"You sure you don't want to fly out West—maybe study on the flight, attend your Dad's party, then catch the red-eye home?" Marcia prodded gently.

"No!" he said a little too loudly. "No," he repeated, this time more quietly. "We already decided." He looked with exasperation at his wife, as if she were no longer his friend. "I can't leave anything to chance the night before the finals. That's just crazy." He paused, emotionally drained. "Why are we going over this again?"

"Okay. Okay. I'm with you," she said, sorry she had even broached the subject. Michael was strung out with the pressure of preparing for the bar exam, and she had inadvertently made the situation worse. "You're doing the right thing," she added lamely, although she sincerely believed it.

Michael shook his head sadly. "It's such lousy timing. How can

I be in two places at once," he said miserably.

Marcia was worried. Her husband was starting on a downward slide. What was needed was a plan of action. She had one. "Listen, Sweetheart," she said, her voice full of a confidence she hoped was contagious, "let's order a large pizza, you go back to studying, and I spend some quality time with Scraps."

'Scraps' wasn't his real name, of course. He actually had three official ones listed with the Canadian Kennel Club where he was registered as a miniature wire haired dachshund. He earned his unrefined nickname during his puppy days when he would strategically position himself in the kitchen and remain on stand-by alert. That way, if any table scraps should happen to fall to the floor, he was ready to make his move. He was just crazy about scraps—hence his new handle.

Now all grown-up, the dog was tunneling head first under the thick comforter where he wedged himself firmly against Marcia's thigh. She often wondered how the tiny dog kept from suffocating under all those heavy covers. But there was no point in trying to figure out Scraps. He was his own little 'person.'

Michael's mood was beginning to lift. "You're the best," he said softly. "I'm sorry for my outburst." He sat down on the bed beside her.

"Forget about it. I have."

Marcia knew her husband was not normally given to tantrums, but Gordon had pushed his buttons. The decision not to go home for his Dad's retirement party had been a tough one for Michael, especially since he realized it might make him look like an ungrateful SOB. The fact was Michael truly did love his parents and he wanted to be with them for this milestone, but the bar exam was crucial. He had to make a choice, but disappointing his Dad tore him up inside. That was what Gordon didn't understand, but Marcia did.

"Do you think it's wrong to hate your only brother?" he wondered out loud.

"Why don't you ask Gordon?" Marcia suggested with a wry smile.

Michael lay down on his back, folded his arms beneath his head, then stared up at the ceiling. Marcia's question had him thinking. Scraps backed out from under the covers and nuzzled against Michael's side. The pack was together again. What could be better than that?

"I guess Gordon has a right to hate me," Michael sighed.

"Don't be silly." Marcia hesitated. Should she point out how his parents had financially rescued Gordon and his wife for most of their long tumultuous marriage? "You've both benefited from being the sons of your parents," she said presently. "He made choices, and so did you. Why look for someone to blame? That's Gordon's game, and, if you ask me, he's not a happy man."

Michael was silent for a moment. He flipped over onto his stomach and propped himself up on his elbows. "If there was any way I could have been there for the retirement party, I would have. Dad and I talked about it last week, and he said he understood." Michael paused. "Do you?"

"Of course."

Michael sat up and faced his wife. He gave her an earnest look. "Why don't we go out there, say in July, when you're finished teaching and I have some time off. What do you think?"

"I don't know. I was planning on teaching summer school this year—we could use the money. On the other hand, I could use a break." Marcia pressed her lips together in a thoughtful pose. "Maybe we should ask Scraps," she said, half-jokingly. Whenever either of them had to think through a difficult decision, Scraps was the one who usually held the answer. They focused a fixed stare on the dog.

Sensing too much of the wrong kind of attention, Scraps launched himself off the bed, gave his ears a quick shake, then made a bee-line for his crate.

Michael and Marcia laughed together.

Then the phone rang.

Michael looked at the 'call waiting' display and groaned.

"So, what have you decided?" From the thickness in Gordon's voice, it was obvious he had continued drinking since his last phone call.

"I told you when you called earlier, we can't make it," Michael said wearily. He wondered why he had bothered to answer the phone.

"Oh, tha's right, you have to study," Gordon slurred his words heavily. "Gonna be a big shot lawyer!"

"Listen, if you're going to be a jerk, I'm going to hang up right now." Michael's shoulder muscles were starting to twitch.

"Oooh, a 'jerk.' That hurt. Well, you know what? I was 'admitted to the bar' today ... tha's right, me ... and I din even have to study for it." He chuckled into the phone.

"I already explained everything to Dad. Give it a rest, why don't you?" Michael made a mental note to himself. From now on, Gordon would be speaking to the answering machine.

"Well, okay," Gordon sneered. "No pro-plem-mo. I'll be your stand-in at the party." Suddenly a thought occurred to him. "Say that's a good one, huh? Me standing in for you."

Michael had had enough. "I'm going to hang up now. You're drunk."

"Wait ... wait, kid ... wait. Gotta say somethin' .... Then we're through talking. Okay?"

Michael thought for a minute. "Okay. But then don't call me again."

"Listen, little brother, you don' need t' come home—guess why."

Michael let out a heavy sigh. "Okay, I'll bite. Why?"

"Cause there's no need." He started cackling like a half-wit. "Dad ain't who you think he is."

"What does that mean?"

Gordon smacked his lips. "You really wanna know?"

Michael was fuming. "I don't have time for this. Get to the point, or get off the line."

"Well, okay, Bro, if you insist." The weird cackling suddenly ceased. Gordon cleared his throat. "Dad is not your Dad."

"Don't be stupid," Michael said in disgust. "If he's not my Dad, who is?"

"I am," Gordon replied. Then he hung up the phone.

Rebate
by Maria Cecilia Nicu

"I'm telling you, all the problems in our life are questionable, but if you store those questions and don't try to find some answers you're in trouble. You live on a see-saw of confusion, and intelligent or not, ignoring doesn't help."

"Do you think so?"

"Of course I do. Otherwise I'd run around like Dakota after his tail...a vicious circle of temptation and assumptions, maybe even a dream but with clarity."

"I see! Your interpretation of life is an uninterrupted search for understanding and I don't agree. Sometimes it's better to accept or to just let everything flow."

"Listen!"

She was not beautiful, she was not ugly. An aura of fragility surrounded her with something resembling innocence, she didn't have big eyes "as a cow" if I remember correctly. O'Neill's heartfelt saying in his The Moon for the Misbegotten – she was keeping them a little closed. I think that she was afraid to see what she didn't want to see or that maybe she was only a product of her own vulnerability. Who knows!

Even more, for me she's quite scruffy looking, she doesn't care much for a decent appearance. I think she kept all her dresses – though there weren't many - on just one coat hanger, they always look wrinkled. She had a pair of high-heeled shoes but they were always dusty or even soiled. The streets, if you remember, were not quite clean in the Bucharest of our youth and her walk was in a constant rush, she would run like something followed her and I wonder what could it be?

She talked in chanting French and when I got to Paris I thought about her. She would've felt at home with her trilled R...

Sure she didn't have any chance to get to Paris. I think it's absolutely idiotic to even entertain the idea of a voyage to Paris or anywhere else for that matter.

When she met him, I can't recall his name, she was in the third or fourth year at University and he enchanted her reciting Villon with his dip, rather hoarse voice of a heavy smoker and/or drinker. Her own world started to shrink around her and of course she didn't have any idea. Everywhere she turns "Mais ou sont les neiges d'antan?" blurs any communication, percolates interventions or attractive curiosities. She's been arrested by a painful imagination of solitude suddenly muffled by this intruder, armed "up to his teeth", as we say in Romanian, with Villon melancholy.

She loved him with the passion learned from books, and she didn't know that taken out of their stories the romantic heroes lose their glitter and vanish in the triviality of life.

Maybe I'm wrong, maybe he had to come into her life. You can't live in a lethargic state, you have to assume the risk of failure as a song I love says: "I will sail my vessel till the river run is dry".

Anyhow she was happy, and for a while she had that unmistaken glow of love. Those hot nights when any poetic waves become agitated tides gave her beauty and assurance of her femininity.

Villon was sent somewhere, she couldn't ask for his help all the time. I remember her telling me once that his poems kept her captive, obstructing her desire to look outside their splendor. "Our life," she said, "seems to be controlled by the moment, you know? It forced us to observe and accept without question and I don't like it, it scares me."

Summer was short, as it always is, and she tried to appear busy by telling me that she was working on a translation, some French book, she said. I'm pretty sure it wasn't

Villon and to tell the truth, I suspected she wasn't doing anything. She's been sprawled out in a fancy laziness from where you have no chances to get up and not pay the price of a broken dream.

Maybe you realized the moment when her decline started but I didn't.

"Decline, you say? Are you kidding? She plunged headfirst into the unknown, that kind of steep nose-down descent (as father told us about)? ...Pure and simple, she collapsed!"

"Right! For him "the magic moment" passed away. A second of attraction, a tiny curiosity and a boring "nothing is new under the sun" sums up his interest for her.

To turn his back to her was part of his normality of life: not a glance, not a word, not even a thought.
For her, resetting herself in reality was no longer possible. She shut the doors and let herself be overtaken by the dark shadows of madness.

"Do you know Eminescu* was here in this hospital?" she asked me. Of course, I said: Yes he was!"

*Mihai Eminescu - the Romanian Bard.

The Other One
by Elizabeth Banfalvi

My father had two daughters. One daughter loved make-up and fashion and the other didn't care. One daughter stayed in and read books and the other shovelled snow with her dad. I happened to be the other one. I wasn't a tomboy but I just wasn't about prettying myself up at all because I had too much to be curious about.

I was the baby, the second daughter. I had the red hair and green eyes and nobody in my family had been a red head for over 5 generations. My blue eyed father suspected the doctor and the baker but I ignored him. He was stuck with me. He teased a lot and I was my father's daughter. My mother was a dare devil and I was also my mother's daughter. I had the worst of both of them but that was how I was. Don't dare me and I won't do it. Don't be serious around me and I won't tease you. I was the type that when I was finished pulling your leg, I would start gnawing on the other one. Children and animals loved me and I loved them.

My parents lived on a tobacco farm and would take my sister and me into the fields when they worked during the day. I would eventually disappear and they would find me sleeping under the tall tobacco plants on the warm earth. In the summer, they would be harvesting and the outside tobacco gang would have the horse working in the hot summer sun pulling the boat with the load of tobacco leaves. At the end of the day, they would unbridle the horse and put me on its back and then it would be off to the barn for the evening. Halfway to the barn, I laid down on its back and fell asleep on the hot sweaty horse. The workers had to hold me on so I wouldn't slip off. I was called by my Hungarian name, "Bozsi", and I had the pride of knowing milk cows were named after me like all my female cousins. I watched the milking of the cows and the cats sitting waiting for the fresh milk. This was my young life living on the farm so close to nature.

I grew up and we moved to Azilda outside of Sudbury. It was such a cold dry country. I became a teenager there and lived next door to my cousins and the arena and baseball field were in our backyard. My first taste of hockey and baseball was in that back field. My favourite team was Montreal Canadiens because we saw more of the French television than English. I saw Maurice Richard, Jean Beliveau and Boom-Boom Geoffrion play and Montreal winning the Stanley Cup.

The sky was beautiful there – so clear and blue and so were the many lakes in the area. I played baseball in recess at school and then volleyball and broomball in high school. I acted in the high school play and I played the mother who was tied up and screamed for help. Boy, I didn't realize I was so loud until the audience cheered when he gagged me. I was always the one everyone came to when they had a problem with their schoolwork. I was the resident student teacher no matter what the subject was but especially French and Latin. This was my life.

One night when I was sixteen and I wanted to go next door to my cousins, I walked out into the evening. It was a cold winter's night and it had snowed but there the snow was like sparkly white powder. We couldn't have snowball fights there but that was lucky because I had great aim – still do. In the backyard, it was quiet and cold. It was so dark that the only light was the window lights laying across the snow. It was so quiet like the earth had stood still and I felt alone but not alone. I stopped and looked up. The stars were a canopy of sparkling dots above. There were so many in the crystal clear night. I stood there looking up surrounded by the snow, the quiet and the stars. There was such a feeling within me and still is when I remember that moment.

Many years later, I would share that feeling with my grandson. There was a hydro black-out in southern Ontario and everything was dark. The moon was out and my grandson and I walked across the roadway in the townhouse complex we lived in. He had a flashlight and I told him to shut it off and look at the stars. When I held his hand, he had the courage to turn it off. I told him to look up and he did. It caught his breath seeing the canopy of stars above. He pointed and asked if that was the Milky Way and I said yes. We stood for a few minutes longer and enjoyed it. I shared my moment with him.

When I was seventeen, I finished high school and came back to southern Ontario to live. There were no jobs in Sudbury at that time. I eventually met my husband and married 6 months after we met. He was what my mother wanted for me – Hungarian like our heritage. He was almost ten years older than me and I was supposed to listen to him because he knew better. That didn't work well with me. I miscarried not long after that and then got pregnant again and had a daughter nine months later. I held her for the first time and even though I had always wanted children I didn't realize what a difference it would make for me. I was a mother. I felt like a warm wave had flowed over me with the feeling. I would never be the same. I would eventually miscarry 3 more times but then have 2 sons. My older son was like me and his birthday was within days of mine. My daughter was the perfectionist; my older son laughed and made fun; and my youngest just did everything perfect and faster. They were all so different. They were perfect targets for my sense of humour and there are still many pot holes in them.

My older son was diagnosed with diabetes when he was fourteen and had a very hard time with it. He died when he was 25. I still feel the loss and I have watched my other two get married and have children and he would have loved to be like them and also see their children and be an uncle and father. I visit his graveside every year which is in the same plot as my parents. When we had the burial for my son, his best friend came along and we laid roses across the plot. His best friend laid a puck with the Montreal Canadiens' emblem on top of the roses. We were silent but then we started to chuckle. It made it lighter and I knew my son would have enjoyed it.

I left my husband six years later after 33 years of marriage and then the next year I was diagnosed with cancer. I do it up well. The three worse stressors in anyone's life is death, marriage break-up and health problems. I covered them all in ten years. Leave it to me to do it up well.

Now came my once-again single life. Ok, that was short. Going with men that wanted to go for a coffee and then skip the coffee and have do the back seat shuffle didn't exactly appeal to me. I guess now I had to find myself once again. I get lost often.

I really had to use my sense of humour for my single life. So I kept on working and eventually I bought my home and started to write. What my life will still bring me, I don't know but I keep motoring on trying to find the comedy in it and so far I have been really successful in it.

In the Neighbourhood

Murder
by Rashmi Pluscec

The bus came to a resigned
halt as the amber light bled
into red. My groggy eyes glanced at
the time. 6:36 a.m. And only Tuesday. Ugh.

I glanced at the sky and witnessed - in that
fleeting moment which sits on the cusp
of dawn and morn - a murder most wondrous!

Safely ensconced in a sea of cobalt, sat a
charcoal cloud. But not for long… First there was
a stab right through its heart. Then the gash

widened and a ray seeped through. Changing
its hue from an innocent pink to a whorish
red. Morphing the cloud from a sleeping giant to

a golden boy. And then in a final act of
glorious defiance, the sun ripped through and
rose to rule the sky.

The fragile dawn gave in to the fierce
day, leaving but few witnesses who would
go on to tell the tale. The red surrendered
to the green and the bus moved on.

A Dark and Stormy Night
by Nicholas Boving

You could have cut the atmosphere in the bar with a blunt knife. Outside, the weather had clamped down with a vengeance in the way it sometimes can on the west coast of Scotland, and the fishing boats had taken shelter: the result being that fifty boisterous, raucous and slightly fuddled fishermen were crammed into a room meant for twenty at a pinch. The bar was on the other side of the hotel, away from the guest quarters where I was supposed to be. It was my own fault: I should have known better.

I was perched in a corner holding a whisky the size of which you'd never get served anywhere else in the bar without seriously endangering your credit limit, watching the barman dispense drinks and witticisms with equal rapidity. There were more genuine characters per square foot in that small room than you'd find anywhere outside its counterpart in some port like Halifax or Honolulu. Seamen all over have a way of enjoying themselves that's unique, usually involving trying to drink a bar dry and find a face to smash in. I was content to make myself very small and just watch and listen.

The evening wore on, the noising level increasing in logarithmic proportion to the volume of whisky consumed, and inevitably I found myself watching a particular couple of fellows hunched over a table looking as if they were solving the riddles of the Universe. Maybe they were at that, but the puzzled frowns and expressions of intense and pained concentration indicated I.Q.s about one level up from the average house plant.

The smaller one, only about six foot two and two-twenty pounds felt my gaze in the end. You do that, don't you: feel someone looking at you. It's something to do with E.S.P. I imagine, or a guilty conscience. Anyway, he swung round slowly, baby blue eyes traversing the length of the bar like twin hawks looking for a juicy mouse, until they settled on me. I looked away sharply, but not sharply enough. Talk about across a crowded room! I wish he'd been called Sheila, or Morag, but I had a feeling it was just Jock because he couldn't spell anything as complicated as Hamish.

Funny how simple actions can bring instant attention, like pushing back a chair and standing up. He stood up, the chair scraped back, and there was instant hush. Just like that, magic!

Jock came through the crowd like Moses parting the Red Sea: it sort of parted as he moved, another bit of magic that made me wish I could do the same with the wall at my back. He stopped a yard away, swaying a bit and surrounded by a miasma of whisky fumes that must have really kept the flies away as I had a feeling it was semi-permanent. But perhaps I was being unjust: maybe working on a fishing boat made you want that kind of personal deodorant.

"Who are ye starin' at?" The tone did not make it a polite enquiry.

I smiled in what I hoped was a disarming manner. "Certainly not you."

"Ye damned well were. An' ye were listenin' tay a private conversation, Mr Nosey Parker."

My smile evolved from disarming to placating. "How could I possibly hear anything in this noise?" There was no noise. Sprint would have loved it.

"How could I possibly hear?" The man mimicked my English accent and moved closer. I tensed and put my glass on the bar. What had been totally innocent looked like turning ugly if I didn't do something to create an atmosphere of calm and brotherly love, and all eyes were turned in our direction in delighted expectation. Jock finally realized we were the focus of attention and decided to push it.

"Look, I'm sorry if I've offended you," I said. "And I'm sorry you think the way you do. Let me buy you a drink to show there's no harm meant."

I might have been talking to the wall as things suddenly came to head when he grabbed a fistful of my sweater, thrusting his reddened face in mine. I reckoned I had a couple of seconds before the inevitable happened.

Then the barman came to my rescue. He placed a full glass on the counter and leant across.

"Whoa there," he said."'What d'ye want to be fightin' this fella for, Jock? He's never done ye no harm. Leave it be an' take a drink: that way ye'll no be sorry."

"It'll nay be me that's sorry," Jock replied. By God, I was right. "I'll smash his face in."

The logic of the thought process escaped me, but the barman just shrugged and beckoned with a conspiratorial air.

"Jock," he whispered loudly, "D'ye ken James Bond?"

"Aye," said Jock, with a puzzled frown.

The barman jerked his head at me and hissed urgently. "Yer man there; yon's James Bond."

The effect was little short of miraculous. Jock's baby blues widened as he went full astern, and there were a couple of snickers from the audience. Then someone at the back of the room struck up a tune on a battered accordion and moments later the bedlam was again at force ten, the incident forgotten.

Church Lets Out
by Bev Bachmann

Dec. 23rd 11:30 a.m.

Willy Saunders was in no hurry as he leisurely guided his taxi along a stretch of Bathurst heading north. Lost in his own thoughts, he barely noticed the row housing lining both sides of the street—grey windswept structures snuggling shoulder-to-shoulder against the dreary December cold.

When he reached the bustling intersection of Bathurst and Bloor, he made a right turn onto Bloor Street and steered his taxi towards Jarvis where he turned south in the direction of Lake Ontario. A few seconds later his cab was cruising past a popular steak house that had once been an elegant mansion at the turn of the 20th Century before becoming a top-rated restaurant.

A few blocks further down the road Willy spotted the headquarters of the Salvation Army, or as it was affectionately known, the Sally Ann. Around town there were plenty of reputable charities to service the needs of the less fortunate, but the Sally Ann was the indisputable first choice of the hard core drifters, drunkards, and junkies—those innumerable lost souls who wandered the streets in an constant quest for whatever it would take to get them through the long days and even longer nights.

Keeping the cab well within the speed limit, Willy continued his journey through the eerily empty street. A wadded up hamburger wrapper bounced across his windshield and landed on the sidewalk when a sudden blast of air sent it sailing high above the rooftops where the wind sent it plunging back down to earth.

Willy shivered in his cab, but not from the cold. He could feel fear creeping up his spine with each minute that brought him closer to the end of his shift. He had to think.

His mind went over every possible traffic violation that he could have committed, but always he came up empty. Damn police anyway! Why the hell aren't they tracking down the Mafia instead of bothering him? Willy shook his head as if he could dislodge the worry nesting there and send it packing.

It was probably nothing, so why fret? Still, his dispatcher had told him that the police wanted to see him—and not just the police—the Chief of Homicide! Willy gripped the steering wheel with both hands, took a deep breath and waited for the light to turn green. Gently he eased the cab through the intersection. The last thing he needed now was a speeding ticket.

He figured he had about one more hour of freedom left, and then he would go see the police and get it over with. He even used his turn signal. He often didn't bother with such 'niceties,' but this time he was careful. He was going to do everything by the book.

The cab turned to the left and headed east on King Street. Willy had something on his mind. A beer. That's what he needed, a beer. But just one. It wouldn't do to meet the Chief of Homicide with alcohol on his breath—but one beer couldn't hurt.

King Street was bleak and deserted. He glanced to his right at the Safety Supply Company, closed for Sunday. Inside its big picture window two bright yellow hard hats had been placed side by side. Willy snorted. He had done construction work in his day and he was damn glad to be driving a cab. Shiny hard hats indeed! The light turned red. About two blocks ahead he spotted what he had been looking for—The Bull's Eye Tavern.

As he pulled up to where King met Parliament Street, he glanced up at the cathedral spires of St. Matthew-in-the-Field, situated on the King Street side of the intersection. The Bull's Eye was located on the Parliament side of the corner facing the church. Separating the respective establishments was a shared parking lot used by these two unlikely neighbors who had had the good grace to ignore each other for years. The arrangement had worked out remarkably well. Until today.

Willy parked, yanked on his gloves and got out of the cab, slamming the door shut behind him. Within minutes he was sitting at the bar and watching Sergio, the good-natured Italian bartender, wipe a glass dry and place it on a tray alongside a collection of others just like it.

Willy glanced around nervously, then picked up one of the bar's circular paper coasters and used it to blot the sweat on his forehead. Damn, he wished he didn't feel like this. Why did he have to speak to the police, of all people? Why couldn't he just kick back and enjoy his one lousy day off?!

"What'll it be, Willy?" Sergio asked politely. Willy was a good customer—not sloppy or stupid like so many he'd seen.

"Get me a Molson Canadian, Serg."

There was a quiet Sunday crowd in The Bull's Eye with only a few patrons hanging around inside the dark warmth of the tavern.

"Somethin' wrong, Willy?" Sergio pushed a frosty mug across the counter.

"Ah, it's nothing, Serg. At least I think it's nothing." He gulped down the beer and swiveled the bar stool around. "Business is bad, eh?" he said.

"Yeah. It's the rotten weather. The thermometer dips too low and nobody wants to get out of bed—even to get drunk," he said in disgust.

Willy shook his head in agreement. "God! How I hate Sundays!" he blurted out suddenly.

Sergio stashed his dish towel under the counter and placed both hands palm down on the bar. "You sure nothin's wrong, Willy?"

"It ain't serious, Serg," he said quietly before grabbing his mug and lifting it to his lips. The wide mouthed glass covered most of his face, leaving only his eyes and the ridge of his nose exposed.

Sergio didn't say anything. He had been a bartender long enough to know when to leave a man alone.

Willy continued to drink in silence.

Just then a nerve jarring crash exploded in a dimly lit corner. Both men jumped, their eyes riveted in the direction of the noise.

"You god-damned whore monger, I'm gonna cut your throat!" A beet-faced bull of a man staggered and swayed like a swinging chandelier. He had in his hand a broken beer bottle, the sharp, jagged edges pointed outward.

"Bastardo!!" cried Sergio. "You'd better get out of here! It's George and he's a mean SOB when he gets rolling!"

Willy stared, openly fascinated. The three men who had been sitting at the table with George backed away from their drunken companion and scrambled quickly out the front door. George looked around stupidly. A bit of froth oozed out of the corners of his mouth. He lumbered over to the bar.

"Who you staring at, you son of a bitch?"

Willy looked steadily into the man's blood shot eyes. "Hit the bricks, Bud," he said in a level voice.

When Willy was a kid, he had been knocked about by a brutish father who respected only one law: the power of the fist. But Willy had survived and survived well. He was not a man to be pushed around.

"What'd you say?" Fire raged in George's bulging eyeballs.

He lifted an arm the size of a python and brandished the teeth-like edges of the broken bottle close to Willy's face.

Quick as lightning, Willy grabbed George's arm and pinned it tightly behind the big man's back. Then he guided his pinioned captive towards the front door, and with one mighty shove, sent the bum flying into the street.

George stumbled onto the sidewalk. He glared at the tavern door, then turned and started weaving clumsily towards the curb. The bells at St. Matthew-in-the-Field rang out several times to announce the conclusion of another service. He stopped to listen. Church bells. People. George staggered off to greet them.

"You really handled that guy. Have another one on the house." The bartender was grateful and wanted to show it.

"Thanks," said Willy. "But I have to be going."

"Damn church bells," remarked Sergio wiping up a spill on the counter with a swipe of his rag. "Bad for business."

Willy laughed. Grabbing his coat from a bar stool, he sauntered out into the cold, damp air.

A long line-up was collecting inside the crowded vestibule of St. Matthew-in the Field. Everyone wanted to shake hands with the popular minister, Reverend Lassiter, a warm hearted man who was so tall he had to stoop to look into their faces as they stopped to say their good-byes. He patiently took each hand in his and beamed a smile of benediction on every man, woman, and child before they filed out the front door—exactly as he had done every Sunday for the past thirty-five years.

The good reverend hadn't always been a man of the cloth. There was a time, long ago, when he had been a math instructor at a local college where he coached a highly successful intervarsity basketball team. Of course, that was before he found his true calling and became a coach of a different sort. However, he had no regrets. If anyone had asked, Reverend Lassiter would have said simply that he was a very lucky man.

Setting foot outside the sanctuary, the older adults exchanged pleasantries and some made arrangements to meet for lunch at a nearby waffle house while others—mostly groups of university students—mingled on the sidewalk reluctant to leave the comfort of each other's company in spite of the chill in the air.

There was the usual bantering and good natured ribbing among the bachelors hanging around a cluster of girls smiling shyly beneath an assortment of woolen tams and faux fur hoods carefully adjusted to keep their delicate ears from being bitten by the wind.

Several blocks away a police cruiser was gliding along King Street heading west towards the heart of the city. A pale, dusty cloud drifted across the sun, casting a grey pall on the grimy streets below.

Willy Saunders strolled towards where his cab was parked, but then hesitated. He thought he had seen the flailing figure of George stumbling in the direction of people pouring out of St. Matthew's. Willy knew in his bones that he should just jump in his cab and take off, but an unseen force kept him from opening the door. He ran a hand through his unruly hair. Part of his brain warned him not to get involved; another part told him that George was like a rabid dog loose among unwary children. He paused for a moment, trying to make up his mind.

A young married couple was threading their way among their friends and church acquaintances, making gradual progress towards the parking lot separating the church from The Bull's Eye. It was their misfortune to be the first of St. Matthew's parishioners to encounter the inebriated George.

"Hi-yah, pretty lady!" He weaved like a swaying cobra dangerously close to the woman's face.

At first, the couple tried ignoring him by side-stepping around him, but he would have none of it. George wanted attention, and by god, he was going to get it.

"Wassa matter, honey? Ain't I good enough for ya?" He jeered loudly at the embarrassed couple beating a hasty retreat in the direction of their car. George spat contemptuously on the ground. "Thas for you, ya high and mighty slut!" he shouted after them, letting go with a stream of scathing obscenities.

Several shocked churchgoers started moving in closer to get a better view. George sensed he was getting an audience and wheeled around to face the gathering crowd. He grinned widely at the gaping parishioners. He had their attention. He was a star!

The young husband deposited his wife in the front seat of their subcompact, closed the door, and turned to face their assailant. His wife reached out of the hastily opened front window and pressed her hand down on her husband's arm with a grip that pleaded for him to forget the nasty episode and get in the car. But he was in no mood to 'turn the other cheek.'

"C'mon, college boy," George taunted. He was bobbing unsteadily on his feet. "You wanna fight? Prove you're a big man. Huh! Well, c'mon then. Even sloshed, I can whip the pants off ya!"

"Don't dirty your hands by touching him, Hank," someone in the crowd yelled out.

George spun around and snarled. "Stay out of this, whoever you are—ya chicken-shit Sunday-go- ta-meetin' pantywaist." He stopped as if in a daze. Stringing that many words together seemed to have short-circuited the synapses in his brain. George looked around dully. Who were these people?

"Why doesn't somebody call the police?" A woman was heard to say. George's bleary eyes tried to make her out in the crowd.

"Why don't you do it, you whining cow?!"

The young husband whose wife had been insulted had heard enough. "Okay, buster. Apologize for what you said to my wife and to this poor lady here, and I mean right now!" He had formed two fists and was testing his balance by bouncing gently on his heels.

Just then the Reverend arrived on the scene and sized up the situation quickly. "Hank," he called out gravely. "Get away from that man." When his words had no effect, he tried a different approach. "Don't give in to temptation, son," he admonished kindly. "Turn your back on the devil and walk away."

Incensed, George wheeled around. "Say! Who you calling the devil?"

The Reverend opened his mouth to speak, but it was too late. George was already rushing at him with the force of a freight train. Within seconds he had the front of the reverend's robes clutched in his oversized fists, the foul stench of his breath fanning the minister's face.

The congregation stared in mortification.

All at once, as if on some preordained cue, the crowd surged forward, hell-bent on rescuing their minister from the grip of this deranged drunkard. Suddenly what had been a peaceful parking lot full of churchgoers heading for their cars had become the scene of a full blown riot.

The patrol car that had been closing in on the area was now within sight. Normally St. Matthew-in-the Field would be deserted by now, but what the police officer saw amazed him. He didn't wait for an invitation.

"Move back! Everybody, move back!" the policeman ordered. He reached the center of the commotion and started separating the mob. "Break it up! Everybody! Back off!"

One by one the crowd disbanded, leaving George standing alone, disheveled and panting. "Ain't my fault," he said, gasping for air. "Damned minister here called me a devil and then his thugs jumped me," George huffed indignantly.

"Sure, sure." The policeman was not impressed.

"Excuse me, Sergeant." Willy stepped forward. "I saw the whole thing. George here was drunk and insulting people comin' out of church. I saw him lunge at the Reverend and grab his frock. Me and some other guys didn't like him manhandling the Reverend, so we tackled him. That's when you came along."

"What this gentleman says is true," said the Reverend, smoothing down the front of his robes with the palms of his hands. "Would you like me to make a statement?"

"Ahhhh!"

A terrible moan shook George's powerful frame. Tiny threads of broken blood vessels in his face merged into one flaming mask of red while little bubbles of perspiration popped out along his brow. He clasped both hands to his chest.

"I don't feel so good," he said feebly. Without warning he slumped forward like a building caving in from the blow of a wrecking ball. Hastily the Reverend and the police sergeant grabbed an arm each, the two men forming the end supports of a sagging bridge between them.

Then, for one sickening moment, George's body quivered and jerked in uncontrollable spasms. Suddenly all motion ceased. George's glassy eyes focused blankly on a point far off in the distance, and, with a violent headlong plunge, he pitched forward and hit the snow covered ground with a thud.

No one moved.

Visibly shaken, the police officer looked down at the man sprawled at his feet. "Get up, Buddy," he ordered in an unsteady voice.

The Reverend knelt down next to George and felt for a pulse. "Poor tortured soul," he shook his head sadly. "I'm afraid there's nothing this side of the grave anyone can do for him now."

The sergeant moved quickly to his parked cruiser. He reached inside and put the black police telephone receiver next to his ear.

Stunned St. Matthew's parishioners stood around aimlessly, speaking to each other in hushed tones. Most were disturbed by what they had seen; some were disturbed by what they had done.

"It's all right," said the Reverend, addressing the scattered remnants of his parish. "Go home. Get some rest. We'll talk about this next Sunday, but for now, please everybody, go home."

Slowly the crowd dispersed, each moving in the direction of their waiting cars and heading back into the worlds from which they came.

Willy himself had been stunned by the sight of George's death throes. He felt more than a little unsettled. If the rest of the day was going match the morning, he'd just as soon go back to bed.

"Probably," the police sergeant was speaking into his mike. "Looks like a heart attack. Yes, sir, I've ordered an ambulance." The officer stopped to listen. "Right." He turned to the Reverend. "Would you mind coming downtown. We're going to need a statement from you."

"Of course."

"What about me?" asked Willy, trying not to seem nervous.

"What's your name?"

"Saunders. Willy—William—Saunders."

The policeman spoke into his phone. "The witness is a cabbie who was on the scene. . . .William Saunders. . . .What?"

The cop walked a few steps away and lowered his voice. Willy couldn't hear the rest of the conversation. He didn't have to. He knew it wasn't good.

"What's this?" The minister bent down to examine a peculiar stain he noticed on the dead man's jaw. His naked fingers reached out to touch the brown smear.

"I wouldn't do that if I were you, Reverend," said Willy. "The police don't like anyone messing with the body. Keeps 'em from figuring' what went wrong," he suggested helpfully.

"You're right, of course," the minister said, drawing back his hand.

Just then two cruisers arrived along with an ambulance. Blue clad officers and paramedics hastened to a clearing where the police sergeant stood guarding George's body on the ground.

One of the medical attendants who was crouched over the corpse, called over his shoulder. "You need to see this," he said to the policeman watching the proceedings.

"That dirty patch?"

"It's not dirt, Sergeant." The paramedic and his partner exchanged glances.

The cop bent over to get a closer look. "You know what it is?"

"Forensics will have to run some tests, but I've seen this kind of thing before."

The policeman stared at the peculiar smudge and shook his head. He didn't want to think what he was thinking. Abruptly he turned to the Reverend. "You can ride with me downtown . . . and you, Saunders, can follow in your car. The Chief specifically asked for you."

Willy's left eye began to twitch. He felt like a kid who had been called to the principal's office. "You don't know why he wants to see me, do you?" he asked, doing his best to appear nonchalant.

"I couldn't say," the policeman offered in response. "Let's go."

Wordlessly Willy fell in behind the Reverend as the three men marched to the curb where the police cruiser was parked next to Willy's cab.

By now all the excitement had drawn a crowd from the neighboring houses. Curious groups of onlookers stood around in little clusters with their arms folded across their chests, staring with obvious fascination at the tarp covering George's body. Meanwhile law enforcement personnel and television crews had quickly arrived, adding a certain element of macabre entertainment to the crime scene now cordoned off with yellow police tape.

As the wind picked up, a few fresh flakes began to fall, dotting the newly cleared sidewalks like talcum powder. Soon a light coating of white covered the ground, burying all traces of the morning's mayhem under a thin blanket of soft, unblemished snow.

My Neighbour
by Veronica Lerner

we come across in the elevator
I see a joyful elegant salesman
in a man's suits store
an unpaid advertiser for it
retired - he works on Sundays

the pet's lover has two
shaggy Charlie is sensible
and willingly accept the other dogs
when their masters leave them
in the neighbours care

illness won't stop his wife
to glide the newspaper and leaflets
under my door
on Thursdays

John drinks coffee
cracks jokes and laughs
with all other neighbours
our elegant John our courteous John our friend John

recently the suits went into hiding
a shadow appeared instead
in the elevator

yesterday
with the speed of light
life's been severed for
our elegant John our courteous John our friend John

when the death scythes around
the greatest reverence
can be made
only by silence

The Kallus Next Door
(Kallus is pronounced as Cull-loose)
by Jasmine Sawant

Cast Breakdown

SHANTI – 43+
She can be plump or slim, but she's always well-dressed and carries herself very well. The kind who'd sail into the room and expect everyone to stand at attention. Wears both kind of clothing – Indian and Western. Has a full-time job. Strict. High expectations. Adores her son, so lets him get away with certain behaviour that in others she finds unacceptable. South Asian. Lighter-skinned.

MOHAN – 46+
He may be a bit heavy set or lean, but he is a gentle soul, with a philosophical attitude to life, likes nothing better than to read books, newspapers, etc. Should be taller than his wife. Wears reading glasses. South Asian. Wheatish complexion.

RAHUL – 24
Lean, agile, sharp as a tack and a scamp. Irreverent attitude, and behaves younger than his age. Indulged by his mother and doted on by his grandmother, this irresponsible-seeming young man has more depth and dimension to him than is apparent at first. South Asian. Lighter-skinned.

SONIA – 21
Pretty, slim, vivacious, well dressed, and shorter than JORDAN. Lives in her own world, which is a world of justice, equality, honesty and love, but does bend the rules a bit when it is to her convenience. Not as light-skinned as her brother.

BIJI – 65+
Grey-haired, sharp repartee, but dreamy at times, floating in and out, warm-hearted, caring. She is from MOHAN'S side of the family so skin colour is not important, but she should not be too dark-skinned.

JORDAN – 26
Tall, good-looking, athletic black male, older than RAHUL'S. Very well-spoken and well-mannered, is well-educated and is doing well financially. Can be of Caribbean or African descent.

Minor roles for the wedding scene only:
JORDAN'S parents
His uncle and aunt
Couple of cousins if possible
A grandma or pa or both
One Asian girl
A whole lot of Indians dressed for the wedding

ACT ONE

SCENE I

Present day Mississauga. It's night-time. SHANTI is pacing up and down. She has not yet changed into nightwear, whereas MOHAN is in relaxed wear, sitting quietly, absorbed in his book.

SHANTI: (worried) It's almost midnight and she's still not here. We should call the police.

MOHAN: (gently) SHANTI, stop that pacing and sit down. There's no need to call the police. Just sit down.

SHANTI: (annoyed) What do you mean, sit down! What sort of a parent are you, Mohan? You must have a heart of stone.

MOHAN: SHANTI, I am as concerned a parent as you are. I just happen to be …

SHANTI: In fact, you do have a heart of stone. All my appeals always fall on deaf ears!

BIJI: In that case he has ears of stone not a heart of….

SHANTI: BIJI! What are you doing here at this hour?

BIJI: You haven't exactly been whispering you know.

SHANTI: Thank you very much, BIJI! I can do without your sarcasm! (Turning to MOHAN) And you, sir, what are you doing? How can you sit and read at such at time! And where is that RAHUL? He's never here when he's needed.

MOHAN: If you are ….

SHANTI: But of course, that is exactly what you will do. Sit and read. Why do I even expect you to think of something I don't know. After 25 years of marriage I should know better! You are no help at the best of times. Either you're away, or you have your nose buried in a book!

BIJI: No wonder his ears have turned to stone, he's buried! Actually he's dust, but stone, dust, all the same, once you're buried.

SHANTI: BIJI, why don't you get back to bed? I am in no mood to…..

MOHAN: Can I complete my sentence?

SHANTI: There you go, interrupting me again. The moment I say something, you have to interrupt me. I don't know why you keep doing that.

MOHAN: All I am trying to say is, if you are that worried then call her on the mobile, but stop this crazy pacing!

SHANTI: (coldly sarcastic) How utterly brilliant! You don't think I would have done that already!

MOHAN: But of course! You would have done that already! (faintly mocking)

BIJI: Careful MOHAN, she's like a caged tigress, even more dangerous, MOHAN…(A look from MOHAN, and BIJI lowers down to a mumble)

SHANTI: She is not answering her phone. I have called her several times. Oh my God! What if she has been abducted! I am calling the police right now.

MOHAN: Wait, SHANTI, I just heard a vehicle pull into the driveway.

Everyone expectantly looks at the door.

BIJI: Maybe that's a cop coming to tell us that SONIA…SONIA'S had an accident!

SHANTI: BIJI!

Everyone waits in total silence and keeps looking at the door. Seconds tick by, but nothing happens.

SHANTI: Should have guessed! Now you're hearing things that don't …..!

BIJI: Told you. Ears of stone. (SHANTI stares at BIJI angrily.) That's because his nose is buried. You said so.

SHANTI: BIJI!!!

SHANTI: OK, MOHAN, enough is enough. I can't deal with this. I am calling 911 right now.

SHANTI is about to call 911 when RAHUL enters, singing a lilting number, grabs his mom, the handset goes flying as he waltzes her around to the number he's singing while SHANTI is struggling away saying:

SHANTI: Stop it you, idiot! I said stop.

RAHUL stops so suddenly and takes his arms off that SHANTI keels over, and RAHUL comments:

RAHUL: Tsk, tsk. Haven't I told you not to hit the bottle, Ma. Women from decent families should not …..

SHANTI: Stop being idiotic. Here I am out of my mind with worry, and you're being the stand up comic. Look at the time!

It's past midnight and ....

RAHUL: Mom, mom, there's no need to worry. Every night at this time it's always past midnight, but if you are out of your mind then you should be worried.

SHANTI: You....you are impossible. When will you ever take your responsibilities seriously? You are not a little boy now. You are a grown man and you have to ...

RAHUL: Pa, she's talking to you. Do take your responsibilities seriously, Pa. You need to make more money so I can retire.

MOHAN: (with a faint smile) RAHUL, what Mom is trying to tell you is that it's past midnight, SONIA'S not returned, nor is she answering her mobile. So Mom is about to call the cops.

RAHUL: You mean, she has called the cops.

MOHAN: No, RAHUL, I mean she's about to.., uh oh…

SHANTI: (On the phone) I am sure something terrible has happened to her. You've got to find her. What do you mean calm down? My daughter's missing and you want me to calm down. Police, yes I want the police, I already said that.

RAHUL grabs the phone from his mother's hand

RAHUL: I am extremely sorry, Ma'am. My apologies. The lady is sometimes delusional. She is quite senile and forgets…yes, we take good care of her. No, we don't need a doctor. Thank you, very much.

SHANTI: How dare you call me delusional?

RAHUL: Please calm down, 'Mataji'.

SHANTI: (at her screechiest best) Tell me to calm down just one more time and I am going to scream.

RAHUL: You already are screaming, but if it makes you happy, calm down just one more time.......

SHANTI screams, and screams and screams

FADE TO BLACK

SCENE II
Fashback. Daytime. MOHAN and SHANTI are new immigrants. Their rented house is a bit run down and there's hardly any furniture. Opens with SHANTI screaming. In this SCENE a visibly younger looking MOHAN and SHANTI have pronounced Indian accents.

SHANTI: Stop that infernal sound! I just can't take it! Close the curtains, Mohan. It's too bright!

MOHAN: (Looks up from his reading and asks) Are you having a migraine?

SHANTI: Can't you tell? Am I this irritable otherwise?

MOHAN: That's debatable, so we won't go there. (MOHAN gets up, gets a pair of sunglasses instead of drawing the blinds and hands them to SHANTI)

SHANTI: Hmmmph! Never can do what I ask you to. MOHAN just shrugs. (SHANTI grudgingly puts the shades on) What **is** that sound? That continuous thump thump.

MOHAN: RAHUL is outside playing basketball.

SHANTI: (She pushes her glasses to the top of her head) Outside! In this terribly cold weather? Is he out of his mind? Ask him to come in right now. I don't want him catching a cold just before his exams.

MOHAN: Relax, SHANTI. It's a beautiful day. And don't mollycoddle him. Let him be a…..(strong, tough boy)

SHANTI: A Man? I didn't think a runny red nose and smelling of Vicks vaporub made you manly. Oh dear, I hope he has his jacket on (this sentence is to herself). (To MOHAN) Does he have a jacket on? Mohan, Go check.

MOHAN: SHANTI, please....

SHANTI: There it is again. That horrible thump thump. (SHANTI covers her ears, closes her eyes and grimaces). (Then opens her eyes and says sharply) It sounds like there is more than one ball.

MOHAN: (smiling slightly) It sure does.

SHANTI: Is SONIA outside too? (worried, high-pitched)

MOHAN: She is. Calm down, SHANTI, it **is** a beautiful day.

SHANTI: SONIA'S playing basketball?! I thought she didn't like playing basketball anymore.

MOHAN: No, she's just watching.

SHANTI: (irritably) So, if Sonia's watching, who's playing with the other ball? Mohan, why do I have to ask you so many questions just to get one little piece of information? Can you not tell me who is playing with RAHUL? Why are you so mysterious?

MOHAN: There's no mystery, SHANTI. Why are you so curious? (Hastily) If you are, that's perfectly OK, but take a look outside and find out for yourself.

SHANTI: I would, but it's too bright and I have a migraine.

MOHAN: You do have those sun glasses, though it would help if you had them over your eyes.

SHANTI: (SHANTI pushes them down to the bridge of her nose) (Not very aggressively now) Are you going to tell me or not? Oh God, all this talking is making me more sick. I feel like throwing up. (Looks as though she may throw up but doesn't).

MOHAN: (Hastily) RAHUL'S playing with the neighbour's son.

SHANTI: And SONIA is there too! (pushes shades back up on her head) MOHAN, what kind of parent are you? You should be outside keeping an eye on her. We don't know who they are, how they are, and you're letting her play outside unsupervised. I knew it! We never should have come to Canada. Boys and girls playing together! That's just not done back home.

MOHAN: SHANTI, RAHUL is there with her. Calm down! And she's barely ten years old. Stop getting so hyper. Why don't you get back to bed? Can I get you… a cup of tea?

SHANTI: Mohan, in this country, it doesn't matter if she is ten or twenty. Don't forget she's a girl. And yes, I would go to bed, if that thumping would stop. (Sarcastically) Burying your nose in the book is going to stop it? Do something! Talk to the neighbour's kid. Oh, you have met the neighbours. Tell me, how are they?

MOHAN: They're fine.

SHANTI: There! You're doing it again! Go on…tell me, how are they? What's their name? Where are they from? How many kids do they have?

MOHAN: Oh boy! So many questions! It sounds like the Spanish Inquisition.

SHANTI: It's your fault. If you gave me all the details then I wouldn't have to ask. So tell me, who are they?

MOHAN: They're the Andersons and…

SHANTI: (with a smile) Ohhhh. So they're 'goras'. That's not bad, though it would be better if we had our 'desi' people for neighbours. Anyway, now I know why I never get to see any of them. Goras are not a very friendly type of people, like us. (Reflective pause). Well, go on. Why did you stop? I finished asking you all those questions.

MOHAN: If you keep interrupting how can I go on? (with a twinkle) So, what's your next question?

SHANTI: (gestures as though she wants to throttle him)

MOHAN: (with a laugh) OK. I really don't know where they are from. Haven't asked them yet...

SHANTI: And how many children, not counting the one playing outside?

MOHAN: He is their only child.

SHANTI: Just one. 'Bechara'! No wonder. The poor kid must be so lonely. It's good he has RAHUL to play with now.

MOHAN: (puts his book aside and rises and in dulcet tones): I think I should call RAHUL and SONIA back in, it may be a bit cold and... they might fall ill.

SHANTI: (quickly) Let them be (says it twice). It's good for them to make some Canadian friends. It will make it easier for them to settle into this new place, you know.

MOHAN: They're doing just fine. They have taken to the Canadian way of life very easily. (Pause, then continues in a reflective tone) It's only us who are finding it difficult...(to adjust to these new ways).

SHANTI: Yes, I know (quiet for a moment). This Canadian experience that they keep asking you for...(pause again) When **they** come to India, we don't ask them for Indian experience.

MOHAN: That comparison does not really hold SHANTI. They are not immigrating…..

SHANTI: I don't care. What sense does it make for a highly qualified engineer like you to be serving doughnuts at Tim Hortons?

MOHAN: Calm down, SHANTI, I am not the only one. All new immigrants face this problem. It's only a matter of time before….

SHANTI: (irritably) I don't care about all of them, and stop asking me to calm down. Calm down! How can I calm down when you still don't have a proper job? Calm down? When I am cooped up in the house all day! I can't drive the Canadian way, we can't afford to buy a car, you don't have a job, and I don't have a job! We need to have a car to go looking for a job that we can't get, because we don't have Canadian experience, that we can't get, because we don't have a job, that we can't get because ….aaagggh! (clutching her head in agony) Owww.. my head. It's awful. (Loud sounds) Are they having a party? That sounds like a lot of people.
MOHAN: It's quieter upstairs. Let me help you. Wear some ear plugs and a mask and just take it easy.

SHANTI: (rises) (As she passes the window she glimpses something that makes her go closer to the window. Looks outside, makes some choking sounds and then whirls around to face her husband shrieking) Black! Kallu, Kallu, Kallu. They are black! You lied to me! We have black neighbours! (Accusingly) You told me they are 'goras'.

MOHAN: SHANTI, **please** calm down. You jumped to conclusions. I just said they are the Andersons.

SHANTI: You led me on. That's lying. Kallus! Oh my God, we're in a Kallu neighbourood. Do you realize how dangerous this neighbourhood is? Anything can happen. Guns and drugs and ….(shudders) I can't even bear to say it.

MOHAN: Then don't say it, and don't make such sweeping generalizations. You can not lump them all as criminals just because they are black.

SHANTI: Just look at you, taking up for them as though you're related. What's so wonderful about them?

MOHAN: They have been wonderful. Wonderfully neighbourly. They have helped me with snow shoveling, and they often drive me to the grocery store and back, and also...(show me how to repair things)

SHANTI: So what? The Mahans down the street are helpful too. They took us shopping for comforters the day we landed. And Rita Mahan has been so wonderful, introducing me to all her friends. She keeps saying that if we need anything, all we have to do is call her. Why didn't you go grocery shopping with them?

MOHAN: How strange! If I tell you something, you find it so hard to believe it. And here you are, so ready to believe that Rita Mahan really wants to take us grocery shopping. She was only trying to ....(impress you with all her goody goody talk.)

SHANTI: You just cannot bear it when I make friends with people who are smart, settled and connected.

MOHAN: SHANTI, please do calm down, or the migraine will worsen and then .....

SHANTI: Don't try to change the topic. We cannot have a Kallu family for our neighbour! We have to move. I am going to start packing right away.

MOHAN: SHANTI, stop, (goes after her and brings her back) sit, and let me explain.

(SHANTI sits but not quite at ease.)

MOHAN: Listen, we cannot move right away. I have ...

SHANTI: I don't see why not.

MOHAN: First of all, it is not right to be prejudiced about any race or group. And why should skin colour matter? It's not something that….

SHANTI: Don't start lecturing me. My head hurts…..ow…Oh God…..

MOHAN: (grimaces) And secondly, we cannot move right away, because (pause)…….

SHANTI: (arms akimbo) Go on, why did you stop? Complete your sentence now! Why can't we move right away? Don't you care about SONIA?

MOHAN: (a bit impatiently) Of course, I do. The problem is that we have paid a year's rent in advance, and there's no way they are going to return that, so we have to stay here till the end of the year.

Total silence.

SHANTI: You – gave them – a year's rent in advance? What's wrong with you? If I ask you for $2 you kick up such a fuss, (MOHAN says 'SHANTI' here very quietly, but of course she goes right on) and here you go handing out such large sums of money. Did you even stop to consider that we may need…

MOHAN: SHANTI…

SHANTI: What?

MOHAN: Did you stop to consider that no one will rent you an apartment when you have no job, no guarantor and no credit history in this place.

SHANTI: Oh….oh… sits down.

MOHAN: We cannot afford to move until I get a proper job, and you get one, too. So….I don't know how long it will be ….

SHANTI: I cannot think of taking up a job right now. I will not leave the children to come home to an empty house, no, that I cannot bear. (Pause) We have to think of something, though, I don't know what......

The phone rings, SHANTI picks it up and says:

SHANTI: Hello, yes, yes, SHANTI here. Yes, Namaskar. I am fine, thank you. How are you? I, yes of course, I do recognize your voice. Yes, that's wonderful news, when? I am not sure if we can ...yes, sure I will call him.
SHANTI: (Turning and calling out MOHAN) MOHAN its BIJI. She wants to speak with you. Charu's getting married to Prasad, and ...

MOHAN: (taking the phone) Hello BIJI, how are you? Yes, we are all doing well, by the grace of God. (Pause) This is great news! Congratulations! So when's the wedding? (Pause)Yes, ok, I see. Well, the boy is from a good Brahmin family, doing well...(Pause) yes, that's important. (Pause)You know we would love to be there, but at the moment..... we have yet to settle down, we are so new here...yes, yes, do not worry, (pause) I will let you know ....yes, I know, we will miss that too. OK, BIJI, I will do what I can... but I want you to start thinking about it. No, you're not old. Promise me you will think about it. OK, come on a visit first. Of course, after the wedding....ok, ok, bye. Take care and our respects to all, and our blessings to Charu....ok, ok, bye.

(All this time SHANTI has been pacing about, frowning, but when MOHAN asks BIJI to come on a visit, she perks up and soon as he's done speaking she says)

SHANTI: This is fantastic, MOHAN! Sheer genius!

MOHAN: (Very puzzled) Talking about me....

SHANTI: Who else? Definitely not that 'Kallu' next door. This is great! I can't believe you thought about it so quickly.

MOHAN: SHANTI, what are you talking about?

SHANTI: Calling BIJI to Canada. That is genius! Amazing! How did you think of it?

MOHAN: (is about to open his mouth to explain that he did not really think of it, then shrugs his shoulders, smiles) Oh, that. Nothing to it my dear. No big deal.

SHANTI: I still can't get over how quickly you thought of it. Oh you clever man.

(SHANTI gives him a hug and MOHAN of course just happily accepts it all. For once she's so delighted with him, so he just goes with the moment. His face is turned towards the audience with a look that says let me enjoy this attention whilst it lasts)

FADE TO BLACK

SCENE III
Back to present day Mississauga. A continuation of SCENE I, so we hear the tail-end of SHANTI's screaming.

RAHUL: Phew Mom, that beats the wailing Banshee stuff hands down. Are you a member of the Ontario Screamer's Association?

SHANTI: RAHUL, for once can you zip up your wisecracks and focus on the problem at hand. You interrupted and dismissed my 911 call, you and your Dad are just sitting here, doing nothing, and BIJI insists on coming back to join the party. (To BIJI) Welcome, welcome. (sarcastic).

BIJI: Well, you don't think I can fall asleep with all your screaming and shouting, do you? Now what's the problem?

SHANTI: (Has resumed her pacing, turns to glare at her) What do you think? (then turns to RAHUL) If only she would answer her mobile, I would not be so worried.

RAHUL: Sure you would. Even more for what I am about to say. SONIA does not have her mobile with her.

SHANTI: What?!

RAHUL: (a little louder) SONIA does not have her mobile.....

SHANTI: RAHUL, I heard you the first time. Don't be crass! Where is her mobile? Why does she not have it? Who has it?

RAHUL: Ma, one question at a time. One – Where is her mobile? In my pocket; Two - Why does she not have it? Because she loaned it. And, as to who has it? I do. I asked her for it.

SHANTI: (very coldly) And why would you do something like that? (between gritted teeth) And why would you not have mentioned that before? I will...(as though she's going to throttle him)

RAHUL: No Mom, you won't, I am your 'pyara baccha', your darling child, the one and only RAHUL Vedi.

SHANTI: One of these days you will have gone too far....Why didn't you tell me this earlier.

RAHUL: Aww Mom, I forgot I had it in my pocket...

SHANTI: You forgot! When you were the one who asked her for it?! Really RAHUL, if you have to make up stories, at least make them credible! Now tell me, why did you take her mobile?

RAHUL: To play games.

SHANTI: OK, RAHUL, out! Enough of your games. However darling a child you are, at this point I do not want to take any more of your silliness. (Turning to MOHAN) And you sir, if you don't get up and make a stir, I am going straight to the police. I have borne more than enough.

(MOHAN slowly gets up, by which time SHANTI has already turned to BIJI)

SHANTI: And you had better not...

BIJI: But I have not uttered a word....

SHANTI: Oh. Yes, fine, fine (and turns away)

SHANTI: (To MOHAN) So she does not have her mobile, but at least she could have called from a payphone. A dinner with friends can't take that long.

BIJI: It did in your days, I don't see why it's any different.....

SHANTI: BIJI! Kindly don't try my patience. I am ready to scream.

RAHUL: Not again, Mom. We are convinced you are a champion screamer. (And hurriedly looks away, before his Mom can say anything).

(BIJI and MOHAN have faint smiles on their faces. MOHAN looks as if he is about to leave when he stops and goes towards the exit looking very intently, then turns around and says)

MOHAN: SONIA's home, I just saw her pull into the driveway.

(SHANTI, BIJI and MOHAN are all standing as though frozen. RAHUL continues to sit)

(SONIA enters humming a tune and with a little twirl. The tune has to be a soft, popular, romantic number and Western, not Bollywood. She's in her own world and does not realize that she has a welcoming party waiting for her. Suddenly she pulls up short and notices everyone)

SONIA: Oh! (uncertainly) Hello, (then looking at each one of them) what happened?

RAHUL: You happen…to be late.

SONIA: How is this late? It's just a little past midnight.

RAHUL: Exactly! You should have been here way before that. Remember, even Cinderella was not allowed to stay beyond midnight.

SONIA: But she did! And that's what made the difference!

BIJI: And Snow-White had no curfew time, and Sleeping Beauty just slept…

SHANTI: (To BIJI) Enough of the bed-time tales! (To SONIA) You can not be out so late on your own. Girls from ……

SONIA: I don't buy that. The same should apply to RAHUL.

SHANTI: RAHUL is a boy, so there is no comparison.

SONIA: You cannot discriminate…

SHANTI: That's just the way it is. Young, unmarried girls cannot be out so late. And you do not even call!

SONIA: Sorry Mom, I was…..(SHANTI's cue to explode)

SHANTI: Sorry, that's all you have to say, sorry! I am out of mind with worry, on the verge of going to the police and all you have to say is 'sorry, Mom'.

SONIA: Mom, I am trying to explain….

SHANTI: What? You are what? You don't call when you should. And now you want to explain. I think it's a little too late for that. This is like trying to shut the stable door after the horse has bolted.

RAHUL opens his mouth, but his mother is quicker.

SHANTI: No, RAHUL, I am not interested in your modern expressions like what's the use of buying a mouse when you have voice-activated computer….or whatever else it is.

RAHUL: (with admiration) Wow, Mom, that sounds neat!

(While the above exchange was going on, SONIA pleads with her Dad non-verbally to come to her rescue. MOHAN gives one of his soft smiles and turns to SHANTI).

MOHAN: That expression makes no sense, SHANTI, but I digress. Look its really very late, can we address this tomorrow? A good night's rest will make a world of difference.

SHANTI: There you go again, taking up for her. Now, who's pampering her? You are going to regret it one of these days.

MOHAN: Whatever you say m'dear.

SHANTI: Hmmph.

(Everyone is slowly moving away, towards the exit leading to the bedrooms, except for SHANTI, who's standing as still as a statue, in the middle of the stage)

SHANTI: (Suddenly) Stop! (Loud as a whipcrack).

(Everyone halts in their tracks. MOHAN turns around, a bit impatient)

SHANTI: Come here, SONIA. (At the word 'stop' SONIA has not turned, now she bites her lower lip and turns around)

MOHAN: Cut out the drama, SHANTI. We are all a bit tired.

SHANTI: Come, here SONIA. (Repeats even more coldly than before)

(SONIA reluctantly complies)

SHANTI: Who were you out with?

SONIA: I told you, Mom….I was out with friends.

MOHAN: SHANTI, you already know she was out for dinner with her friends, stop dragging this scene out…we need to…

SHANTI: Go on my dear....which friends?

SONIA: This is really so....

SHANTI: Which friends?

SONIA: If you have to know, it was Tara (tayraah), S....

SHANTI: So now you are lying to us? Tara (taaraa) called for you this evening, so you were definitely not with her. Who were you out with?

SONIA: It is Tara (tayraah) not Tara (taaraa). She is a colleague from work.

RAHUL: Can we go to bed now?

SHANTI: I am not done yet.

MOHAN: Thought so.

SHANTI: Put out your hands, SONIA.

RAHUL: Here you go, Mom (holds out a ruler to his mother)

(Everyone ignores him)

SHANTI: I'm waiting, SONIA.

SONIA: This is ridiculous! You are treating me like a child. You can not...

SHANTI: SONIA

SONIA, puts out her hands and there glittering on her left hand is a beautiful solitaire.

SHANTI and BIJI gasp.

MOHAN looks on with a tight look on his face.

RAHUL's eyes narrow and he whistles.

RAHUL: Does this mean what it normally means?

BIJI: Is it real?

SHANTI: Oh my God, you....

SONIA: Yes, Mom, I am engaged.

SHANTI: You should be ashamed of yourself!

SONIA: Because I am engaged?

SHANTI: Because you stand there and say 'I am engaged'. That is not our tradition. Girls from our families do not behave so shamelessly. Never mind us finding a suitable match for you, you just go ahead and get engaged! We don't know who the boy is, what his background is, who his parents are. And you go get engaged without even telling us!! This is not how we raised you, Sonia.

SONIA: But this is the way it is. You can't be living here for so long and clinging on to those old-fashioned traditions of yours.

BIJI: Do your horoscopes match?

MOHAN: But why didn't you tell us? Why so secretive, SONIA? Why?

SONIA: How could I tell you, when I didn't know it myself!

RAHUL: You were seeing someone, but you didn't know it!!!

SONIA: I didn't know if this was the real thing. If this is what we both wanted. It's a huge commitment. (To RAHUL) Something you wouldn't know.

RAHUL: Whoa!

SHANTI: That's exactly what I am saying. It's a huge commitment and you don't get into it without discussing this with your parents, or knowing the boy's background, or meeting his parents...

BIJI: Is he a Brahmin?

SHANTI: (a look or a gesture for BIJI). How could you, SONIA? How could you take such a big step without telling us? (Turning to MOHAN) This is all your fault! You have spoilt her with all your pampering.

MOHAN: I was wondering when we were getting to that.

SHANTI: She has become so independent that she does not even ask us before taking this momentous step. Never mind us finding a suitable boy for her.

RAHUL: And to think that you wouldn't have told us if Mom hadn't been so insistent. That's what bothers me.

MOHAN: They are right, SONIA. Marriage is a major milestone. However independent you are, you do not decide to marry someone without consulting your parents and elders. This is just not done.

SONIA: That is strange, Dad. You have always encouraged me to be independent and make my own choices and now you're telling me it is not done! That's just not right!

SHANTI: Listen to yourself. You do something wrong and turn around and tell us that we are not right. Do you even know what you're saying? Do you stop to think about us?

SONIA: Getting engaged is wrong? I don't think so. If you said 'living together is wrong', I can understand. And I have not done that, so you see, I do think about you. And I will be consulting you when we start planning the wedding.

BIJI: Is it in June?

SONIA: I haven't got married and turned up at the door, so I don't understand what this fuss is all about.

MOHAN: That is so kind of you, SONIA. I encouraged you to be independent, not arrogant.

SONIA: I am not. I am asking you to look at it from my perspective. It's my life after all, and I have the right to decide who I marry and when I marry.

MOHAN: Sure you do, but not without consulting us. As your parents, we have the right to do our best to ensure your happiness.

BIJI: Is he rich?

MOHAN: (This time MOHAN gives her an impatient look). But how do we know that this person is right for you when we don't know anything about him and you go get engaged to him.

RAHUL: I still don't get it. Why would you not have introduced him to us? To me?

BIJI: What is his name?

SILENCE (For 5 counts) Everyone is frozen.

RAHUL: Right sis, what's his name?

SHANTI: Yes, what's his name?

SONIA looks at each one, but has not yet opened her mouth to speak.

MOHAN: Well....

SONIA: JORDAN.

SHANTI: A Gora!! Oh my God!

BIJI: SONIA becomes Gora too?

(MOHAN is quiet and so is RAHUL for a moment. There is a stillness about him that is not comfortable)

RAHUL: (in a very quiet tone) JORDAN what?

SILENCE (For 3 counts)

SONIA: (quietly) JORDAN Anderson.

BIJI: The babies will have blue eyes?

RAHUL: (Deep intake of breath and then hissing) Not **the** JORDAN Anderson

SONIA nods.

RAHUL: (really mad) Goddammed bastard! Some friend! I going to kick his ass. (Turning on his heel to walk out).

SONIA: RAHUL, stop, try to understand…

RAHUL: What's there to understand..

SONIA: Wait, listen to me!

RAHUL: Just leave me alone. I can't deal with this right now. (Walks out)

SHANTI: Who is JORDAN? What's happening? MOHAN?

MOHAN: (very quietly) It's our Kallu neighbour, from Brampton.

SHANTI: (stunned) Oh my God! That Kallu boy! After all these years! He's back in our life. BLACK!!!! Oh God! What did I do to deserve this? What will I tell everyone?

SHANTI collapses. BIJI just stares. SONIA's standing still. MOHAN is beside SHANTI murmuring inaudibly in a soothing way.

FADE TO BLACK

INTERMISSION

ACT TWO

SCENE I

This consists of mini scenes. SONIA is the common factor. It's her and her interactions with the three most important men in her life. Her father, her brother and JORDAN. Nothing is rushed. The silences are there to say what's been left unsaid.

<u>Only **SONIA** is on stage</u>. A spot on SONIA. Rest of the stage is dark.

<u>Soliloquy</u>

Mom's taken to her bed with a mysterious ailment, Dad's not speaking with me and RAHUL (pause), he's been avoiding me. And BIJI is BIJI as usual. Well, well! What did you expect SONIA darling? It's not like they would have said, wow, SONIA, this is so exciting! JORDAN is just the guy for you.

He's tall, dark and handsome. Highly educated, a professional, doing extremely well for himself and to top it all he loves you so much. Perfect! You have our blessings, let's all dance at your wedding. Cheers!

FADE TO BLACK

SONIA and Dad

SONIA: We can't go on like this, Dad.

Dad: Like what, SONIA?

SONIA: Dad, you do know what I mean. Can we just sit and talk it over?

Dad: What's there to talk about? You have made your decision, so there is nothing left to say.

SONIA: Why are you being so dismissive? Why can we not have a rational, objective conversation? I thought as grownups we don't sulk about stuff, but sit down and talk.

Dad: Sulking!? You take my silence for sulking? Do you know what it is to be in pain? Do you know what it feels like to be shut out of your daughter's life when it matters the most?

SONIA: Dad, I feel a similar pain, a hurt that you of all the people are not supportive. Why, Dad? You have always credited me with making intelligent choices, so why is it so different now? What's wrong with JORDAN?

Dad: Nothing is wrong with him, SONIA. But you kept your relationship a secret. And that's what hurts. You have always been so open. When you were little, you came running to share your exciting discoveries. Even as a teenager, we have shared your highs and lows. And today…..(turns away)

SONIA: How could I say anything, until both of us were sure of our feelings.

Dad: But could you not have told us about it once you were sure? Did you have to just go and get engaged? You've shut us out, Sonia.

SONIA: And, Dad, tell me honestly. If I had come to you and told you about JORDAN, what would you have done? Would you have supported me?

Dad: Sonia, your safety, your future, your happiness, your success, that's what has always mattered.

SONIA: No circumlocutions, Dad! Would you have said he's smart, he's good and that's what's important?

Dad: Sonia, I…

SONIA: Would you have said he's educated, he's successful and that's what's important?

Dad: Listen, Sonia, I...

SONIA: Would you have said he loves my daughter, he makes happy and that's what's important?

Dad: Sonia, I...

SONIA: And not the colour of his skin!

SILENCE

SONIA: Tell, me Dad, would you?

Dad: I...I don't know, Sonia. I don't know...if only you had not shut us out...

Dad looks away in the distance. SONIA keeps looking at him.

SLOWLY FADE TO BLACK

SONIA and RAHUL

SONIA: Got ya! So this is where you've been hiding out. C'mon buddy, what's up? No, let me rephrase that, why are you avoiding me, huh?

RAHUL: I needed some time to understand all this. This is huge, sis! Huge!!

SONIA: Explain.

RAHUL is quiet for a moment.

SONIA: RAHUL?

RAHUL (turning around): How could you? I just can't get over it! How could you?

SONIA: Get engaged? Simple, boy puts ring on girl's finger.

RAHUL (unhappy and irritated): Don't be facetious, SONIA! Two things, how could you not tell me? That really bothers me. Whatever is going on in your life, I have always been a part of it, until now. I just can't get over that.

SONIA: And two?

RAHUL: My friend! Of all the people in the world, why would you go and get engaged to a friend of mine. Never mind the fact that he's black. You didn't even think how Mom and Dad would take this.

SONIA: So what are you saying, RAHUL? That's he's good enough to be your friend, but not good enough to be your sister's husband? You don't think that because each one of us knows the other so well, it would be easier to get along, maybe?

RAHUL: You're not going to get it, sis. Getting married to your friend's sister is against the code. That is a rotten thing to do, and I don't think I can forgive JORDAN for that. You're lucky I haven't kicked his ass yet.

SONIA: You're right. I am not going to get it because I'm thinking if you were to marry my best friend, I would find that wonderful. So why can't it be the same for you?

RAHUL: That's just the way it is! Call it a guy thing.

SONIA (slight pleading): But for my sake, RAHUL, will you not…..

RAHUL (pause): I don't know…

SONIA: Please, please try…

RAHUL: I am not promising anything, but I will try.

SONIA stands still staring at RAHUL. He does not look at her.

SONIA: Rahul…

RAHUL refuses to look at SONIA. She waits some more, sighs and exits.

SLOWLY FADE TO BLACK

<u>**SONIA and JORDAN**</u> on a park bench on Queen's Quay with the CN tower in the background (if possible to project the tower in the background with the sound of water)

JORDAN: What's up?

SONIA: Nothing.

JORDAN: Nothing? Why would you say 'nothing' when obviously it's 'something'

SONIA: There's always something or the other to deal with, ever since my family know of our engagement. So why would you even ask 'what's up'?

JORDAN: SONIA, this is as difficult for me as it is for you, so can we sit back, take a deep breath and see how best we can work things out.

SONIA: It's Dad. (Pause). Actually, it's all of them, (pause) except that my arguments with Dad leave me feeling terrible.

JORDAN: Why?

SONIA: Because what he's saying is so illogical. That's very unlike him. He agrees you are a great guy! But he goes on about how hurt he is that I did not tell him all about it way before getting engaged. (Pause) If he really thought you were a great guy, by now he should have got over not being told.

JORDAN: I think he is a dormant racist, SONIA.

SONIA: What?

JORDAN: Well, he thinks he's not a racist, but actually he is. It only gets activated when something like this happens in his own life.

SONIA: Then why can't he explain that to me?

JORDAN: And how logical is that? He's always thought that he is not racist, he knows you are proud of him because he is open-minded, but now that his daughter is marrying outside, his prejudices surface. Only how can he admit them to you now?

SONIA: Why not? He prides himself on being a straight shooter, so what's so different about this?

JORDAN: It's a guy thing. You will not understand.

SONIA: What's this guy thing? At home RAHUL is going on about it, and here you've begun to say the same thing.

JORDAN: We are different you know.

SONIA: I know that. Mom's been going on and on about how different we are.

JORDAN: That's not what I meant, but do go on. I would like to hear what your mother has to say. I am surprised that she's been talking about us. I thought she was sick and in bed and not meeting anyone.

SONIA: Not anymore. Whatever it was, it has disappeared very quickly. Now she's full of all the reasons why our marriage cannot work out.

JORDAN: She's dead on, Sonia. There are so many reasons why this marriage cannot work out.

SONIA: What! You can't be serious! Are you having cold feet now? Do you want to back out?

JORDAN: (amused) SONIA, jumping to conclusions?

SONIA: I can't think straight anymore, JORDAN. This is supposed to be the happiest time of my life, and all that's going on are sulks and arguments and reproaches. I can't take this anymore.

JORDAN: What did you expect, SONIA? Thought they would love me as you do? Stop and think for a moment. They have not seen me for a long time. They do not know what I do, or how my parents will welcome you. Even in the past your mother never did encourage my playing with Rahul. So don't you think this has shocked them out of their mind? You need to give them some time to take it all in.

SONIA: Your parents didn't need time. And I don't really agree with you. My parents may not know you well, but they know me. They need to have more faith in their daughter's ability and intelligence. I am not going to bring home some loser.

JORDAN: Yes but there are all these differences between us too.

SONIA: Nothing two rational people cannot resolve. I think they've had enough time. They are too busy worrying about what other people will say. And I don't know why that should matter more than my happiness.

JORDAN: I still think you need to give them more time. You're being impatient. Look at it from their perspective too, even if you don't agree with it.

SONIA: Whose side are you on? Instead of supporting me, you're busy putting up a defense for them.

JORDAN: Yours, sweetheart, I am on your side, (tongue-in cheek) but didn't you just say something about two rational beings, and resolving, and all that good stuff…

SONIA: You are unbelievably annoying at times.

JORDAN: And you are undeniably appealing at all times. (Pause) Come on, sweetheart, lighten up. It's all going to work out fine.

SONIA is not entirely convinced but the tension in her shoulders gently eases. She looks at JORDAN for a while then rests her head on his shoulder.

JORDAN is gentle, loving, caring.

SLOWLY FADE TO BLACK

SCENE II

Wedding shopping, Indian style.

First saris, then jewellery, then bags and shoes.

SONIA and SHANTI – BIJI too

SONIA hugs SHANTI.

SONIA: Oh, Mom, I'm so glad; you are happy about it now.

SHANTI: Now, now, SONIA, I won't go so far, but let's just say that we are reconciled.

BIJI: Happy is better. Reconciled sounds like recoiled.

SHANTI: A look towards BIJI. Then turns back to SONIA.

SONIA: OK, Mom. Whatever the word, you're smiling, and Dad's kind of come around too. Only RAHUL....I wish he would be a bit more supportive.

SHANTI: Give him some time, SONIA. He'll be fine.

SONIA: OK, Mom, but I don't know why you and Dad had to give me such a hard time. After all, you also chose your own husband.

SHANTI: How can you compare? You and JORDAN have nothing in common - different religion, different culture, different traditions, and he's....

SONIA: And he's black? Is it so terrible to be black? Are they not human? Don't forget Mom that Africa is the crucible of all humanity. The genome research project....

SHANTI: OK, SONIA, let's not go into genetics and all that.

BIJI: She doesn't want to talk about it because **she** probably has descended from the Persians and she has a touch of the Huns in her.

SONIA: Have you really, Mom. That's so cool!

SHANTI (with a smile ignores BIJI's statement): Never mind that, SONIA. What do you think of this saree, BIJI?

BIJI: Hmmmph (on being ignored) (then looks at the saree), it's beautiful! SONIA will look like a princess.

SONIA: (holding up a dark chocolate coloured kurta) Mom, what do you think of this kurta for JORDAN?

SHANTI: (sharply) Chocolate brown!!! Whatever are you thinking of SONIA? (Then with a smile in her voice, enunciating slowly) Well...if you want everyone to keep asking where's the groom, (then quickly) then that's perfect!!!!

SONIA (part exasperated, part amused): Mom! Stop it!

SHANTI: Maybe we should get him an ivory coloured kurta, to match his teeth.

BIJI: Ivory and chocolate brown. Vanilla and chocolate. Ice-cream anyone?

SONIA: Mom, BIJI, puhlease, that's enough!

SHANTI: OK, dahling.

Now jewellery

SONIA: Isn't this the most stunning set?

SHANTI: Ummm. It doesn't look expensive though.

SONIA: But I like it. What hypocrisy, Mom! Why does it have to look expensive?

SHANTI: What will people say? They will think that we didn't want to give you real jewellery because you're…..

SONIA:…marrying a Black guy? It just amazes me how everything keeps coming back to that. Can we not give this a rest?

SHANTI: You'd better get used to it. It's something you will have to deal with all your life. Just because we've come round does not mean the rest of the community is going to be that forgiving….

SONIA (explosively): Forgiving indeed! Just what crime have I committed, huh? Go on, tell me…

BIJI: Come on you two… look at this, it's so beautiful…

SONIA and SHANTI exclaim over it, and the difficult moment passes.

Now bags and shoes

SHANTI: Let's hurry it up. Hardly any days left and so much to do still

SONIA: (pointing to red, gold and silver footwear) All right, let's go with this, this and that.

BIJI: Take the other one also, it will match your turquoise dress.

SONIA: Sharp, BIJI, really sharp.

SHANTI: Girls, cut the cackle. I still have some more invites to do and check with the caterers one last time, and call the garland person....

SONIA: We get the picture, Mom. Let's go. (Rahul has entered and overhears SHANTI)

RAHUL: What, Mom! Still planning? What about my shoes?

SONIA (playfully): You're a guy, who cares what you wear

RAHUL: Now sis.....
SONIA runs off, RAHUL after her with SHANTI and BIJI following slowly carrying bags and boxes.

SHANTI: Typical. Leaving us to look after the shopping

BIJI: Never mind. SONIA is happy now.

FADE TO BLACK

SCENE III

Shehnai music playing softly. SONIA's parents are centre stage greeting their guests.

AUNT (comes up and says): Chalo ji. Enough gupshup. Let's have some dancing. (Claps her hands for change of music).

The music changes to a Bollywood/Bhangra number.

Choreographed dance follows.

Everyone joins in, SHANTI a little hesitatingly.

Dance music ends.

Everyone stops dancing and starts talking, except for AUNT who is upset that she can't keep dancing.

AUNT: Arey, DJ, bhai, kya kar rahey ho? (What are you doing?)

Just then, enter SONIA and JORDAN in their wedding finery, Hindu style. They go around shaking hands and doing namaste. Hugs and congratulations all around.

AUNT: (delighted to see Jordan in Indian clothes, makes a gesture to ward off evil and impulsively says) Wah! You look just like us now.

JORDAN smiles.

SHANTI smiles with a grimace.

SONIA (ignores it and says to her Aunt): He dances like us too! (turning to JORDAN) Come on darling, let's show them.

Music begins.

Choreographed Bollywood dance sequence with SONIA and JORDAN.

Everyone cheers.

JORDAN"S parents are present too. They are very well-dressed, but a bit awkward in this sea of South Asians. SHANTI ignores them, but MOHAN is very warm and welcoming.

Music softens down to wedding music.

Just then RAHUL approaches SHANTI with an Asian girl (Vietnamese, Korean, Japanese, etc. but not Chinese). She is a guest with whom he was dancing earlier. SHANTI had not paid much attention to her.

SHANTI turns to RAHUL, her face wreathed in smiles. Holds out her arms for a hug, but RAHUL introduces the Asian girl.

RAHUL: Mom, let me present Jen….your future …..(daughter-in-law)

SHANTI takes one goggle-eyed look at the pretty young girl, points to JEN and then to RAHUL registering that they are a couple then screams: 'Oh, no. Not Chinese' and collapses.

The End

To use this play or a part thereof, in any way, or in any medium requires the written permission of the playwright. Email ***jasminesawant@yahoo.com***

The Old Man
By Elizabeth Banfalvi

Over the crimson hills he comes
With head and shoulders bent
Weary from the long day's work
And spent from the worries
Of many a long year.
Each weary step an effort
Till at last the familiar path of home.
Home, where memories are kept still
As the years come and go.
Home, where no longer a loving voice welcomes
Or laughing voices ring.
Gone are all these but still their memories linger
Entwined in an old man's heart
And revived as thoughts go astray and tears begin.
Soon he shall meet them again
As he climbs the well-worn path to the Golden Gate
But now he is content with memories of old.
Ah, to sleep and to rest his weary bones
His eyelids slowly droop only to be awakened
By a small child tugging at his sleeve
And a lovely woman as he remembers her last.
He smiles as she beckons to him.
He rises, no longer weary but blest with a new life.
He walks to his beloved and together
They go to join the Lord.

Salma

By Chitra Ayyar

Salma woke up because the baby cried nonstop, shrill and demanding. Her mother picked him up and fed him some thin milk from a glass. The crying subsided gradually. Salma brushed her teeth with the *neem*[1] stick and asked her mother for some tea.

She found a slice of bread, mold growing on the fringes, but that didn't matter, she was used to it. Food was food, whatever grew on it. Taking the bread and the half glass of tea, she went outside, sat on the roadside and devoured it. This had to hold her till lunchtime. If her mother got paid, there would be something to eat then or else she had to find some food by herself.

"My Salma Rani, you really are my queen, that's why I like to call you Rani", her mother used to say when she was a little girl, cuddling her. Not anymore though, with the arrival of other children, her mother barely had time to talk to her, except to bark out orders. During the tedious babysitting forced on her, she liked pretending that this huge slum was her kingdom and in her perpetual hunger, the only thing she thought about was people bringing her good food to eat- *puri, tandoori murg, halwa*[2] and other delicacies which she had only heard from other people and got to eat very rarely.

They had moved to this hut with a tin roof just a year ago. Earlier, when her father was still around, they slept under a bridge in Parel[3].
Then something happened and her father did not come home. Some said he found a job in a construction site in another city, other times she was told he got something called TB and was in hospital, dying. Even her mother wasn't sure about his fate.

Salma did not know how old she was or when she was born. All she knew was that she was old enough to take care of her sisters

---

[1] *Neem: A tree with medicinal benefits. Puri: deep fried Indian bread tandoori murg: clay oven baked chicken*
[2] *halwa: rich Indian sweet sprinkled with cashew and almonds*
[3] *Parel: neighbourhood in central Mumbai*

Rehana, Parveen and the baby boy while her mother worked. She was about four and half feet tall, dark and scrawny. Her hair was rough and dry and itched a lot. She walked about with a pair of torn slippers, held together with safety pins. She was lucky to have that. Rehana walked about barefoot.

Her mother was a rag picker for some time, these days she was selling things in the local trains, cheap plastic things, combs and hair bands. She did not give up rag picking, because she sometimes found treasures, like the time she found a very nice girls bag which she gave to Salma. It was a beautiful cloth bag, shaped like a cut watermelon, with a zip. Another time, she had found a perfectly wearable red frock, which is what Salma usually wore these days.

"*Aye* Salma, see what I have", her best friend Saira came by, swinging something. It turned out to be a fancy pair of goggles, pink frame. It was so funny to see her wearing it- with her dark green skirt, yellow blouse and pink framed glasses, she looked a sight.

Salma thought she needed one too, handy against the glaring sun.

"Where did you get it?"

"Raza gave it to me"

Raza was a local boy, their friend who looked out for them. He was only a little taller than them, but was already working, selling handkerchiefs and odds and ends on trains. When hunger gnawed her, she would go in search of him, hoping he would get her something to eat, at least some tea.

"My name is Raza and you are Salma Rani, so I have to help you", he would say, pronouncing his name *Raja*. If he was in a good mood, it happened when sales were good and he got money from his *seth*[4].

---

[4] *seth: employer*

When sales were not so good, usually on weekends, he would snap "What, I am your father or what, pestering me for food? Go ask your mother"

And Salma would stay hungry. Lately, she had taken to begging for food. She was quite successful, especially in the evenings. When it was lamp lighting time in the evening, the cashiers in the tea shops and small hotels were kinder. The most usual food given to her was *pao*[5] or *batata wada*[6], but some festival days, sweets were distributed- *pedas, milk barfis*[7].

That's why she looked forward to festivals, even Hindu ones like *Diwali* and *Navratri*[8]. Because of the evening generosity, her dinner was sometimes taken care of. But nowadays, other children were encroaching on her territory. A store person will be generous only once.

"Go, go, just now I gave to a kid who came before you. If I keep giving like this, my *maalik*[9] will sack me.

"Please, please, I am so hungry, haven't eaten for days"

Depending on his mood, he would give her some leftovers or shoo her away. Sometimes, when many children were gathered around, he would just throw something in their direction. There would be a mad scramble and scuffle then. The children would fight, bite or hit each other to get the food. "I'll stop giving any food then, go and fight somewhere else." the cashier would scream. That would be bad for everyone, so they would go elsewhere and the fighting and snatching would begin again.

A few rare days were bumper days- she would get *pao* from one store, some *pakoras*[10] from another. She would bring them home

---

[5] *Pao: baked Indian bread*
[6] *batata wada: fried fritters with spicy potato filling*
[7] *Peda, milk burfis: types of Indian sweets made of thickened milk*
[8] *Diwali /Navratri: Hindu festivals*
[9] *Malik: male boss/owner*
[10] *Pakoras: deep fried fritters made of flour and onions*

and sit outside and eat hungrily. Dabbu, the scrawny stray dog would come wagging his tail at the smell of onion *pakoras*. They would sit side by side, munching, enjoying this brief moment of contentment.

But she wouldn't share this booty with Rehana.

"You go and ask shopkeepers yourself, they'll give you"

"But I don't know how to ask, show me how"

"Just do like this", she said, making a begging motion with her hands "and plead with them to give something to a poor hungry girl, not eaten for a long time"

"Why are you feeding the dog, but you won't give me?"

"Because he loves me, he wags his tail, see? And he can't beg, they would only kick him"

"I'll tell ma when she comes, that you are giving food to a street dog"

"You do that and I'll knock your head off when she's not looking"

She didn't have any feelings for Rehana, she was sure they were not real sisters, because she vaguely recalled there was a different man around the house when she was a baby.

One morning, Salma was kicking her legs about and screaming. The reason was her mother's objection to her new found addiction to ride the trains. Their slum was near the tracks, so she had taken to abandoning her post as babysitter and was caught going up and down local trains, aimlessly and needlessly, at the risk of falling off or worse, getting caught by ticket checker.

"What if the TC catches you, you'll go to jail"

"No, because I can see the TC from far and jump out in time. I have done it so many times"

"And who will be home with the baby?"

"Baby has grown. And let Rehana mind the baby now"

"Rehana is small and whiny, how can she take care?"

"No, if I can't go, you can't go either. I won't let you"

Salma liked the trains because she was excited by the sights and sounds of people in it- a kaleidoscope of people, scents of their perfumes mixed with their jasmine *gajras*[11], the nice clothes they wore and the things they talked. There were also the bhajan singers, the card players, the singing beggars, the *hijras*[12] who annoyed the ladies, it was a whole world unfolding in front of her wide, curious, innocent eyes.

She was struck by the unfairness of being deprived of all that and screamed even louder. A stinging slap from her mother stopped her in her tracks. She could see Rehana was pleased. It was a matter of pride now, she became more defiant.

"You can't stop me. I will go"

Her mother clutched her hand and shook her "Okay, I will give you to the beggars, let them cut off your hands and feet and have you begging on the trains day and night"

Raza happened to pass by then, along with his father, Amir uncle.

"Raza, Raza, save me from this witch"

"Did you call me a witch? Take this, and this" her mother rained blows and Salma was flailing away.

---

[11] *Gajra: string of flowers women wore*
[12] *hijras: eunuchs*

Some neighborhood women stood around to watch. But, they approved the beating. Life was hard enough without giving in to children's tantrums.

"Why are you hitting her?" Raza asked, taking a big risk of getting pummeled by this berserk woman.

"Up and down, up and down, she goes in the train. Doesn't do any housework, nothing."

"She deserves it, needs to be punished, the saucy girl, doesn't wear a scarf yet and grown so big now" said another woman.

Salma hated everyone that moment, her mother and Rehana the most. 'I will run away, far away', she resolved.

"Okay, okay, you go to work. I'll talk to her" said Amir uncle.

Her mother tried to show anger in her eyes, but they were just weary and sunken. She made her way outside, feet dragging, laden with her box of things to sell.

Raza removed a *samosa* from its wrapping and gave it to Salma. "You eat this"

Dabbu came running, wagging its tail. Amir uncle tried to shoo it away,

"Go, go, dirty creature", he glared at Salma with anger, thinking 'taking up with this dog, didn't her mother teach her anything?'

Unconcerned, Salma gave the *samosa*[13] covering to Dabbu and ate the potato filling hungrily and hurriedly. The fight had made her hungry.

"How old are you?" asked Amir uncle "I don't know"

"Can you count money and change and all?" asked Raza

---

[13] *Samosa: spicy potato filled pastry, a popular Indian snack*

Salma felt annoyed by this questioning, but she can't be angry with him, not when she was eating his *samosa*.

"Maybe I can. I know everything"

"So, if something is four rupees and the customer gave you ten rupees, how much change you have to give back?"

She counted on her fingers and said "Five"

"Stupid girl, learn some counting fast, then I can make you work selling *bindis*[14], my *seth* was looking for a girl"

Wasn't that nice! She loved looking at *bindis*, they came in so many colors and shapes, with stones and gold and silver powder, and they looked so pretty. But, she didn't wear them. What an irony- a Muslim girl selling things she can never wear.

"I can count, I will sell *bindis*" she nodded her head.

"If you go around making mistakes in the accounts, the *seth* will hand you over to the police saying you are a thief, remember that"

"No, I'll not make mistakes, I am ready to work now"

"And wear a better dress, wash your face daily, put oil on your hair and comb it. Even the ladies in second class will not buy things from a dirty girl"

She nodded her head, but she thought 'He is a fine one to talk. Thinks he is better than us, just because he sees some money'

Though, she would do anything to get out of here and be in the other world of trains.

"Ok, in three days, make sure you are cleaned up. I will test you once again. If you answer correctly, I'll take you to the *seth*"

---

[14] *Bindi: a dot or design worn by Hindu women in the center of the forehead*

"But he may hire somebody else by then", she knew all about competition from her begging experience.

"There are so many trains and so many people, they will find something for you to sell"

Amir uncle voiced his displeasure over all this "Raza, I don't think girls should be exposed to the cruel world outside, Salma should become a servant in somebody's house."

"Is that so? Then why is my mother going outside and selling things, she should be doing housework too", she resented all elders today, they were all the same.

"Haven't you learnt how to talk to elders? Impertinent girl! Now I know why your mother has so much problems with you, fighting and screaming all the time, we can hear you way over in our house", he spat and walked away.

Salma knew it was the usual adult talk, if they could not explain things, they trotted forth the speech on 'respect for elders'. She was fast losing respect for the 'respect for elders' speech.

Raza reprimanded her too "Now you have made my father angry, he will tell me not to talk to you anymore"

"Please Raza, you are the only one who can help me. I promise I'll hold my tongue, I'll be very polite to the ladies in the train, I'll learn counting, anything"

"Okay, we'll see. Get yourself cleaned up, you smell awful"

So, the first step was to get cleaned up. Salma and Saira went about looking for soap.
They would ask Farzana didi, who always looked neat and clean. "What, you think I will give my expensive soap to you riff raffs or what? I don't even share it with my sister. Run away," she shooed them out, her nose in the air.

It was time to try something else. They went to a nearby corner store and hung about, waiting. When the store person disappeared to a nearby bathroom, leaving the store in the hands of a small boy, Saira distracted him, while Salma took a bar of soap and slipped away, heart thumping. Later, they laughed deliriously at this caper.

Ah, how nice the soap smelled, of fresh blossoms, a whiff of jasmine and rose and fresh earth. Tomorrow, they would find out when water flowed in the common tap and then bathe in it, lathering soap over their bodies and hair. They went home excited.

That evening, Salma had no luck with her begging at restaurants, not even a stale *pao* she got. Her mother was asleep in the corner, exhausted. She found some stale, moldy *roti*[15] in the kitchen and stuffed it into her mouth, to silence her hunger pangs.

Today was a big day for Salma. She had scrubbed her face clean and wore a better dress, salvaged from another rag picking foray. She held a box of *bindis* for selling on the train. She had persuaded Saira to be with her, Saira's mother had still not allowed her to take a job. Later on, if her mother agreed, Saira would get a route of her own. Her own mother had not liked the idea, but Salma just didn't care anymore. Rehana was sulking because now the baby was in her care.

Salma and Saira walked out, carrying the precious box, a skip in their step, talking excitedly, their first steps into the adult world. They had to account for every strip of *bindi* given to them, if she had to keep the job. She was already planning what she'll do with the money earned today- a nice full meal, pick up some food for baby and Dabbu, nothing for Rehana and her mother.

---

[15] *Roti: Indian flat bread made of wheat flour*

She couldn't forgive them for her public humiliation that day, in front of everybody. If Raza had not intervened!

A whole day was spent going up and down on the train, as her mother would have said. But this was no aimless jaunt; she would get some crisp notes at the end of the day. Enough to keep her stomach happy. She found she liked this work, thrusting the box at the women on the train, helping them pick out good *bindis*. Saira was learning the business quickly too, soon they could form a pair and do the rounds together. She felt luck had finally started turning in her favor.

Once, she tried to get into first class ladies compartment, but was pulled back by Saira.

"No, no, if TC catches you, it'll be a big fine. And the ladies in first class will not buy anything from us"

"But they all wear *bindis*"

"They buy it from big shops, they won't like to be seen buying things from us, they think it's cheap stuff. They will insult us and ask us to get off rudely. Raza told me"

How come Raza never told me all this, Salma felt a moment's anger, which disappeared quickly when a woman in the second class bought three packets of *bindis* for ten rupees.

A few days later, Saira had a box of cheap earrings to sell. They loved the routine, setting off at eight in the morning, their faces shiny, eyes bright, a big smile of expectation on their faces. Going from Andheri to Bandra to Dadar and back, back and forth so many times, they lost count. In a month's time, they had learned some crucial business facts, not to get into first class, commuters in fast trains are not good sales prospects, how to spot a ticket checker from afar, who was interested in buying and who was just looking.

They felt they were on the way to becoming good sellers. They had seen it all, the singing group, college students with their trendy clothes, the harried working mother in a rush to get home, life long train friends who kept seats for each other, pregnant women vomiting, leaning precariously outside. On weekdays, they watched awestruck, as the *dabba wallas*[16] performed their relays with precision. This was a whole life time of experience, a feast for their senses, they had never felt so alive.

And the money was welcome too. Dabbu was better fed, he had put on some flesh on his bones. And so had she and the baby. She still begged occasionally, but only at festivals, for the kind of food that was still out of her reach, sweets and such like. The frantic snatching and grabbing days were behind her. Even her mother treated her better and Rehana feared her anger. But for some reason, her mother was getting more bent, thinner and was coughing all the time. She heard the word TB mentioned on and off among the other women, God knows what that was.

As the months rolled by, they were going greater distances. Many times, they rode till Churchgate and back, selling their wares. What a big city this was, and the rush of people, going here and there, like busy ants.

At train stations though, it looked like they turned into rats, scrambling to get in, for a place to sit, stand, get fresh air, get off, always scrambling, clawing, fighting. This panorama of raw life was much more complex and interesting than a megastar Bollywood film. She felt she had finally found her place in the world.

The day dawned bright and sunny, after five days of grey, depressing rain. Salma knew business would be brisk today, the sunshine will make people open up their minds and purses, discover a need for *bindis* and buy them. So will they buy ear rings! They set off as usual, planning to do the long route, Churchgate to Borivali.

---

[16] *Dabba walla: carriers of lunch containers from homes in suburbs to offices in business districts*

On the way, they passed Amir uncle. The girls tried to avoid him, he was always saying something nasty. Amir uncle beckoned them over.

"Are you off on your shameless work?"

'His son does the same thing, that's not shameless', thought Salma, but kept quiet, for Raza's sake.

"It will be better if you don't go on trains today, it is not good"

"Why not, today it's not even raining?"

"I don't have time to sit around explaining to disrespectful girls like you. It's not safe, that's all I can say"

He walked away. Saira asked "Should we go back now?"

"What, he's just trying to scare us, it's his usual talk"

"But what did he mean by not safe?"

"Who knows? Come, let's go. Today, I am sure we will earn more than fifty rupees"

Saira walked on, looking back over her shoulder repeatedly to see if anything was going on, but it all looked as usual. 'Maybe Amir uncle just said such things to frighten us'.

"Beautiful *bindis*, colorful *bindis*, for weddings and festivals", Salma said in a sing song voice. She had a fresh stock today and they were really dazzling, she had already selected her personal favorites. She had a new set with colored crystals on them and that would be a hit with buyers, she hoped.

By evening, their boxes were half empty. Their selling together had its advantages- a woman trying to find matching *bindis* and earrings for her new outfit could get both together. They knew that today's payout would be good, maybe they could spend the money buying something decent to wear from the market near the station.

"*Aye*, we'll sell till late today, business is good"

"No Salma, I am tired, I want to return the box, collect money, have good dinner and sleep"

"Let's do this, sell till seven, collect money and go to hotel to eat a *thali* dinner. Then home and sleep, come on, don't say no"

"No, no, I am tired. My feet are aching"

"Are you an old woman, my feet are aching!!" Salma mimicked her.

"I am going back to Santacruz. I am so tired that I cannot go over the bridge, am just going to jump trains"

In a few minutes, two trains running in opposite directions came on platforms one and two. They got into one train, moved quickly to the other side, Saira gave her box to Salma to hold while she jumped further onto the train going in the opposite direction.

Before Salma could jump over, the train started moving. So, here was Salma, holding two boxes, in a train, moving away from Saira. She got off at Jogeshwari and was walking along the platform towards the bridge.

"Hey *bindi* girl, hey you……." a group of young girls, wearing what appeared to be party
clothes, silk Indian wear, was calling out to her from first class. She didn't think twice, but just climbed in. Here was her theory being proved, ladies in first class did buy things from girls like her, and they had more money to spend. And here she was, holding boxes of *bindis* and earrings too. Why not sell both?

She extended the boxes towards the eager hands of the girls.

"Ooh, this one is nice"

"Look at the nice shape on this"

"Hey look, I found matching earrings for that dress of mine, perfect"

Salma noticed that some of the girls were showing the *bindis* and earrings to some boys in the adjoining gents' first class, probably their boyfriends, for approval.

They were grabbing stuff, Salma found it difficult to keep count of how much they were buying. But she knew that most people were honest about their purchases, they wouldn't cheat a poor girl out of a few measly rupees. Kandivli had come and gone and they were now approaching Borivli. She thought since she sold Saira's stuff, she should get a part of that commission too, after all, she didn't run home, saying her feet ached. She took risks getting into first class.

The final sales was sixty five rupees total and the girls were digging into their purses to get the money. Today her *seth* would be pleased. Maybe he would give them a bonus, a few extra rupees.

She was counting the money when the train lurched sideways and there was a loud bang, like an atom bomb firecracker set off during Diwali. Within seconds, the two adjacent first class compartments were torn apart, a bloodied mass of people thrown here and there. Cries of pain, anguish and fear were heard all around, along with the rumble of trains on other tracks. Some who had been thrown onto tracks were run over by trains speeding on those tracks.

Hours later, railway police and fire department walked along the tracks, clearing wreckage and looking for survivors. Years of rescue efforts had hardened them to all kinds of disaster, but even they were moved by the destruction caused by this act of hatred. They worked in silence, in honor of the dead and the dying, who would now find eternal peace. Peace that was probably denied them during their lifetime.

During their search, they found a box of colorful *bindis* and earrings, scattered over some of the bodies, a kaleidoscope of color, youth, beauty and all the things that made life worth living. Ah, these young girls and that little slum girl, who lay lifeless, their bodies mangled, they would have no need for them anymore.

Matters of the Heart

Rewind
by Rashmi Pluscec

I see it now. a crooked lane of pink dots
tentatively raising their heads on that dry
flesh. first a thin scratch, a question unto
itself. then a thick line, rich with colour.
finally: red joy, bubbling over in sheer
abandon! peace. at. last.

but where are the friends they said would
come with strong shoulders? where is the
knight in shining armour? for fuck's sake,
where is the home-sweet-home they keep
framing and hanging on walls galore?

People greater than I have stood undecided
at a fork in the road. People more insane than
I have let destiny pick a path as they dithered
at the start. I too waited nervously to see what
glorious wonders life has in store for me!

From the ashes of a murky past, a brand new
day had just risen in a brand new life. From a
world of options and in a world of decisions, I
took my first steps,

Putting Loving Sex Back Into Your Relationship!
by John Henderson

Every week another potentially loving couple arrives at my office, distraught over their dissatisfied sex life. Couples complain their relationship and sex life isn't what it used to be when they were first married. Between having children, juggling two careers, family and personal commitments, stress filled commutes and providing a taxi service to kids hockey, soccer games and music lessons – it's no wonder many couples find the spark has gone out of their love life.

Henderson's Four Warning Signs:

1. The first thing to disappear in a relationship seems to be loving communication. Complaints, frustration and criticism of one's partner increase as dissatisfaction grows. Communication becomes tense, critical, judgmental and tragically filled with sarcasm. Hostilities and disinterest often abound. Sadly, couples in this situation stop sending each other the loving affirmations, appreciations, and the caring compliments that keep the relationship wheels turning.

2. Next to decline is affection. It's hard to feel attractive and interested in someone if they are dumping on you. When unresolved anger increases, affection decreases. With fewer hugs and less hand holding also comes the loss of good feelings toward one's partner and even oneself!

3. One or both partners can become depressed at this point. Negative self-talk and blaming your partner (or self) closes the door on developing intimacy. Misperceptions, frustration and anger often erupt. In the worst cases, this can lead to explosive anger and even inappropriate aggression, hostility or violence.

4. Stalemate – In this stage, conflicted couples have often made numerous unsuccessful attempts to rekindle their intimacy, only to meet with rejection or failure. To protect themselves from even greater emotional hurt, couples "stale-mate" each

other – and wall themselves off from their partner. Stalemate, cold fish, stonewalling, and glazed over smoldering stares are all signs resentment has come home to roost. Each person is no longer able to initiate simple compliments or affection because the darts of rejection and rebuff have become too entrenched. Like a stale-mate in a chess game, no one makes a move, and this makes for very "stale" – mates!

Other factors in the breakdown of a couple's sex life include: alcoholism, drugs, affairs, Internet addictions, work-aholism, financial worries, stress, family problems and difficulty re-engaging sexual relations after the birth of a child. Complex issues such as touch aversion, loss of desire, male & female sexual problems (erectile difficulties, painful intercourse etc.), may require a referral to a doctor or Registered Sex Therapist.

While the following tips may seem simple, many couples find that to get them to work, they are best to see a Registered Marriage & Family Therapist or counsellor for detailed guidance.

Step 1: Increase and Improve Your Loving Communication: – Using your tongue to send loving words of appreciation to your partner is still the best 'oral' technique. A trained couple therapist can really help you restore positive communication to your relationship. Saying and doing loving things for each other is the basic first step to restoring intimacy. It can be something simple as bringing your partner a cup of tea/cold drink or writing them a 'missing you' or 'thinking about you' note and leaving in their appointment diary, briefcase or cell phone calendar. Don't take your partner for granted. Thank them and be specific saying: "Thanks honey, – I really appreciated your help getting the kids dressed today." The task is to consciously develop a list of 5 or more compliments and appreciations for your partner and communicate them to each other in genuine and loving ways. Couples often need professional assistance jumping over the hurdle of starting this task. A trained Registered Marriage & Family Therapist or counsellor is an inexpensive investment in your relationship future.

Step 2: Add Holding Hands & Hugs Slowly: Loving Touch is a basic human need. We need gentle loving touch and hugs that don't always lead to the bedroom, in order to feel safe and good again with our partner before a sex life can be rekindled. It's all about soothing and feeling safe with your partner. Ask your counsellor or Registered Marriage & Family Therapist for exercises to restore affectionate touch to your relationship.

Step 3: Can Antidepressants be added to the drinking water? Well not really, but talk to your family doctor about whether one of the newer antidepressants (SSRI – serotonin reuptake inhibitors) is appropriate for you in your situation. Getting regular exercise is one of the best ways to help you cope with changes in mood. Eating healthy, going for a walk 3 times a week, and getting a good night's sleep can help in regaining your emotional balance. Don't be afraid to talk to your therapist and family doctor about your moods and feelings. Unresolved anger often makes rekindling touch difficult. Be honest with yourself – it might just save your marriage.

Step 4: Consider seeing a Counsellor – If you're sleeping in separate beds, watching TV late at night to avoid going upstairs, or spending 5 minutes in a refrigerator feels warmer than spending 5 minutes in a room with your partner, you probably would benefit from seeing a OAMFT Clinical Fellow/Therapist or counsellor. I tell my clients that counselling is just like getting the oil changed regularly in your car – every relationship needs an emotional oil change from time to time.

Step 5: Go Out on a Date: Remember what it felt like to anticipate going out on a date? Be creative and invite your partner out on a date. Think of someplace they would like to go. Write them a note, call or text them on the phone and ask them if they would like to go out on a date and are available. (Prearrange babysitting). Keep it fun and easy going. Don't expect sex on the first date! Simply appreciate the opportunity to talk, listen, hold hands and enjoy being with each other. As you become more comfortable with your partner, pay attention to your body's signals of desire and arousal.

Remember that if you can't talk about sex in your relationship, it probably is a sign you are not ready to do it – and that applies to a lot more topics than just sex. Some couples have unrealistic expectations about how often sex should occur and think everyone is having more of it than they are. It doesn't matter if it's twice a week or twice a month, what matters more is that both partners are comfortable and content with the communication, quality, timing, frequency, emotional sensitivity, connection, trust, respect and affection they are able to share with one another. Enjoy and be content with what works for the two of you and build on your successes from there. Don't try for the sexual Olympics right away.

Remember sex is as much about enjoying being with each other as it is about having sex. It's about making love more than making sex. Remember the most powerful sex organ is the brain, and the largest is the human skin. Get reconnected there first, and a healthy sex life will follow.

Felt By the Heart
by Angela Ford

Constant tears streamed over her cheekbones like a river running dry. A sharp pain pierced her heart. It felt like her heart had been ripped from her entire being. There had been trials in her life but this was different. This one she could not describe. A part of her heart was missing, the part that could only be filled by the same person she cried for.

Faith Taylor's mind raced persistently around the thoughts of how she got to this point. Confused and desperate to understand how and why, only kept the tears flowing. The past couple of years had not been great. There were a lot of ups and downs in the family but life seemed to be normal. Well, as normal as life can be. It's not a perfect world. But the past year had knocked the breath out of her, crippled her with great sadness and emptiness.

It just seemed like yesterday there was laughter and enjoyable times together. There were so many special times. Special memories made that were felt by the heart. Faith had sacrificed everything; her career, her time, her love, and in the end her dignity was in jeopardy. The sacrifices she chose without regret and never looked back, for her treasures were all she wanted when placed before her. She gave her heart completely, without a thought. There was no other love that could match what she had been blessed with.

Faith always loved generously and protected her life's treasures. She refused to defend herself to the choices she made and the reasons why she made them. Her choices were made out of love and for their safety. If the past had just been left where it was, and he hadn't interfered; maybe now it would be different. It only created confusion and hurt but for the wrong person. There is right, and there is wrong; and two wrongs don't make a right. Yet, sometimes, doing the right thing ends up creating something wrong, very wrong. Never live with regret; no one can ever change the past. Faith knew she made choices and then had to live with them. Her safety and that of her treasures was most important; it was all she had left. He had taken everything from her but her priceless treasures.

It was time to regain her strength and rediscover who she really was. Blessed with support from those closest to her, they were the ones who held her hand, lent a shoulder to cry upon, and gave her back her strength to take care of those treasures. Nothing else mattered but them.

He did promise to make her life a living hell. What he didn't realize was that her life had been a living hell while she was with him. Since she left him, there was instant peace. It only got better with every day she stayed away from the abuse. The conflict continued, of course, it would linger for some time; basically the conflict was his anger relentlessly looking for attention. It was a game to him, one he had to win and over time it became apparent that it did not matter who was in the way or who would get hurt. Fogged with his own bitterness of losing, so he thought, he hurt the ones he should have loved and protected the most. She tried for years to protect them and have him direct his rage at her. She was not successful.

The reason to leave was made out of fear. It took forever to leave; he did not make it easy; for he knew the love she had for them always made her stay. The constant threats of playing her into believing she could go only ended up forcing her to leave. Now he could blame her for leaving and convince them to believe she was in the wrong. She only told them when they were young that sometimes two people do not get along, and that you should always treat people the way you want to be treated. It was best to keep it simple and not confuse, but reassure them that they were loved and that's all that matters. In today's society there are broken families everywhere, everyone adjusts. Then there are some people who want to try to make your life a living hell instead of living themselves. When they use the people they should love and protect the most, it just becomes sad. Yet, those hurt by these people are still so deserving of love.

Faith survived the past and wanted nothing more than to live with love, peace and serenity. Her mother had always told her to

Live Simply and Love Generously. There was an abundance of love in her life. There was instant peace when she left, and now she worked on her serenity. It was like the three went hand-in-hand; love, peace and serenity. *God grant me the serenity to accept the things I cannot change, the courage to change the things I can, and the wisdom to know the difference.* She had left the past where it must stay, accepted it without regret, and had the courage to save herself and live; for them. There had been so many bumps in the road along the way but she felt like she had made it through the worst of the storm. Confident to live, to love, to laugh, to hurt; it was all part of living.

The unbearable pain she experienced now was part of living; it was hurt. For one to love there is the possibility that one will hurt. It's been said that time heals everything. She will hurt. She will survive. She will continue to live and love and laugh. One day, she hopes that the tears she cries now will one day be laughter again.

Faith watched the day come to an end. The ocean before her appeared as a sparkling sapphire kissed by sunlight. Soon it would become a sea of darkness. No matter how many times she had seen a sunset, every time mesmerized her. The golden rays of the sun stretched across the ocean and slowly disappeared beyond the edge. A deep breath and then a peaceful smile formed upon her face. Completely relaxed by this simplicity and a touch of comfort for her saddened heart, she raised her wine glass to the incredible view before her.

Her love of the ocean gave her the peace she so desired. She had been through so much over the years. Her heart was pure and real. She loved deeply and the hurt ran just as deep. She released a sigh but uneasiness still lingered deep within her soul. Her thoughts travelled around the love she carried in her heart for her treasures, her children.

Faith survived more than her fair share of heartache. Her warm smile and the genuine love that showed in her eyes made many wonder how strong one woman can be. After times and trials, heartaches and hardships; it is difficult to open your heart to trust another soul. Though she did; she opened her heart to a man who came into her life unexpectedly. It took a few years, but she did eventually open her heart completely to him. He was gentle and comforting to her pain as the dams opened up and her heart poured out. He reassured her that he was there for her and understood.

She believed it was forever. Forever did not happen. He hurt her deeply when he told her he regretted their time together and referred to it as "wasted time". She left with whatever dignity she had left. He told others he was *clued out* as to why she left. Truth was not a part of his morals and values, if he had any. In the end, he had chosen the bottle and his selfish ways over her, their family, and the home they both had so desired at one time. Leaving him gave her peace. In time, her heart would heal.

But it was not him that her tears had been for, or the man before him. The tears were for her daughter. Her treasure, her gift; it was her she needed to be there for. Not herself. Not her lost love. But for her Brooke; the one she shed so many tears for. There had been so much suffering. Now it was time for all to heal, her son Tyler as well. He too, had suffered from those who were not there for him as they should have been. Memories were held close to the heart. Time together was now the best gift. Better communication; one with trust.

The past had crept up upon them all, separately and had hurt them individually in different ways. Matters of the heart were hard enough for Faith to deal with; yet, for Brooke, only life experience will teach her about matters of the heart. Broken promises, broken families, broken hearts and for a young adolescent; broken fantasies of relationships that never formed, ones that broke along the way, and ones that had only existed in one's fantasy on how it should be. What matters the most is the unconditional love and bond between mother and child. There is comfort in knowing and feeling a love so strong, and when it breaks, even for a little while; the heart suffers and nothing else matters. It is now a time to live, to love, and to laugh. Memories are being made; the kind that will always be held dear to the heart; the kind that means *forever* can never be broken. Simply put, it is the love between mother and child.

Turn Back The Clock

This short story is dedicated to Georgette Heyer, P. G. Wodehouse and Jane Austen, the three brightest stars in my life.

by Samna Ghani

I had a feeling something was buzzing nearby. Bzzzzzzz. Bzzzzzzz. It was my cell phone - probably Max calling me. I groaned and opened one eye. The first thing I saw was 8:25. 8:25! Oh shit, I am going to be late for work. Rushing into the bathroom, I managed to get dressed in record time. As I ran down the stairs, I could hear Mum humming in the kitchen.

Ok, back up! Mum and I had a little tiff last night. Oh, you know, the usual. How long will you continue living with Max? When are you getting married? When are you getting pregnant - yada yada yada… Yeah my Mum is a modern-day Mrs. Bennett [1].… long story short, I do not want to restart that discussion. So, I had to figure out my exit strategy.

Considering the fact that there was only one exit door, my options seemed quite limited. Ideally speaking, Harry Potter's Invisibility Cloak would be really useful right now. Yes, I am 28 years old and talking about Harry Potter [2]. Get used to it!

"Catharine, are you up?" Mum called out. Busted!

"Yes Mum but I'm really late. I've got to get going!" I said, running downstairs quickly and gulping down a glass of orange juice.

"But I thought we could talk," she began but I was out the door.

"Later Mum," I said and I was home-free!

---

[1] The character of Mrs. Bennett was originally created by Jane Austen in "Pride and Prejudice".
[2] The character of Harry Potter was originally created by J.K. Rowling in the Harry Potter series of books.

Jeez, it was raining. This day couldn't get any better now, could it? Flipping my umbrella open, I ran toward the bus stop. If I missed the bus, I would miss my train and if I miss my train, I am going to be late for work. That is not going to be pleasant. Since Eleanor would look down at me with those menacing eyes making me feel like some kind of fool.

Eleanor, yes my boss. I am one of her slaves in the Creative Writing Department at Vintage Digital. She's one of those bitches who can never be satisfied, no matter how hard one tried. Nothing is good enough for Ms. Eleanor Cromwell.

Mum was right. My life was a big mess. I was living with a man I did not love. I mean I did love him but I didn't *love* him. Yes, I know. It sounds crazy. But the thing is, nobody has ever really clicked for me. You know, that "click"? When everything around you stops and you can't hear anything, see anything, feel anything but him? No? You don't know the feeling. Neither do I and till I do, I am not marrying anybody! Plus, I was working in an organization where I felt my creativity was always being stifled.

Lost in my thoughts, with the rain pouring like cats and dogs, I didn't even realize that a guy was running past me. Within seconds, he had snatched my purse and was fleeing off with it.

"Hey! Stop! Help! Thief!!!!" I called out, looking around but no one seemed to care. Jeez that's why I wanted to beam back to the 18th century. Chivalry was completely dead today! Where is Doctor Who[3] when you need him anyway??? Well, since I didn't have any decent male specimen willing to help out a damsel in distress, I had no choice but to chase that moron myself.

"Stop you asshole!" I saw him turning into an alley and was right behind him but when I got there, he had just disappeared. Poof! Just like that. What the hell??? Panting like crazy, I struggled to catch my breath. Suddenly, I saw a whirl of green

---

[3] Doctor Who is a British science-fiction television program produced by the BBC.

clouds. It seemed like something out of Once Upon a Time[4]. I thought I would see The Evil Queen walking out of that mist. Suddenly with a thud, a blue British Police Box landed on the pavement.

I was blown away. I mean, are you serious??? Does wishing for Doctor Who actually make him appear? Suddenly, the door opened and out walked a tall, skinny guy in a black suit and bowtie. Kind of cute, I must admit, except for the nose.

"Who the hell are you?" I cried out.

"Oh hello, I'm the Doctor!" he said, in a very sexy accent.

"As in Doctor Who?" I must be dreaming.

"Yes yes, now come along, I don't have much time!" he said, looking all around as if twenty spaceships were flying around us.

"How can you not have time? You're a Time Lord aren't you?" I questioned him.

"Yes, well, it's complicated. Now are you just going to stand there and yap all day or are you coming along?" he said, irritatingly.

Not exactly as charming as David Tennant[5] was, this one. Nor did Tennant's mantra "the laws of time are mine! And they will obey me" apply to this one apparently.

I shrugged. Whatever! Only an idiot would decline a ride in Doctor Who's time traveling spaceship and I for one was not that big an idiot. So I ran toward him and as soon as we were inside, TARDIS[6] started to twist and whirl. Within minutes, it landed

---

[4] Once Upon a Time is an American Fairy Tale drama series aired on ABC.
[5] David Tennant is a Scottish actor who played the tenth incarnation of Doctor Who.
[6] TARDIS (Time and Relative Dimension in Space) is a time machine and spacecraft used by Doctor Who.

again with a thud.

"Well go on. Get out. You earthlings really are sluggish!" he said, handing over my purse to me. When did he recover this????

"What? Where are you leaving me? What am I supposed to do?" I asked in desperation.

"Well, do what I do woman. Hold tight and pretend it's a plan!" he declared and with that he opened the door of the box and pushed me out.

As I steadied myself, the green cloud had appeared again and poof... he was gone. Just like that thief. Well, I guess if earthlings in the 20th century had forgotten chivalry, so had this time traveling humanoid alien! Leaving a woman in the middle of nowhere with no advice but to pretend that she has a plan! Awesome! Remind me NEVER to watch another episode of Doctor Who again when I get back home!

Focusing on the present, I realized two things. For one, it had stopped raining and second, I was standing in a very big and beautiful garden. There were beautiful roses and a very pretty and serene lake. Wow! Very nice. At a distance, I could see .. well,.. it looked like a castle, I suppose, or a huge house.

Suddenly, a girl rushed out of one of the bushes, sobbing and shaking her head. The fact that she was wearing a hobble skirt did not make it easy for her to run and she crashed right into me.

"Calm down lady. What's going on?" I asked, steadying her.

"I am mortified. Simply mortified! I made a declaration of love and he told me he was busy studying newts. Oh, I feel so humiliated. So ashamed! Mother would be so disappointed with me," she said, sobbing uncontrollably.

Wait! Newts. Rose Garden. Castle. No. It couldn't be. I couldn't possibly be standing at Blandings Castle! I surveyed my surroundings again. Yep. This was it- Lord Emsworth's beautiful rose garden. And this girl, who was she? Was she talking about

Gussy Fink Nottle? Oh my God, as Bertie would say, she was in love with that newt-nuzzling blister![7] Eww!

Information overload people, information overload! If this is a dream, I'd better wake up soon.

"Why are you dressed like that?" the girl asked meekly.

It was at this moment that I realized what a sight I must be. I mean, hey, I was very nicely dressed but in this time... whatever this time was... I probably looked like some kind of hooker. I was wearing a knee length black skirt with a white silk top with a plunging neckline. What can I say guys? I work for an advertising agency. I can't very well go around wearing a hobble skirt, now could I? Jeez, give me a break! It didn't help though that my clothes were also quite wet since in this entire running after the thief and boarding the TARDIS episode, I had somehow misplaced my umbrella.

"Er.. well,... my clothes... they got dirty while I was traveling. I met a lady on the way and this is all she had," God, what a singularly idiotic story. She seemed to buy it though.

"Oh you poor girl. Come with me. You cannot go around town like this. People would take you for a commoner!" she said.

Commoner. That's what I was but hey, who was I to argue. I was told to pretend I had a plan and getting dressed like an Austen heroine seemed just fine to me. In fact, nothing could be better! I grinned like a little school girl and she giggled with excitement as she dragged me toward the castle.

Blandings Castle was a magnificent and stately home with a beautiful rose garden, a lake and God knows how many rooms. Charlotte, yes that was her name, took me upstairs to her room. Weird. I don't remember a Charlotte from the Wodehouse Blandings Castle series of books but then who the hell was I to

---

[7] Lord Emsworth, Gussy Fink Nottle, Bertie Wooster are characters originally created by P.G.Wodehouse. Blandings Castle is also the original creation of P.G. Wodehouse.

object? The Literary Police? If she wanted to be here, she bloody well had the right to be, I thought as we entered a huge bedchamber. Oh my God. The Victorian bed, it was something out of a Savoir catalogue. Her room had those French windows that opened onto a huge balcony overlooking the lake. Amazing!

But what was even more amazing was her walk-in-closet. This dream was suddenly looking much better. Day dresses, ball gowns, hats, shawls, gloves, fans, purses, you name it and she had it.

"The dinner gong will ring at 6. You should dress up," she said as she fished around in her wardrobe. "This blue gown will look perfect on you," handing me a spectacular blue chiffon dress with a full skirt. It had a beaded bodice with matching silk gloves and a pretty little bonnet. Wow, If Mum saw me in this, she would faint!

"You want me to wear this?" I asked incredulously.

"You don't like it? Here, I have another one which is even better."

"No no, I love it! I just wanted to make sure you were comfortable with me borrowing your clothes," I said.

"Of course, and you're not borrowing it. Please, you can keep it," said Charlotte.

I was as excited as a girl attending her first prom.

"You must hurry up and get dressed. Lord Emsworth hates it if we are late for dinner," and with that Charlotte directed me toward the bathroom.

I gulped. I am going to have dinner with Lord Emsworth. I splashed water on my face. Come on Catharine, if this is a dream, it better end now. Splash! Splash! Splash. Nothing. I was still there.

I took off my ridiculous clothes. Yes compared to this glamorous dress, my clothes looked utterly ridiculous. As I put on the dress, I felt like Cinderella. Jeez, I was looking good! But my hair! Oh God, my hair. Shampooing and blow-drying may work in the 20th century but it was definitely not the norm in this part of the world.... I mean in this time-space.... I mean... oh hell, I don't know what I mean. You get it anyway, don't you?

So, what should I do about my hair? I looked around and found some ribbons. I tried to copy Charlotte's style and made a high knot at the back tying a blue ribbon around it. Then using a comb, I curled up the front layers of my hair dropping them like ringlets over my forehead and some over the neck. I must say, I looked quite nice.

I had already noticed that Charlotte wasn't wearing any make-up and still looked really pretty. But for me, I was so pale I had to put on some color on my lips. I decided my light brown shade would work just fine and would not be considered vulgar. Turning around to take it out of my purse, I froze. Holy shit! My purse! Where the hell was my purse? I realized that when Charlotte had crashed into me, the purse must have fallen down and in my excitement to dress up, I had forgotten all about it. Talk about stupidity!

I had to go back to the spot where Doctor Who had left me and get back my purse. All my stuff,. driver's license, my credit cards, my debit cards, was in it. I couldn't just leave it all lying around. If somebody from this era found it, they would freak out! Besides, I had photographs of Mum and Max and also my cell phone. It was settled then. I had to go get the purse back.

I opened the door and walked out.

"You look beautiful," Charlotte exclaimed.

Beautiful sheutiful whatever. I had more important things to deal with right now. But since she had been so nice to me, I had to approach it with caution.

"I was wondering. You have such a beautiful garden. Would it be ok if I went for a short walk before dinner? I just love roses," I gushed. Yeah sure, I didn't give a fig about roses but hey, whatever works.

"Of course, I would love to go with you but I have to change. My maid should be here soon," she said, appearing quite distressed.

"Oh, it's perfectly alright. I will be back in a jiffy," and without another word, rushed out of the room. Climbing down the magnificent staircase, I realized that if I had been here under different circumstances, I would be on top of the world but too much was happening all at once. And none of it was making any sense!

"May I be of assistance, Madam?" I heard a voice. I turned around and saw a man with slicked back hair wearing a black suit with a bowtie.

"Oh hello Jeeves[8], "No, I doubt even you could figure this one out," I chuckled and then I realized I had just called this stranger, Jeeves.

"I believe you have the advantage over me, madam?" Oh God, it was Jeeves. Now all I need was Aunt Agatha[9] and this Wodehouse dream would be complete!

"Er... well.... Charlotte... she mentioned you," but even as I said it, I knew Jeeves wasn't going to buy it. Now if it had been Bertie, that would have been another story altogether. I had to get out of there but I didn't want Jeeves to start snooping around so I decided to use another approach.

"She is devastated you know," I started.

"I don't quite follow you, Madam," and he was now on red-alert. Shit, this wasn't going so well.

---

[8] The character of Jeeves was originally created by P.G. Wodehouse.
[9] The character of Aunt Agatha was originally created by P.G. Wodehouse

"Well, you know, don't you? About Gussie and Charlotte?" Surely, he knows. Jeeves always knows everything.

"I am agog to learn, madam," he said, dryly.

I looked around conspiringly and then slowly whispered in his ear. "You see, Jeeves, Charlotte is in love with Gussie but....we all know how Gussie is right? Women don't stand a chance against those newts of his,"

Jeeves was thoughtful for a moment. "A most illuminating story, madam. You will pardon my asking how you came about this vital piece of information?"

"Well Charlotte of course. She told me!" Duh. Seriously?

"Indeed," said Jeeves. Ok whatever. He's not buying it. I had no more time to waste. He could snoop all he wanted. In fact, maybe he'd be able to tell me what the hell was going on in my life!

I ran back to where TARDIS had dropped me off (yeah I know it sounds really cool – I hitched a ride with Doctor Who ....wohooo!) but this was no time for jokes. And sure enough I saw it lying there, safe and secure. Phew. I grabbed the strap but wait! It jumped – the purse jumped nearly two feet ahead of me. No, I am not making this up! And NO, I don't need a shrink! Will you shut-up already? I am telling you it jumped! I tried to grab it again and this time the purse dragged me with itself into that bloody green smoke (yes it was there again!) and within seconds I was whirling around like Dorothy[10] and slam, I was on a dusty road.

Where the hell was I now? Seriously man, this dream had now officially become a nightmare! Suddenly, I heard the sound of horses and to my horror, a carriage or curricle or whatever the

---

[10] The character of Dorothy Gale is from the Oz novels and was originally created by L. Frank Baum

hell they call them, was being driven at a frightening pace right at me. Ok, this is it. Sayonara people. I am mince-meat! But with a screeching halt, it stopped. I was still alive and in one piece. Holy shit!

"My dear girl, if you really want to obliterate your existence, you could choose an alternative option. Arsenic, for example? Or maybe drowning? Committing suicide in the middle of the road would be extremely tiresome for others," a voice said.

Are you kidding me? The nerve of this guy, whoever the hell he was.

"Obliterate my existence! Did you notice the speed at which you were driving this thing! Who do you think you are? Lord Worth?[11]" I screamed through the window of that awful carriage.

"Your attire indicates that you are a lady of quality but your insolence and words you utter contradict the very notion," that damning voice continued. Jeez, English please!

I was about to respond with an equally acidic comment but I stopped as I saw a gentleman walking toward me.

"You mentioned a Lord Worth I gather? I'm afraid I am not acquainted with the gentleman. Pray, enlighten me with his whereabouts?" he asked, his eyes now very much penetrating mine.

I stared at him. Holy shit! Stop the presses! Click. I mean, click, click, click. This was it. This, for the love of God was it! His eyes! I couldn't look away from those eyes. Brown? No, coffee brown. But they twinkled. They actually twinkled. He had beautiful black hair, slightly dishevelled giving him an "oh so sexy" look. He was wearing one of those long flowing coats with several layers – what does Heyer call them? Caped greatcoats? Yes, that. His vest had gold buttons, beautifully engraved and his

---

[11] The character of Lord Worth was originally created by Georgette Heyer in her book "The Regency Buck."

pants, well.. let's just say they fit him quite well.

Come to think of it, people in this century wore too many layers. Must be a real pain taking them off when having sex. Shit, did I just say that out loud? No. Oh, thank heavens. Why was I suddenly thinking about sex anyway? On second thought, don't bother answering that!

My heart was now beating at a rampant pace. No, I didn't just read that in a romance novel. It really was! And my pulse was racing like crazy. And all that talk about women panting when they meet the man of their dreams? Not true. I felt I had stopped breathing altogether.

"Well? You would observe I have yet to receive a response from you?" he insisted.

Ok, hot dude. Hold your horses. Let me get my heart to stop pounding and my pulse to …what.. stop pulsating? Whatever! It's called regaining one's composure. Ever heard of it?

This was the time to think, Catharine. Think. Think Georgette Heyer. Think Regency Buck. The fact that you've read the book a thousand times should surely prove useful at this moment. What do you remember about Lord Worth? Come on you dimwit! Make up a story!

"Lord Worth is my guardian. I am Ms. Johnson," wishing for the first time in my life that my last name was a little more … extraordinary. Johnson? I mean come on!

The gentleman continued to stare at me with those twinkling eyes. He had a slight smile on his face.

Suddenly, he bowed. "Enchanted, I'm sure," he declared.

Huh? What does that mean? Are you enchanted? Are you sure you're enchanted? Or are you saying I'm enchanted? What? Jeez, people in this century not only dress funny but they talk funny. And what the hell am I expected to do? Curtsy? Do ladies curtsy to every gentleman or just the King and Queen? I really need to brush up on my history when I get home.

"Is he accompanying you on this ...er... journey?" he asked, glancing around as if expecting a carriage or two to materialize out of thin air.

"Um... no. I'm actually going to visit him," I improvised.

"And where may I ask is your chaperone?" he inquired.

Jeez, enough with the questions already! I am 28 years old. I don't need a bloody chaperone.

"Chaperone?" I repeated, like an individual with a zero IQ.

"Yes, a chaperone. You know, a lady of genteel background who accompanies a young lady when she is out of the protection of her home." His eyes were now examining my lips. I blushed. Did I just blush? I didn't even know I could blush! Why is he looking at my mouth anyway? God, I want to kiss him.

"I hope it is not too presumptuous of me to assume you are unmarried?" he continued while I continued to gawk at him like a total bimbo. "Since you mentioned that this...*Lord Worth* is ...er... your guardian?" His tone indicated he didn't believe my story but hey, what did I have to lose? He was either going to dismiss it, get into his carriage and drive on or I could play along with this charade and see if I could manage to keep him by my side for a few more hours... or days.. or years... or maybe forever.

"She's not here," was all I could come up with. Yeah I know. Lame, really lame but my friends, I had just fallen in love. Give me some time to recover, will you?

"Good Lord. Are you suggesting that you have been traveling all the way to London without a carriage, without a chaperone and without any luggage except for this ...this hideous reticule?" he demanded, his eyes now glaring into mine with shock and disgust.

Hideous reticule? Oh my purse. Are you kidding me? I paid an arm and leg at Harrods for this purse. Hideous, my ass!

"My purse is not hideous. You really don't know how to talk to a woman, do you?" I cried out.

"Please do not address me in such vulgar overtones. It does not become you at all," and now his eyes were flipping from my eyes to my mouth and back to my eyes again. Lord, he was sexy.

Vulgar huh? I cannot possibly let the man of my dreams think I am vulgar. Catharine, this is really the time to utilize all those Heyers' and Austens' you've been reading all your life. Seriously!

"I apologize sir." I said quickly. "I've been through a terrible ordeal. You see... um... I had a chaperone ... and a carriage... and my luggage.. but then ... um... a band of smugglers.. yes... a band of smugglers attacked us. They stole my luggage ... and my chaperone... er... she ran away.... She was scared." Oh dear God, bless Georgette Heyer. That actually sounds plausible. Doesn't it?

This sexy chap... I didn't even know his name..... looked at me thoughtfully. My heart started to race again. Get a grip Catharine! It's not like you're a sixteen year old virgin. What the hell is the matter with you?! Breathe. Breathe.

"It breaks my heart to hear about your... *terrible ordeal*. I'm afraid there is no other option but to take you to my sister." he suddenly said.

Sister? Excuse me? I don't want to go to your sister. Take me to your place. Hell, take me to your bedroom. But sister??? God, these people were beyond boring.

"No, I best be on my way," and I started walking on but he grabbed me by my arm and pulled me close. Oh lord, don't do that. His scent was intoxicating and he was standing so close to me, I thought I would faint.

His lips were now dangerously close to mine. "If you have some sort of a hubble nubble notion that I would allow you to travel all alone in the middle of London like some brass-faced hussy, you will be so good as to think again," he said in an extremely menacing tone of voice.

Hussy? Did he just call me a hussy!? Oh of all the insufferable and arrogant individuals to click for me!

"Have I made myself clear?" he asked, raising his brows. Sheesh, this guy has seriously walked out of the pages of a Georgette Heyer book.

I nodded. Yeah I know. You see, my IQ had taken a hike as soon as I laid eyes on this man. That's all I am going to say in my defence.

He guided me into the carriage and then sat down opposite me. I decided to remain quiet throughout the journey. No point in upsetting this dude. He was way too serious. Besides, I had to figure out what I was going to do next. Who was this sister he was taking me to? What would I be expected to do there? And to top it all, why the hell was I going along on this joyride with him? What if he was some axe murderer or something? I didn't even know his first name, for God's sake!

"My name is Alexander. Alexander Seymour," he suddenly said, as if reading my mind.

Nice. Alexander, had a nice ring to it. I could live with that. I gave him a smile. I knew there was no way I could be one of those *fluttering your eyelashes type* but I have been told I had a terrific smile.

He seemed kind of amused at my response. Oh alright, maybe my smile is not all that mind-blowing but hey it was worth a shot.

"Tell me, this …. *invisible chaperone* of yours…. aren't you the least bit concerned about what might have happened to her? After all, your …. *band of smugglers* could have done anything to her by now,"

Ok, I might be dense but I could clearly see he didn't buy a word of my story and yet, here he was taking me to his sister. Or was he? What if he planned to abduct me or something? Surely he was too cute to be a criminal right? A little reassurance please!!!!!

"Where are you taking me?" I asked.

"To Lady Cavanaugh. My sister. I do remember stating that before," he said calmly.

"And I am just supposed to take your word for it? What if you kidnap me and lock me in some tower or something?"

"I would be eternally grateful if you would refrain from addressing me in this detestable manner in the future," he snarled.

Enough already, I am not going to sit here and take any more derogatory comments from this Lord and Master!

"You are in no position to tell me to do anything," I replied with as much courage as I could muster.

He looked at me and continued to do so for what seemed like an eternity. His gaze was causing havoc in my brain and my body was feeling all tingly.

"You really are altogether quite refreshing," he said, finally.

Refreshing? Is that a compliment? He was making me sound like some detergent but what the heck, I'll take it. I had the elegance to blush. In fact, I'm really glad I can blush. Not that Max or anybody else before him has made me feel like this and Alexander wasn't even making an effort to charm me. Which I guess made him more charming.

I was totally unaware that the carriage had stopped. I was busy admiring this altogether refreshing male specimen. Who knew how long I had? That poof of green cloud better stay the hell away from me till I have at least managed to get a kiss from this gentleman.

Lady Cavanaugh's mansion... (yes, mansion)... was breathtaking. We were shown into the parlour where the butler informed us that her ladyship will be in shortly and walked away. I was alone in this big room, with this intensely sexy guy, and somehow the space seemed too cramped. My heart started to race again.

"Make yourself comfortable Miss Johnson," he drawled as he poured himself a drink. "May I offer you some refreshment?"

My throat was completely dry, so I asked for some water. He rang some kind of bell and in an instant, the butler appeared. "Water for my lady, Alfred," he commanded. "At once, my lord," said Alfred and was out in an instant.

Suddenly I heard some hustle and bustle and Lady Cavanaugh entered with much panache! "Alex, my darling brother. To what do I owe this surprise visit?" she gushed.

I stared. Yeah man, I stared. She was one of the handsomest women I have ever set my eyes on. Her resemblance to Alexander was unmistakable but her entire demeanor was quite marvelous. And her clothes! Wow! It seemed as if she was wearing diamonds, the way her long, flowing gown sparkled. Did she dress like this all the time? God, these women had too much time on their hands!

"Julianna," Alexander said as he kissed her on both cheeks. "I am very much in need of your services."

Lady Cavanaugh had now finally caught sight of me. And the way she looked at me, I wished she hadn't. She appraised me from top to toe and it suddenly dawned on me how Elizabeth must have felt when those Bingley sisters had looked down upon her muddy gown.[12]

"Alexander, pray tell me this is not one of your......," she left her sentence hanging as she glared at her brother.

"Julianna, before you make a fool of both us, please permit me to explain the circumstances in which Lord Worth's ward has had to be brought to your doorstep," he snapped.

"Lord Worth? I have never been introduced to any Lord Worth,"

Sheesh. Not very hospitable, this *Lady Cavanaugh*. Besides, these people placed way too much importance on acquaintances and introductions. If somebody came to my house with nowhere to go, the last thing I would want to know would be where they came from or what their family background was. I would ask them if they were hungry! Which I was - famished, actually.

"This is really too much trouble for both of you. If you would be so kind as to drop me off at the nearest train station, I would be out of your hair in an instant." I got up to leave.

"You will do no such thing Miss Johnson. Julianna, what the deuce is the matter with you? Do you really think I would bring some lady of low-birth to your abode?" Alexander was now very angry.

"Oh pray, Alexander, do not be cross with me. I didn't mean to imply.. I mean, any friend of yours is welcome in my home," she said with much effort. It was altogether too insulting and I had had up to my ears of this royalty crap! I ran out of this house and into the garden.

What the hell was this? Why was I being made to suffer in this intolerable manner? Shit, was I talking like these people? Alexander was suddenly right behind me.

---

[12] The characters of Elizabeth Bennett and the Bingley sisters was originally created by Jane Austen in her book "Pride and Prejudice."

"Where do you think you're going?" he demanded. "Miss. Johnson, while I acknowledge that you are quite spirited and extremely beautiful, I would not hesitate in restraining you if you continue to act against my wishes."

"Against your wishes? I am not your slave Alexander!" It was another thing altogether that I was delighted that he thought I was beautiful.

His eyes flickered dangerously for a second. What, because I called him Alexander? Should I be put on the guillotine because I wasn't polite enough to bow down to this Earl or Baron or whatever the hell he was.

"I am very much capable of taking care of myself," I stated, a little less aggressively this time. He was looking so handsome and I … I just wanted to run off into the sunset with him. That of course was not possible because I was completely out of place here.

"You queer creature, when will you understand that I want to take care of you?" he said in exasperation.

What was it about this man that he seemed to make my pulse race even if he is referring to me as some queer creature?

"Is this some kind of wooing strategy of yours? Calling women queer?" I asked.

"I usually do not have to employ any wooing strategies," he said nonchalantly.

Oh, of course. You are such a sex god that women just fall at your feet. Jeez! Get over yourself already. I turned around to walk away from this altogether crazy scenario.

"Miss Johnson, I find it quite repellant, this manner in which you keep walking away from me," he said.

Repellant? Seriously. This guy had no clue how to talk to a woman!

"I repel you? Then why in the name of God do you keep following me?" I screamed.

"Because I love you!" he shouted.

I froze. He was now standing right in front of me, looking at me with so much adoration I was mesmerized.

"Miss Johnson, I know this seems a trifle irregular... and I am aware that I should be presenting myself before ... Lord Worth... before declaring my intentions to you. But it appears that these feelings I have for you are entirely beyond my control." he continued

I was dumbstruck. I couldn't take my eyes away from his face.

"You ... those eyes... oh damn those eyes," he said huskily and his lips crushed mine with no warning whatsoever. Dear God, I have never been kissed like this before. It was as if he was kissing my very soul. And to give myself credit, I returned his kiss with the same fervour and passion. If this was a dream, I never wanted to wake up. I could remain in his arms till my dying day.

When he finally let me go, I was totally out of breath. I tried to steady myself but this darling man had already encircled my waist and was holding on to me as if he would never let me go.

"I have wanted to do that from the first moment I saw you. Now, you have to tell me where I can find Lord Worth. I must seek his permission to marry you immediately," he continued.

Dear Lord, how was I going to tell him there was no Lord Worth? But you know what, for now I was just going to treasure this moment and fantasize my life with Alexander. After all, they do say, don't they, all's well that ends well?

Loss and Hope

Mother's End
by John Henderson

My name, she recalls only occasionally now
A familiar face gains greater recognition
Hands that knit, cooked, and embraced
Tremblingly shake, tracing unseen patterns
A blanket's edge, a canvas for lost memories
Lost words, dimmed connections

Grasp….. out window……there……who?........I don't know…..
Incoherent phrases expelled by mind and emotion
Searching……….for a word………a thought………that never came
Or maybe her thought came……but the words to express it were lost
Lost in a life of giving, four score and 10, or 15 years
And then some

Mothers. They give birth
To the universe. They give birth to love
Another generation, grandchildren play, hiding
Torment of weakened limbs, fragile bones
There is no tread left for traction on Life's treadmill
She depends on her husband, help-mate

Gone are cookies, piano songs, desserts, school plays and meals together
Mother
Gone too are your worries and fears
Mother………….NOT gone is your love
Carried throughout the years
Father…….devotion and love beyond amazing
Mother. Life's Blessings. Father. Life's Lessons.

Live now. Blessings.

When He is Gone
by Elizabeth Banfalvi

When he is gone
Who takes his place
When he is gone
Who's there to love
My heart is lonely
My eyes are searching
Searching but why
When he is gone

Who can explain
To a lonely heart
The forgotten toys
The empty shoes
The reason why
He is gone

Elegy for the Creative Soul
by Cheryl Antao-Xavier

the light in your eyes
died
along with the poetry
creative inspiration
crushed for mundane profit
blinding vision
to the beauty in life

the loss is ours as well as yours

who will hear the silence
feel the emptiness
notice the darkness
in your eyes
and our lives?

Aniruddh Remembered
by Jasmine Sawant

I long to hear
His bike revving up
His plane overhead
His car onto the driveway

I long to hear
Him call 'mummy'
Him play his drums
Him ask for advice

I long for
His hug
His kiss
His deep dimpled smile

I long
How long?
Hours into days
Days into years....

The tears
The anguish
The pain
Losing a son of twenty-five years

Do not scold me
by Veronica Lerner

do not scold me
Father Time
for my yesterday's apple orchard
quince - pear - walnut
and my dog Goofy

do not scold me
Father Time
for my tomorrow's emptiness
wilted remnants
among children

yet
do scold me

for today's blackness
blind light amongst the hours
that just
wouldn't pass

The Phone Call
by Elizabeth Banfalvi

It was 1999, and more than a year before I had left my husband of over 30 years. I should have left long ago but I didn't so now being over 50, I did. I got my own place and was happy. It had taken over six months before I stopped sobbing each night alone here but finally I did or I ran out of tears. It felt like the latter. My world was starting to right itself. I started to do yoga every night and I was feeling so much better physically. Our house had been put up for sale and it seemed like a buyer was interested and was going through the motions of buying it. But something was wrong. I was definitely going through the change but it was erratic. I finally went to my doctor and she sent me to a specialist in Toronto. That had been the week before.

I had just gotten home from work and the phone rang. The specialist was on the phone. She started telling me that I was lucky and I had to listen to what she was telling me. I had uterine cancer but I was lucky because it was the best cancer to have because an operation would take care of it. I didn't hear that part. Suddenly the tears started again and my world crumbled. I sobbed talking to her and wondered how I would survive this. She kept repeating it again and again but it didn't matter. Eventually I hung up. She had made arrangements for me to go to a famous cancer hospital in Toronto and she told me when the appointment was. I had heard how amazing the hospital was but I didn't really care. I wrote it down.

Our house was in the process of being sold but I thought if I told my family that it would be stopped. I couldn't tell my daughter or son what was happening. I was more alone than ever. I had two friends I told and we cried together but I made them promise not to tell my family.

I told my family doctor and she was upset and knew how upset I was. She told me to get another test just to confirm if the first one was right – it was to comfort me more than anything. She gave me a list of questions to ask the surgeon to better understand my options. So the next week I went to the famous hospital and my surgeon was a female. I gave her the note from my doctor. She looked at it; said she couldn't read it and tossed it aside. I asked to have a second test but she asked me why when it was true I did have cancer. I insisted so she did and when she was taking the samples from within me, she dug deep to make sure she got a good sample. So I left there and was sent to a series of medical tests to find out how healthy I was.

The next appointment came for the surgeon and I dreaded going. I knew I couldn't let her operate on me. I just couldn't. I sat in the coffee shop because I was early. I was shaking – how could I tell a surgeon from this prestigious hospital that I didn't want her touching me. I prayed for all sorts of strength as I sat there shaking and looking at the time. I noticed that a woman was pushing a wheelchair with an older man in it and they were going across the big lobby. Finally they arrived at the door and she pulled the fire alarm instead of the automatic door opener. All of a sudden the lobby was screaming from this fire alarm. Everyone came running from all over and trying to figure out how to shut the alarm off before the fire engines would come. Too late, I could hear them coming. I watched this scene unfolding in front of me. The noise, the people scurrying, the woman apologizing profusely, and the fire engines speeding here all sounding loudly in my head. Then they finally found how to shut off the alarm and everything was quiet. By then, it was time for me to go for my appointment and I wasn't shaking anymore. I realized that I was forgetting how to be afraid. I thanked my guardian angels and said up to them "did you have to be so loud?"

I walked into the surgeon's examining room and sat down to wait. It wasn't long. She said that she got the results back and she held it up in front of my face. The nurse was even shocked. The surgeon said "see, you do have cancer!" I looked at her. "Now are you going to let me operate on you?" In a calm voice, I simply said "No". She was shocked and then said "Well, you don't have to come back here, then." So I left.

My family doctor got a letter from her laying all the blame on me and how irrational I was. It was May. I was tired and wanted to take control back into my hands. I told my family doctor to not bother me with any other appointments for the summer. She was so incredibly worried because she said I couldn't do that to myself but I was tired.

My house sold and I even helped clean it up and got my ex moved into his new place. Nobody knew. I went to a homeopath, read books and did the spiritual path. What they came up with is that so much of what I was still going through was grief. My older son had died in 1992 and my marriage had finally broken down last year. Grief was definitely what I was still going through.

The summer was filled with me changing how I thought. My divorce was finalized late summer. In September, one other friend told me about another specialist in Brampton so I once again started the process. I went and his first question was why I didn't have my operation in the famous hospital. I told him because they wouldn't listen to me. He didn't quite know what to do about me but he examined me and recommended me to his "guru" in Sunnybrook Hospital. I even liked the name. So off I went to yet another surgeon and hoped this would be better.

I walked into the waiting room and the sun cascaded down from the overhead windows. The reception was so friendly. I was taken to an examination room and I got undressed and waited. The curtain was slightly drawn around the bed and I heard the door open. All of a sudden I saw the curtain being hit as someone walked to the end where they could see me. It was the doctor who had playfully hit the curtain. He started taking my information and asked why again I didn't have my operation at the other famous hospital and I told him they didn't listen to me. He went to the only chair in the room, pulled it in front of me and sat down. He said we would stay here as long as I wanted and I could ask him any question I wanted. There were no questions I needed to ask him. He made me feel like he would care. He went out when the nurse returned and got me all sorts of brochures on what would happen to me as a woman after the operation but there was very little and he apologized. What I didn't know was that he was one of the top three surgeons in Canada.

We talked about the surgical arrangements but I asked that we wait till December till my son came home from his tour. He told me that it might not be possible but I insisted. He agreed but warned me about any possibilities. I finally went home and told my daughter.

My son still didn't know. I got a call from him and his future wife. They were coming home early from their tour. I knew then that I would be going in early. November came and I had to go to emergency because I wouldn't stop bleeding. It stopped and I was sent home. My surgeon was on vacation and wouldn't be in till Monday. On Sunday night again I had to go to the hospital and this time, my ex had to drive me because my daughter had to take care of my very young grandson. I didn't go home then. I had lost more than half of my blood supply and needed transfusions. I didn't want them but I calmed myself and imagined who had given the blood. The image came that it was an older man, tall and wore short sleeves in the summer. The other was a short woman who loved the sun. It wasn't till the next day I realized I had imagined my parents.

My surgeon came home the next day but his schedule was full. He said he would have to operate on me at 9:00 that night. I called my son. I told him and he was truly upset but I reassured him like I had been that I would be alright.

Later I was wheeled up for the operation and I was never so frightened in my life. I lay there alone with the nurses coming and going around me. Suddenly it was quiet and I felt someone there but there wasn't anyone. I felt my older son and my parents there and they comforted me. I was operated on and I awoke not long afterwards. I came through my operation and my doctor said it was totally successful.

My roses came the next day. On the card was simply "we love you, your son". I sat and cried.

Afterwards, I put my world back together stronger than ever. Five years later and some other wonderful doctors, I was declared free of the cancer. I told my children first.

Let Him Go
by Jasmine Sawant

Let him go, m'dear

You have to let him go

So they all say.

Yes, yes, I know

I have to let him go.

Did I not let him go

Not too long ago

When he ran around unsteadily

On his two chubby feet.

Yes, yes, I do know

I have to let him go.

Did I not let him go

Just the other day

Riding his wobbly bicycle

In his grand way.

Yes, of course, I know

I have to let him go.

Did I not let him go

Why, that feels like yesterday.

Yes, I let him go

Far away to the north

To cold wooded lands

To fiery Red Lakes

I let him go fly

High up in the sky

Over thousands of miles

Over forests of pines

I let him go fly

High up in the sky

In a piece of metal

Held together

With his dreams, his ambitions

Held together

With my hopes and prayers.

Let him go, m'dear

You have to let him go

This one last time

You have to let him go.

For he has gone!

Gone so far away

He needs not your care.

His spirit now soars

The heavens above

Knowing he has

Your love, your prayers.

Ruins
by Rashmi Pluscec

for an endless space
for an eternal moment
unbroken lay the silent monotony

through the yellow swirls of mists
amid the grey terror of loneliness
rose in the distance, lone and proud

the final remains of a citadel
the last symbol of a brilliant age
a grim cacophony of glory and ruin.

a sad song wafted across the sands
perhaps journeying to touch any sympathetic ear
or perhaps calling out to a long awaited soul mate

somewhere glistened a primordial shrine
scattering its last few blessings
across the crumbling tapestry

some leaves swept in and brushed away the memories
some petals drizzled through and created a withered wreath
and then came the wind; that last official pallbearer.

Suddenly an ancient bell cried out
its high peals, the laughter of a world that was
its deep gongs, the grief of a world that never would be
its wild clanging, the final rage of a dying era.

Creating Success

Today
by John Henderson

To DO: Today.

To BE: Today.

A choice. Pick one. Do one, today. Be one, tomorrow.

All I have is this moment. Act or re-act? Control? Out of control?

I choose to see light today, even if my mind and events are dark.

I chose to be nice to someone today.

I choose to do something affirming for myself.

Today, I will focus on my children.

Today, it's only 15 minutes to walk around the block.

Today, I'll drink an extra glass of water, add a vegetable to my diet (not in the same glass) and laugh more.

Today, I will apply a more serious mind to every task and enjoy.

Tomorrow, I will not take everything so seriously. Laugh!

Today, the world will not end.

Today, I will take time to observe people.

Today, I will suspend judgment and criticism of myself and others.

Today, I will just say "NO" to that demanding person, and walk away.

Today, I will give a little more of my time to someone I believe deserves it.

Today, I will do one more thing.

Today, I will not offer any excuses.

Today, begins today.

Today, is all I have.

The Role Model
by Bev Bachmann

My last class for the year at Queen's had just ended when I decided to drop in on my Faculty Advisor on my way home.

"Hey, Rebecca," he called out cheerfully the moment he spied me standing in his doorway. "What's shaking?"

The startled expression on my face had him laughing. "Sorry 'bout that," he grinned sheepishly. "School's about to end, my vacation's about to start, and I'm a happy camper. Well," he said, motioning me to a chair, "what can I do for you, young lady?"

"I don't know," I admitted. "To tell you the truth, I'm a little worried." I searched for the right words, and then blurted out the question that had been nagging me for days. "So, what do you think? Am I going to make it in the world of in high school hell?"

He considered for a moment. "Tell me," he said, giving me a penetrating look. "Do you think you'll be a good teacher?" I recognized his question as something of a challenge, but he was smiling when he said it.

"I hope so," I replied.

"Not the right answer," he shot back. "You must have confidence." He tapped the tips of his fingers together lightly to form a steeple. "What you need is a role model."

"I have an idea," he said, getting to his feet. I took that as my cue the interview was wrapping up. "Go home," he advised, walking me to the door. "Think about your own high school days," he continued. "See if you can zero in an incident that stands out in your mind. Remember, what we're looking for here is a role model, so give the matter some serious thought. Then come back tomorrow and we'll talk."

"Okay," I replied, "but I went to high school in the States. Does that matter?"

"The States? Didn't know that about you." He stopped at the door. "Well, if truth be told, Americans are a strange kettle of fish," he said, bemusement in his eyes, "but they're still people. So, in answer to your question: no, it doesn't matter."

That night I took my assignment to heart.

* * * *

Fate, which is a generic word for my parents' divorce, had landed me in Texas, of all places, when I was 17 and beginning my senior year. Being the new kid in town, I decided to take a cautious approach as I walked into my English class on the first day of school and found an empty seat.

As I looked all around, I took in everything—especially the rather formidable looking teacher standing at the front of the room. Her name was Edwina Anderson and she was to be our guide through the wonderful world of literature with side trips to the land of syntax and composition.

Whenever I think about Miss Anderson today, I am put in mind of the time a piece of popcorn got stuck between my teeth and my gums and my tongue couldn't stop trying to dislodge it. Today it seems the perfect metaphor for this particular teacher— a tiny irritating presence that poked the tender flesh of youth with the sharp edges of arrogance and authority.

But I'm getting ahead of myself.

I didn't start out with this particular perspective. My impression of Miss Anderson took shape gradually over the course of my senior year. During that time I had ample opportunity to observe this teacher, and observe her I did.

I used to sit at my desk and wonder how this bitter, frustrated woman ended up in the teaching profession. She really missed her calling. Prison matron would have been a better fit.

However, in spite of her sour disposition and rigid mannerisms, I found her fascinating—in a grotesque sort of way.

First of all, there was her size. Short and squat, she wasn't obese—rather she was bulky. She had no curves and no discernable waist. Instead, she was built like a stack of cinder blocks perched atop two slender stick-like legs.

She had a small square head that sat on a token neck which disappeared into an ample bosom under which a narrow belt was cinched as tightly as a tourniquet. From there her dress hung down in lifeless folds to the middle of her knobby knees. Her mouth was a slash of deep scarlet that never entertained a smile and her tiny eyes, the color of cobalt, were forever scanning the classroom like suspicious sentries on standby alert.

Her appearance wasn't the only thing about Miss Anderson that was unique. She originally came from Massachusetts, and she spoke in a clipped Yankee accent, unlike the soft southern drawl of her Texan students. She was very proud of being from New England, and she took every opportunity to remind the class that she came from a state where education was based on high academic standards, unlike those of the schools in the Southern states, where, unfortunately for her, she had secured the only the teaching position she could find

Everyone knew that Miss Anderson was an intellectual snob. She certainly made no effort to hide it. She could be nice to those students who made an "A" in her class, but she was patronizing to everyone else. Since I did well in her course, I was one of her favorites—a fact that did not endear her to me. I found her snobbishness off-putting.

There were lots of great kids in my class, and they didn't deserve a teacher like Miss Anderson. Nobody did.

One day Miss Anderson decided to teach the class a new word. She didn't write it on the board. Instead she gave out clues and made everybody guess. Some of the cooler kids started calling out various words, and soon the whole class got into the spirit of the thing. It wasn't long before lots of different words were being tossed about as my classmates struggled in vain to come up with the correct answer.

I noticed that with each passing minute, storm clouds of disapproval began to gather in Miss Anderson's face. Was it their fault? They were doing exactly what she had asked. But they were failing miserably—those dumb-ass Texans! Miss Anderson looked thoroughly disgusted.

As it happened, I thought I knew the word, but I did not raise my hand. Whenever any of my teachers posed a question in class, I would say the answer silently in my head, but never out loud. Fear kept me safely inside my comfort zone, and I assiduously shunned the spotlight.

Miss Anderson was getting tired of all the commotion created by her increasingly boisterous students, now caught up in the excitement of the chase. She'd had enough. Abruptly she pushed back her chair with a screeching sound and stood up. Silence swept across the room like a blast of cold air. Then, without looking at me, she started addressing the whole class in that clipped New England accent of hers.

"All right, Rebecca," she said in a voice scathing with scorn from which, apparently, I alone was exempt. "What's the word?"

I froze.

Every head in the room turned in my direction. This was bad! If I was wrong, I would look like a first class fool, and my classmates would have good reason to laugh at me. On the other hand, if I was right, I would look like some kind of know-it-all and they would have good reason to resent me.

I had no choice. I had to say something, so I said a silent prayer and gave her the only answer I had.

"That's right!" She pounced on the word the way a cat springs on an unsuspecting mouse. Then she narrowed her tiny eyes in pleasure and puffed out her chest to signify she had, at long last, received some measure of satisfaction.

I, however, felt sick. The whole thing reeked of a set-up—as if I had somehow been part of a diabolical plot to put one over on those backwoods Texans.

I was positive my classmates would shun me after that, but I quickly discovered I was wrong. When class was over some of the kids approached me in the hallway. "Listen, Rebecca," one of them said, looking over his shoulder to make sure Miss Anderson was nowhere in sight, "we want to thank you for putting an end to that torture in there. I didn't think she was ever going to let us off the hook. Yankee bitch!"

I was stunned.

So, no one blamed me. In fact, they were grateful! It seemed my classmates could size up situations accurately—certainly more accurately than the woman assigned to teach them. No, my classmates weren't the ones whose lack of sensitivity betrayed their ignorance. That honor went to their teacher.

And, what was the word in question that had caused all this totally unnecessary uproar?

"Oppression."

I doubt the irony escaped the notice of anyone in the class—with the singular exception of Miss Edwina Anderson.

*   *   *   *

"Well, Rebecca, did you choose a role model?" My Faculty Advisor smiled at me as I stepped inside his office.

"Yes, as a matter of fact, I did," I said, taking a seat across from his desk.

"So tell me about it," he urged. "I'm all ears."

"Well," I started to answer, but then suddenly stopped. There was so much to say—I didn't know where to start.

My poor Faculty Advisor looked puzzled. He waited a moment before nudging me forward. "Don't keep me in suspense, Rebecca," he said. "What did you learn?"

I took a deep breath and started to relay the experience I had had that day in Miss Anderson's class when my back was to the wall and a firing squad was aiming at my chest.

When I had finished recounting my story, my Advisor sat silently for a minute or two while I waited for his response. He appeared to be deep in thought and taking his time before answering. "So," he said softly, "are you sure you want to use Miss Anderson as your role model?"

"Absolutely!"

He seemed taken aback by the force of my answer. "I'm curious," he gave me a thoughtful look. "What makes her so right for the part of role model?"

"That's easy," I replied. "Miss Anderson taught me the most valuable lesson I could have learned."

My Faculty Advisor arched his eyebrows. "And what was that?" he asked.

"What not to do!" I declared brightly.

A Woman's Way
by Elizabeth Banfalvi

I was raised in a traditional European family and the woman, although she stayed at home, was the centre of the family. The family revolved around her. She kept the family stable and working or doing things. She was there to wake them and send them off to wherever they needed to go. Then she was there to welcome them home at the end of their day. There was a comfort in knowing she was there. Front porches and back fences were her contacts with the rest of the world and other people. She wasn't afraid to tell off other children if they were doing wrong and the mothers listened to each other.

There was always a pot of something cooking on the stove and bottles of preserves to enjoy from the summer harvest. We didn't have large freezers or refrigerators either. My mother and grandmother wore aprons with their hand marks smeared on them. They were always the handiest as a substitute for oven mitts or hand towels. By the end of the day, they had to be washed. It was what met our face when we were given a hug and it smelled of food and detergent.

We didn't have steaks and roasts but soups and stews. We had desserts at our suppers and they were full of fruits and sauces. Everyone was welcome to the table and it was set simply. We talked at the table as we ate about what we had done that day and my mother would be part of that. We were scolded and encouraged as the need arose. My friends would crash my birthday parties because they knew my mother's cooking and how good it was.

My mother and grandmother sewed and my clothes were hand made. My grandmother used to sew wedding dresses in Hungary before she came to Canada. They didn't knit or crochet but I learned that from my aunt who didn't sew. My aunt's family lived next door and we shared our mothers between all of the cousins. We were at home in either home.

So this is where I learned to be a woman in their kitchens. I learned to cook, bake and sew. I wasn't fancy but my children knew a home cooked meal and I see them cooking and being comfortable doing it. We sat around a table and talked.

Now I am a grandmother to three children and I see my children grown. As a woman I see them still look to me not necessarily for approval but just as I did to my grandmother. I keep the fires burning to let them know I am as a woman of old - always there. I am proud to be a woman and all it entails. I have a quiet strength that comes of knowing I am the mother and grandmother of my children and grandchildren.

I may not be a modern woman in all the senses although I work and have a career in an office and am an author. I bring my sense of a woman's way to all that I do. It is the way I am.

Golden Age Sonnet
by Veronica Lerner

Priceless "gold" but facing gold is hard,
And when they call it "gold", seems tough to hear,
So then, you play the laughter foolish card,
And feed your inner desert with a tear.
But spending time in silence is a loss,
So, turn to your companions, now old,
They're just the same; try speak to them, because
Your wounded soul needs merely to unfold.
My friend, renew your own familiar beauty,
You're just a tree, remember that, so raise.
Surrender to the growing, it's a duty,
And next to dearest brothers, weave your lace,

So even if your trunk one day should dry,
You'll keep the steady branches to the sky...

Where is YOUR ATTITUDE AT?
by John Henderson

Is it Up?   Is it Down?

Or somewhere below the ground?

IS it HIGH, Is it Low? Or Did you leave it covered in the SNOW?

Where Is Your Attitude At?

DO YOU EVEN KNOW?

They Say: (Whoever They are) and you've been told   - That ATTITUDE is EVERYTHING.

THIS IS ONLY PARTLY TRUE. THIS IS NOT 100% or entirely TRUE.

It can be true that our ATTITUDE determines Our ALTITUDE and how high we can climb.

But it is NOT true that our Attitude is everything. Humans are more complex than that.

It's OUR "Mastery & Control" over our attitude that is everything. You can have a great attitude but if you can't carry that attitude with you every day, you'll slip. You've heard the phrase: "GET A GRIP!" This is good advice. We need to have a masterful grip on our attitude to bounce back and be resilient whenever things go wrong. Get a grip on your attitude. Getting a grip is about mastery and developing thought control. Getting a grip begins with gently recognizing when your attitude has gone out of control and you need to calm down, refocus, get a grip, regain mastery over your thoughts and emotions. You can have a horribly negative attitude but if you can't get a grip on it and see that it won't last forever, if you can't shift gears and raise your hands above your head, do a little dance (ok, be sure no one's watching) and put the negative thought away for a moment then how is space for a positive thought going to creep in? You need to keep trying until you do get a grip on your thoughts.

I developed a simple phrase that helps clients (and myself) 'get a grip', regain control, bounce back, recover sooner, faster and with more energy, each and every time.

Here it is: **"Make Gratitude Your Attitude and you'll have more Latitude with yourself and others."** Repeat this 10 times (22 is ever better), and see what changes. Now go write down whatever you discovered. (OK, this is the point where, before you read the next sentence, if you haven't stopped reading and started repeating "Make Gratitude Your Attitude......" and written down what changes in you when you do that (10x), then please, be kind to yourself and do it now). Gratitude is the secret of mastery. Gratitude for another chance, gratitude that tomorrow will be better, gratitude that you're still alive, gratitude that if you slow down that anxiety attack you might just discover that your worst fears were mostly in your head and there is always something to be grateful for.

"Make Gratitude Your Attitude and you'll have far more Latitude with yourself and with others." So, it's not your attitude, but where your ATTITUDE is AT that determines your attitude and altitude. And it all begins with: Making Gratitude Your Attitude to develop more Latitude with yourself and others.

Yes, I arrived slightly ahead of my time in January 1955, I only know from stories I heard my parents tell and birth records, that I couldn't WAIT TO BE BORN. Yes, I arrived slightly ahead of my time, - 6 weeks premature, weighing in at 3 lbs. 6 oz. and immediately dropped to 2 lbs. 12 oz. (a giant among preemies, who now can survive a birth at 8.5-9 oz.)!! For my parents, it must have been a worrisome time. My weight was precariously low for the period. Life was touch & go. (If you focus on the fearful side of a premature birth, things can go downhill pretty quickly). Others have survived worse beginnings, I'm sure. Luckily for me, there was modern medicine, as isolettes or incubators had arrived. For me, I just wanted food. A fact that by my size today, is self-evident. From Day ONE, I was born to be a survivor. (Even if I wasn't, it's my choice to see it that way and I'm sticking to it). I might Win, I might Lose, but I will always be driven to choose. Something in my infant brain chose life (and the enjoyment of food). You too can choose your "ATTITUDE" right now, in this moment.

Whenever things aren't going right, I recall the attitude in my infant brain of choosing life and re-fire that circuit in my adult brain. It helps me shift gears.

1. Don't be a victim of your own negative thoughts. It may be painful but you can choose to change them. (It's more painful if you don't change them to something positive.) Do something with GRATITUDE.

2. Where our thoughts and attitudes are AT is the silent foundation to our vitality and health.

3. You are not your mind. Your mind can take you places you don't want to go, especially if we remain on automatic pilot.

4. You are the MASTER of your MIND.

5. You can learn to alter your perceptions, mis-perceptions, moods, emotions and behavior.

6. Gratitude is the anti-virus software for the mind.

7. If you choose to do so, you can feel peace in a moment of stress, gratitude in a time of sadness, and energy during a time of fatigue.

8. Notice your thoughts. Challenge your reactive thoughts. There is always another viewpoint.

9. Our primitive brain is wired to appraise the external world for THREATS, and fight, flight, freeze or fib. Our appraisal of our own capacity to deal with a situation (threat) influences our stress level. The more we calculate our personal resources as good (coping), the lower our stress.

10. Believe you have the resources (or can find people who can help you) and change how you feel about any situation. If you don't like the results, make different choices.

LIFE is like an experiment. We get to try different choices to see what works in various situations over and over again.

Earlier I said that: 'Attitude isn't Everything'. Rather, it's Where our Attitude is AT that is everything.

Where OUR ATTITUDE is AT Determines our latitude and direction.

I leave you with this thought. Make Sure Your ATITTUDE is full of ASTOUNDING Timely TRANSFORMATIONS in Thought You Depend on ENYOYING EVERY Day TO EXCEL. Don't worry if your ATTITUDE ever goes negative. Just notice it and make an Astounding Timely Transformation in Thought. Find A Positive Thought You Depend on Enjoying Every Day to Excel.

ATTITUDE = Astounding Timely Transformations in Thought You Depend on to EXCEL and Energize, Every day. (Henderson's ATTITUD3E Formula).

Some interesting events happened around the year I was born. Following the SMOG alert in 1952 where up to 4000 Londoner's died, the Air Pollution Control Act (1955) was followed by the Clean Air Act legislation, introduced in February 1956 requiring a reduction in coal burning fuels to promote cleaner air.

On March 11, 1955 Sir Alexander Fleming died but not before in 1945 when he was awarded the Nobel Peace Prize for the discovery of Penicillin. It saved thousands of lives. Yes, CHOOSE LIFE.

Elis Presley performed in Lubbock, Texas at the Coliseum on Jan. 6, 1955, and June 3, 1955, with Buddy Holley watching the King perform at the June show.

Did you know that it was on June 3, 1955 was the New York GALA opening of Marilyn Monroe's film: The7 year ITCH? Yes, I was born in the same year when Marilyn Monroe's white dress and that updraft of air from a subway air vent, became one of the most evocative images of all time.

These events are all about Air, Health, Music & Sex. Yes I guess my ATTITUDE is in good company. If you want life, keep those four things in mind.

Earlier I said that Attitude isn't everything. Rather, it's where our Attitude is AT that is everything.

Where OUR ATTITUDE is AT Determines our latitude and direction. I leave you with this thought.

Make Sure Your ATITTUDE is full of ASTOUNDING Timely TRANSFORMATION in Thought You Depend on ENYOYING EVERY Day TO EXCEL. Don't worry if your ATTITUDE ever goes negative. Just notice it and make an Astounding Timely Transformation in Thought. A Positive Thought You Depend on Enjoying Every Day to Excel.

ATTITUDE – Astounding Timely Transformations in Thought You Depend on to EXCEL, Energize, Every Day. (ATTITUD3E).

Failure leads to Success
by Elizabeth Banfalvi

So many of us expect everything we do to be successful. We look to success to show us our value or to be the top of the heap wherever we are. It doesn't matter who we beat or by how much but just that we win overall. We show our value by winning. How many times in our schooling did we want the 90 percentile and definitely not be satisfied in the 80s? We want and then feel a failure when we don't achieve what we want. Even when we succeed we still pass that and go onto the next success and then the next – always wanting the picture to stay the same. We are rarely taught how to fail.

For me, failure taught me more than success. Success is of the moment and temporary but failure equates to a do-over. It makes me stop and think. Why didn't it work? Did I support or construct wrong? What did I want to accomplish or succeed in? What would it have meant to me? It makes me re-evaluate. It never luckily made me feel "not good enough". It opened my eyes and brain to different possibilities or outcomes. My usual question was why and then I proceeded to find out "why". I was born with an insatiable curiosity so failure was just a choice in re-doing not in giving up. I looked deeper and further. The success then was more satisfying because it came with a higher value and accomplishment. Failure gave me a deeper sense of instinct in how to make it better and then my success was more personal.

I have a grandson who plays hockey and as all players do, he went through a scoring slump. So I saw he was unhappy with himself and I asked him if he was unhappy which of course he said he was. Well, then I said to him rather than being unhappy why don't you think of it differently. He looked at me as usual like what was I talking about? So I said, scoring is your "normal", right? He answered of course. So you aren't scoring now – so what changed? Was it that you grew; hold your stick differently; or just need a readjustment? All of a sudden he wasn't unhappy – he was pondering what I had just said. So in the next game I saw him reevaluating things on the ice and trying different things to get back to his "normal". Soon of course, he started scoring but I got him to start thinking differently. Now when something isn't the "norm", he takes the time to figure it out rather than just slumping into the "failure" mode.

Look at failure differently. Failure is what gives us impetus to try a different way of doing things. It teaches us to rethink, reevaluate, redo, and then the success will be better. Don't give up but learn to use a different map.

Discerning Thoughts and Beliefs

Epitaph
by Rashmi Pluscec

here rests a desolate world
where humans fear to tread,

here runs a barbed wire
slashing the heart of the land,

here lies a dead body
an offering to flies and maggots,

here sits a puzzled child
scared but not knowing why ...

    a black cloud fondles a heart of fire
    a fiery explosion cradles a final breath,

    gullies filled with the living
    sandbags propped by the dead,

    hoarse commands filter through flying shrapnel
    desperate prayers whisper through scattered
bones,

    rotting flesh adorns the blackened earth
    dying wails fleck the crimson skies ...

Here lie a thousand dreams
Because someone spoke on behalf of god.

CBC Gossip
by Veronica Lerner

Gossip, rumours and scandals always had an irresistible attraction for us humans. Various forms of media have taken notice of this fact long ago and profited handsomely in all ages. We love to know everything about our celebrities' misadventures, their rise and fall, their marriage-divorce cycles and this type of information constantly fuels our fantasies, our desires and especially our envies. Herein lays the extraordinary appeal of tabloids.

Tabloids are a multi-billion dollar business. Gossip columnists are engaged in a relentless search for the ultimate "scoop"; actually *any* scoop will do. Moreover, when running out of "stories", they don't hesitate to "create" some that have absolutely no connection with reality. In doing so, they run the risk of lawsuits and of ruining their journalistic reputation to the extent they still have one. From their part, their consumers, otherwise known as readers or listeners, are equally indifferent to the amount of truth contained in a particular piece of gossip. Sadly enough, untrue stories have proven to be even more enjoyable to read or listen, spread around or endlessly comment on.

As long as rumors, gossip and scandals are confined to the realm of tabloids, I do not see any reason to worry too much. After all, we live in a free, open society where everyone has the right to access the information they are interested in, no matter whether is dirty gossip, literature or scientific research. There is a lot to worry about, however, when the border between tabloid and "mainstream" media becomes blurred. Nowadays, we see more and more tabloid stuff seeping into "serious" papers, TV channels, websites, etc., The reason is not hard to figure out: it's all about sales, sales and sales again.

To illustrate this point, I will tell you about my experience listening to a radio station ostensibly dedicated to airing classical music. Not all their stories are enjoyable; some of these have little relevance to the music piece they precede. I remember the presenter once asking: "Do you know anybody who, during his whole life, had asked for the same breakfast: two toasts, bacon and omelette, taking the same spot on the plate along some carrot juice? Well, if you do not know, please learn now: the person we are talking about is Beethoven himself! He only had coffee for breakfast, and his coffee was brewed from exactly 68 grains, no less, no more!" Immediately after this little revelation, the program followed with the overture to opera "Egmont". Personally, I found a little odd to put so close together Beethoven's breakfast preferences and music from his famous opera.

Some other time, a symphony by Dvořák was preceded by some commentary about the morning aerobics of a movie star, and so on, and so forth. I am positive that lovers of classical music would happily do without such "introductions".

Sometimes, though, the presenters at the station offer personal or even intimate details from the lives of featured composers or performers and these are really nice. At first sight, there is nothing wrong with this; it may be useful or even commendable, especially when considering the research effort involved. Recently I listened to a radio story regarding the Czech composer Karl Czerny, namely, how he arrived at writing *etudes,* those tortuous musical pieces meant to help students refine their piano playing technique. As talented as Czerny was, he had the misfortune of having Beethoven as his contemporary. Under the circumstances, Czerny chose to concentrate on mentoring rather than on composing, in an attempt to avoid competing head on with the illustrious German composer. The *etudes* were a genre in which Czerny felt he could still be considered the best. In the same radio program, I had the pleasure of listening to one of Czerny's string quartets, an astonishing piece of music, which I'd never heard before. In this particular case, the bit of "gossip" allowed me to gain a better understanding of the composer.

Watching another program, this time on TV, I found out that Mozart had had, at one point, a soft spot for a certain soprano who did not return his affection; moreover, she refused to even perform his music. To get even, Mozart used her personality traits to create an unsavory character – the Night's Queen - in his opera "The Magic Flute". Not only was this character obnoxious but the arias that she had to sing were extremely difficult. I remember listening to "The Magic Flute" as an adolescent, and to Elizabeth Schwartzkopf rendition of Night's Queen Arias. I was thoroughly enthralled; especially since I didn't realize then that her character was a villain. I have listened since to many great sopranos in that role but, in my judgment, none of them has ever raised to Schwartzkopf's level.

I truly enjoy such little stories. They put the music I have known for a long time in a different light.

As for me, if I am to listen to some trivia nonsense, at least give me something juicy, something I can keep gossiping about forever. You see, I am just a regular media consumer, like everybody.

Cowboy
Motto: "All choked up again" (song)
by Maria Cecilia Nicu

"Do you think it's important?"

"Do you think isn't it?"

"Oh, stop! The old trick; answering a question with another question! Why do you even try? Anyhow, my mistake, why the heck am I being asked?

Listen, I am drawing, a rough draft, and I can see I'm in trouble. Nothing works, there are crooked lines spread chaotically showing no intention, and nothing has any sense. You very well know I'm not talking about any logical explanation...I can even say that my hand is playing the part of an absurd visual instrument for someone who doesn't want to see. So you could grasp, I make no mistake thinking about what is or isn't important.

"Big deal!

As usual you start to digress and disguise excuses in some stupid cryptic questions so you'll get my interest, my curiosity. Sure you have the ability to put words in some unusual order just to hide your weaknesses but I'm telling you it's a crooked idea to resume to this artificial structure. What the hell am I talking about? Of course, you know the volatility of any explanation, take your pencil, charcoal, chalk, whatever f...g tool you want and draw with!"

"It's convenient for you!"

"It is always convenient for me, don't you remember? Mrs. Vrabie looked at my drawing map, got it closer to her eyes – I guess she was myopic - I recall her nose being white with chalk every time she wrote something on the writing board. Anyway, the horse she looked at was beautiful and she never believed that I drew it and you tell me it is convenient for me!"

"Isn't that so?"

"False cover up, isn't it? Something as heavy as a blanket being thrown over an empty bed or - to help you understand - a piece of translucent paper giving you the chance to accept the error or even better, to try to translate what your eyes wanted to see but couldn't."

"The horse, our old man said, is only an itinerant and if you were smart enough you would watch where he can take you. The road is long, much longer than I can remember now, with age you forget, you know. And he was right, I should think about it but thinking is not enough. The paper is a white field, and trust me, you have no idea how difficult is to get to that magic moment when you can see something in this non-existent colour. Don't interrupt me, white doesn't exist. If you didn't know that, I'm telling you now so you don't die an "ignoramus"! White colour is only an optical ensemble, and I would ask you how the hell I can avoid the strain and what exactly can I collect from it? Do you understand?"

"Are sure I should understand something here?"

"What do you know? The possibility to be yourself is such an insignificance that it seems to be idiotic to simply want to accept the idea, but the wide, panoramic opening is the idea determination, and all these years I felt some kind of incapacity not only as a confused state but as a serious impossibility to finalize my efforts.

Do you know how beautiful the lonely rider could be projected onto this white piece of paper?

You can't relate to anything else: field with no fault, totally depersonalized, plain desert if you wanted, and by the magic move I get a solid image. A horse and a man, and the lines reveal every muscle involved in the precise movement I thought about. Horse and man is a triangular silhouette, which changes the view and implies that I am still able to understand why the man desires to be alone only because he is... alone."

"Picasso! Don Quixote! It is right you missed Sancho Panza, but who cares?"

"Do you think so?"

"Not too much actually, but by doing that you lose the chance to make something convincing from your lonely rider. Are you sure he's not going to float somewhere in the air, maybe virtually hanged? Or even better being thrown into a freakish fly, a butterfly, a balloon, a kite, a slider and so on... sketched by a deranged imagination and a hand exhausted by too many known interferences?

And I ask you, what has happened to your horse, can't he gait?"

"Gaits, flies, floats, are these truly important? The horse is bordering the point, it is an imagistic subterfuge used to put the man into a specific state. In fact, using it isn't the right word, exploiting, to be truthful. "Vis-à-vis de l'homme", the horse is not only his necessity but also his custom habit. He can offer a metaphoric way of expressing the artist's needs. I know in your mind you find that ideal connection love only can make it work, and I am not sure if the horse was smart enough to make it true.

What I want now is not working, the paper still looks blank with this maladroit "croquis", looks like it is playing hide and seek with me, and it's unbearable. You see, you exhaust your energy with some images that can blow your mind. Try liberation, that ideal freedom you've dreamed of your whole life, and the result is only a lousy one hundred years old diapositive"\...shot by an idiot director like Nicolaescu* somewhere on a beach as he learned from a thousand American movies."

"Phew! What you described is an amputee cowboy!"

"Right!"

What is it but just a Game
By Joseph A. Monachino

My favourite team won the league championship. Is it a pivotal moment in history? Of course not.

There are problems in the world with famine, poverty, war, and drought. Are these problems that are unimportant? Of course not.

Sports events are diversions from real life problems.

My favourite team won the league championship. In the grand scheme of things, what does that do to eliminate famine, poverty, war, and drought? Absolutely nothing.

What is it, really, but just a game.

With – Or Without – Entitlements
by Veronica Lerner

We are living in what can be aptly described as "the age of communication" where by messages circle the planet in picoseconds and the news carried and promoted by the media are chiefly violent. We are assaulted daily, in heavy doses, by this kind of information. Email users know well that among the scores of messages we receive from friends or acquaintances – the majority of them are forwarded in many a step. One can indeed find useful info; however, I perceive the mere fact that I am coerced to peruse a selection made by somebody else as just another form of aggression. Upon expressing my displeasure with the growing disease of indiscriminate forwarding, I found out that the distributors themselves where spreading the (unwanted) word without even bothering to check the content thereof. Yet, I still am puzzled as to where this irresistible urge to click on "Forward" comes from. I've been asking myself if this kind of aggression we are subjected to nowadays doesn't come, conceivably, from some weird feeling of entitlement some people may experience.

Of course, education plays an important role in this regard. The newborn, as we well know, claims nosily their 'rights' the moment they come into this world. Though they are unable to articulate what these exact rights are, we assume that they are limited to the basic ones. As the child grows, to the basic needs of breathing space and food, the need of playing with toys or partners manifests itself increasingly strong. Thus, toys, games or partners – when judiciously chosen – indeed can contribute to a harmonious development of a child's personality. However, there is a certain point at which the parents have to draw a line with regard to their offspring's wishes as well as to the way such are expressed. Exaggerated demands of the child have to be rejected by the parent and the reasons thereof clearly explained. Also, there have to be consequences for the child, whenever they persist in their demands.

A child's way of testing us varies depending mainly on the age of the subject. Thus, between three and five years, our beloved are likely to throw tantrums whether at home or in public places. Teenagers' demands mostly focus on electronics (for boys) and clothing (for girls). As for adults, they may claim an (undeserved) promotion at work or equally undeserved recognition of any sort (artistic, etc.).

However, on an adult's case, self-importance doesn't come from education only. The baseless feeling of entitlement may be due to other factors such as temperament, arrogance or pent-up frustration. It is relevant here to dwell into the epicurean philosophy.

Epicurus, the Greek philosopher of old, categorized the human needs into natural ones (whether necessary or not) and futile or pointless desires. Under necessary needs he lists the basic needs for food, drink, sleep or sex. The natural but not necessary needs may include craving for a certain food, drink, etc. Futile desires are the wish to be rich, to live eternally or to be widely celebrated and respected. Epicurus considers futile needs as noxious since these are hard to be satisfied and unlimited in scope and time. Natural needs cease to manifest once satisfied. (I ate so I no longer am hungry.). Pointless desires are based on the endless craving for more and more. The satisfaction thus experienced is short-live and the need for "more" manifests itself again and again. Epicurus' counsel is not to fall prey to pointless aims but to live in harmony with nature.
Plato, also a Greek philosopher, sees the mindset of an individual preoccupied with meaningless aims as a bottomless basket. Epicurean philosophy encourages the pursuit of natural desires – such as the consumption of gourmet foods – but also warns of the danger of luxury becoming habit; and, conversely, of its lack becoming unbearable. His theory does not foreswear abstinence, which – by compensation – is conducive to pleasure.

Why did I venture into these theories? It is because I sense that in the time we live in the information revolution, it has generated a form of pleasure that although unnatural (one can survive without) represents a way of life people have become addicted to; and that is majorly responsible for engendering a perpetual sense of entitlement. Forgotten is a quality named "modesty". In our *modern times* (see Charlie Chaplin) the boastful and the "grabber" have more odds at being successful than the hardworking, modest, fellow who doesn't know – or doesn't realize how important it is – to *sell* themselves.

Well, success is among the pointless aims in Epicurean philosophy, today very few contemporaries live only for their natural needs. After all, we all need a job to put food on the table; and a job that is obtained via competition. Competition, by its very nature, is violent indeed and encourages, again, the sense of entitlement.

To conclude, I must say that I still am optimistic and hope that I will be able to get acquainted with some decent people on whose worthiness I continue to believe.

A Photograph
by Elizabeth Banfalvi

A photograph captures a second in time and how we see things is our perception of what the photograph represents.

I listened to an author describe his new book and how he uses a photograph to transport the character to another place. My question was when and where was the photo taken.

As soon as a photo is taken, things change. Time has changed and so does nature. We change in so many ways. We age in that millisecond and our body evolves. Our skin sheds and replaces itself. Our nails and hair grow. Thoughts are renewed and we function differently doing things like walking, sitting, standing or whatever. If you want a clear concept of this, try walking around in a circle in newly fallen snow. When you come back to the beginning, you have trouble following your own footprints imbedded into the snow. You have already changed.

In the beginning of September, 2011, 2 buildings stood proudly silhouetted against the New York City skyline and then they were destroyed. I remember the original Law & Order show scanning the sky and the buildings were highlighted and then in later episodes they had to reshoot the New York City view to accommodate the buildings not being there.

Think of nature also. The weather and seasons change. Trees grow and leaves either sprout or turn colour and fall. Flowers bloom and fade. We heat up or cool down. Our clothes and footwear change to accommodate the seasons and time of day. Nothing stagnates in nature – it continually changes.

Even our perception is constantly changing. What we see as a child transmutes as an adult. Our heritage and original home life alters what we see and feel originally. Our experiences throughout life change our perceptions. Our relationships or lack or functionality of them alter how we feel and communicate. Our parents, siblings, relatives, spouses, teachers, bosses, community all change how we feel and evolve. As we go through life our perceptions are constantly evolving and what we see as a child is different than us at 10 years, 20 years and through the decades of time. We never stay the same no matter how we feel we don't change. Change is all around us and is constantly happening.

It would be very boring to think we could or would not change even if we didn't want to. Photographs prove this and we can appreciate, dislike, cherish or regret the changes it shows us. We remember the time, place and circumstances either nostalgically or with stronger emotions. Times of old or innocence are remembered and brought back to us. Times of changes were captured in the world like the fall of the Berlin Wall, 9/11, marching soldiers and disasters that changed the face of the world or just us. They also captured the finer moments like Martin Luther King's speaking his world famous speech or triumphs in sports or the Olympics. There will always be these seconds in time.

What would we be like without photographs and the seconds in time they captured?

Aha
by Maria Cecilia Nicu

all my life I've lived reading books
anything else was accidental

valerica is always on the other side of the gate
preventive locked
the streetcar lefts the station and
trust me
the years helped to even understand Heidegger
I'm taking Faulkner with me not quite knowing why
I'm thinking to Castorp and Caulfield
and I'm telling everybody about Rilke

somebody told me that Bible is the book of wisdom
even if I've opened it
it's pointless

all my attempts smells of stable's hey
you closed you luggage
before
and you can't catch the train when leaves
the station

later
repeating has no sense
foggy view
ash thrown from the window

Family, Friends, Lovers

Historia
by Maria Cecilia Nicu

history book fell under the bed
you put it there says mom
sits perfectly
says dad
and i don't like to contradict them

history is for sure a book sitting under the bed
is not important
my father knew what I don't know
now

the trail pass lespedea over the bridge
two steps the door
and the cherry tree
the rest
I forgot to remember

The Fruity Pen
by Elizabeth Banfalvi

Mike walked into the house and dropped his hockey bag and stick at the door. He went into the kitchen and got some orange juice out of the fridge and drank it straight from the carton not wanting to rummage through cupboards to find a glass. His body hurt from the game he had just played and he rolled his shoulder to try to get some of the soreness out of it. George had hit him into the boards, the big oaf, and he could still feel it. The big oaf should learn to play hockey at his age but at least he bought him a beer after the game.

Mike looked at the clock and it was after 1:00 and boy, would he be tired in the morning. He smelled and just wanted to get a shower and go off to bed. He had to write his teenaged son a note about the hockey try-out tomorrow and he didn't want to text him at this hour because he would probably wake him up. He knew his son always left his cell phone on in case Sidney Crosby might have the notion to text him – yeah, right!

Mike got a paper pad and looked around for a pen but all he could see was the fruity little pen his daughter loved. Around and around he looked but no pen or pencil was evident and his gaze came back to the fruity pen. No, he couldn't use that. He probably couldn't even hold it; it was so thin and small. It was pink, fluorescent pink and had sparkles on it and a fluffy pink thing at the end. If he used it, it would smell from his hockey glove. He looked around some more but no, not a single thing was there. Tomorrow he would have to go out and buy some pens for this place.

He picked up the fruity pen and it slipped out of his hand. It was so thin; he had to hold it harder to keep it in his big swollen hand. Oh shit, it even wrote in pink with sparkles in it. No, he couldn't use this. His hockey playing son would just laugh at him. Who would buy something like this? Oh, he had.

He had come home late from the office one night and he was pissed. His project had gone badly and he was told to go back and redo it after all the hours he had put into it. John had shown his and he knew how to kiss up to the big wigs and they went overboard on telling him how great he did and a promotion was being thrown around for John even though Mike had done all the work.

He walked into the house and his daughter had greeted him with yet another one of her pictures of him and her. There it was again. A big piece of paper with happy colours on it and he was in it with long arms and she was holding his hand. In the picture, she had this big silly smile on her face and his was grumpy – like he was usually. She kept tugging at his arm to get his attention but all he wanted was a stiff drink to forget the day. He finally barked at her and she stopped. Suddenly her eyes filled up with tears and now he just wanted to have 2 drinks – one for the office and one for being a bigger oaf than he was normally. He said he was sorry but he really wasn't and she threw her arms around him and then ran away to her room with the picture still in her hand. He went to have his drink but it tasted rotten and he couldn't finish it. They had dinner and his son talked about his school hockey game and his daughter was silent.

Later his wife insisted on going to the mall and Mike went with her. In the mall, he waited for his wife outside of the dress shop she was in. There across the hall was a store with all sorts of frilly girly type things. Mike looked at the things in the display window. Everything was fluorescent pink and fluffy exactly what his daughter would love. His heart contracted with the remembrance of his daughter's eyes. He walked into the store and was surrounded by pinks, white and all sorts of soft colours. He looked like a gorilla in there but he didn't care. What was he doing in this store? What could he buy her? A young sales girl walked up to him. She was petite and had all sorts of different colours in her hair. Her hair was caught back in little ponytails all over her head and he could imagine his daughter being older and exactly like her. She asked if she could help him. She didn't even reach to his shoulder but her smile was so similar to his daughter's. He told her about his daughter and she knew exactly what she would like. They walked around the store and picked out a little bag with a flying horse on it and put so many little things in it all pink and fluffy and soft. The fruity pen was one of them. He thanked her and paid for his purchases.

He returned to the dress shop in time for his wife to come out with her purchases. He stood there with his bag and she commented on it but he said it was nothing. He couldn't explain.

They went home and there sat his daughter still silent and sad at the table. She was making more pictures but they were darker this time. He sat down beside her and asked to see them and she showed him reluctantly. His arms weren't as long in these and she wasn't wearing a smile. He handed her the bag without saying anything and just watched as she opened it and found what he had bought her. She squealed with delight at each item and everything was better than what she pulled out before. She loved the fruity pen the most and she always carried it with her wherever she went. She threw her arms around his neck and this time the tears in her eyes were for joy and in his also. She bounced away to her room to call her friends and tell them about her new treasures. Mike looked up and there standing in the kitchen doorway was his wife and she had been watching him. She just smiled at him but her eyes were soft and full of tears. She walked over, leaned down and gently kissed him.

Mike remembered that night and after that he changed at the office. He did his best there but he never brought the office home again. After that, his daughter's pictures were full of bright colours, his arms got longer and he always wore a big silly grin.

He picked up the fruity pen and wrote the note to his son. He laid the pen across the note pad, put the orange juice back in the fridge, and went to pick up his hockey bag and stick from the foyer. He unpacked his hockey gear to dry, showered and tiptoed past his daughter's and son's bedroom doors. He glanced at each of them and knew his children slept soundly in their beds. He paused with the feeling of it then wearily moved onto his own and with a smile, crawled into bed, wrapped himself around his wife and fell asleep.

Soul Mates
by Rashmi Pluscec

it was cold
the last rays of the sun had long burnt out
civilization in every form had long ceased to exist

she had walked alone forever
the last proof that there ever was life here
some time, countless ages ago

her feet had turned to leather her face had turned to ash
but the pain in her heart made all other aches irrelevant
for she knew she was only one half of what she had been

     * * *

it was warm
the first rays of the sun were getting ready to burst open
the crudest form of life had yet to take shape

he had moved alone ceaselessly
the first hope that there ever would be life here
some day, countless eons hence

he wavered in his pathetic attempt to move
but the desire in his heart made that inexperience
immaterial
for he knew he was only one half of what he could be

     * * *

for far too long she had been haunted by
the memory of something that probably never happened

endlessly he had been tormented by
the longing of something that possibly never would

and yet the recollection was clear
and yet the memory was certain
suddenly out of the blue, a final ember
almost on cue, a tiny spark

* * *

she thought someone was trying to reach out to her
she turned back

he thought he was about to meet the one
he peered ahead

in the distance far behind, she felt him
the first sign of everlasting love

in the distance up ahead, he sensed her
the last symbol of endless affection

* * *

the mists of time lifted
and cleared a path to the past

the sands of the land parted
and illuminated a way to the future

and against all odds she saw…
a void. that filled her emptiness forever

and in spite of all improbabilities he saw…
a space. that filled his yearning forever

* * *

instinctively she knew his face, his name
intuitively he knew her heart, her soul

the wait she had endured had not been in vain
the wait he would have to abide would not be unbearable

she was born after the end of destruction
he was born before the start of creation

yet they were always meant for each other
and someday, somewhere, somehow they would meet

Willie's Last Ride
by Nicholas Boving

"Two thousand crowns! You've got to be joking. We want to rent a hearse, not bloody buy it."

The undertaker; a fat, pasty faced villain with an unctuous expression, shrugged in a 'take it or leave it' way.

"That's what it costs."

"But it's less than two hundred kilometres."

"And back."

"He's not coming back."

"My hearse has to."

"So find a return load. There'll be people dying to do that."

Jan snickered. Milo belched. Pavel glared at the pair of them.

"It's not funny."

The undertaker stood up, adjusted his silk hat and walked to the door.

"You'll let me know?"

"I just did," Pavel replied.

Milo belched again and tossed the empty beer can in the corner.

"So what's the plan now, genius?"

"We could push him, in a handcart," Jan suggested.

"Two hundred kilometres? They'd have to bury us all."

"O.K. You come up with a better idea. "Shut up, both of you," Pavel ordered. "I'm thinking." He peered out of the window into the winter darkness. Fat snowflakes drifted down, and far off down the valley, a train hooted mournfully. He turned to his brothers, grinning.

"Uncle Willie always did like the train," he said.

"Reminiscing about the past won't solve the problem," Milo replied, portentously. Then his eyes widened. "You can't take a coffin on that train: there's no baggage car."

"So."

"Well, you can't prop it up in the corridor, or chuck it in the luggage rack."

Pavel grinned. "Who said anything about a coffin?"

"But . . ."

"But nothing. Uncle Willie wants to go home. So he'll go home. Special treat. A last train ride." He sighed. "Yes, he did so love trains."

"You mean . . ?"

"Yes. Dress him up and prop him in a corner. Dead easy."

"We'd never get away with it."

"Why not? It'll be dark. We'll break a couple of lights, or maybe just take >em out." Pavel didn't want to seem wantonly destructive. "No one'll see."

"What if someone tries to talk to him? Going to be the strong silent type, is he? Maybe a deaf mute? Christ! No one stays dead still for that long."

"They do if they're dead, dead drunk. Look, we slosh half a litre of cheap booze over him, stick a bottle in his pocket and pull a hat over his face. You and Jan can nudge him once in a while, just so he sort of twitches, and he can snore, real loud. You know, the kind of real grunt snore like pigs in . . ."

"Dead man don't snore," Milo objected.

"Sure they do. Jan does, and he's dead."

Jan blinked indignantly. "I'm not."

"From the neck up you are, mate."
Milo popped another beer can, doubtfully "I dunno. What if we get caught?"

"We won't."

"But Uncle Willie. What if . . ?"

"Uncle Willie won't know, and he'll care less." Pavel laughed. "What can they do to him anyway, lock him up?"

Milo slurped noisily. Pavel pointed at the beer case. "You want to go easy on that stuff. Getting one stiff drunk there's gunna be tough enough without you being legless."

"Couldn't we still just rent the hearse?"

"At two thousand crowns! I haven't got two thousand crowns. I've never even seen two thousand crowns, and four tickets on the train will cost about twenty each - a bit less as Uncle Willie won't be coming back. Think of all the beer you can buy with the saving." He poked Jan. "Hey, dopey. You got two thousand crowns?"

"You what?"

"I thought so. See, Milo. No one's got two thousand crowns. You can push him there in a handcart if you like. Me, I'm going by train."

Milo heaved himself out of the chair and belched again. "O.K." he agreed reluctantly. "We'll do it your way. Where do we start?"

Pavel slapped his shoulder. "I knew you'd come around. Come on, Jan; let's get Uncle Willie out of his Sunday best."

Uncle Willie, who had been laid out in the back shed as there wasn't room in the house, was not cooperative. Pavel and Milo, neither of whom had ever heard of rigor mortis, reckoned he was just being his old miserable, bloody minded self.

Granny Hoffa had done a bang up job as usual - she did most of the corpses in the village - but Willie lay in his coffin rigid as a Palace Guardsman, totally refusing to let his nephews remove his one good suit. Jan said he wasn't surprised. Milo reckoned he was embarrassed as he'd never been known to take anything off, even in midsummer, and Pavel thought they both needed brain transplants and said something unprintable when Willie's right arm cracked him across the nose in the struggle.

"Why we taking off the suit anyway?" Milo asked.

"Cos it's a good one," Pavel answered thickly, "And we'll get a few crowns for it at Tadek's shop. Besides, no one in a good suit travels third class. Make the conductor suspicious, wouldn't it. Here, you, grab his arm and push it up while I slip the sleeve off the other one."

It didn't work. It was like pushing a python into a sack. One coil in, one coil out, and the more you fought, the worse it got. They gave up temporarily and sat on a work bench to think. At least, Pavel thought. Jan couldn't, not really, and Milo's sole interest was another beer can. Snow rustled like dry leaves on the ground outside.

Pavel jumped up. Got it, he announced. "What's wrong with this shed, Milo?"

Milo frowned. "Wrong? Nothing's wrong. It's a good shed."

Pavel blew out hard, his breath condensing in a feathery cloud." See that? It's bleeding cold in here, that's what's wrong. Uncle Willie's as stiff as a plank 'cos he's perished. We got to warm the poor old beggar up."

"How we gonna do that?"

"Set fire to the shed," Jan offered brightly.

Pavel wasn't impressed at the suggestion. ">I'd set fire to you, you wally, but you're probably too thick to burn. Hot water, Milo, that's what we need. We'll soak him in a hot bath."

"It'll wet the suit," Milo objected, seeing his beer money slipping away.

Pavel shrugged. "Needs cleaning anyway, and it'll make him all nice and floppy."

"Bit of a problem, though."

"What's that?"

"We ain't got a bath."

Pavel showed his exasperation. "That's the trouble with you, Milo, no imagination. Of course we haven't got a bath. I was speaking - figuratively."

"What's that?" Jan asked suspiciously, as if he thought he was being let in for something illegal.

"Oh Gawd. We use something like a bath, Jan old son. Think of something. No, forget I said that, you can't do the impossible."

"The only thing like a bath's the duck pond, and it's frozen over. Won't warm him much in that." Jan was on a roll.

Pavel threw a lump of wood at him. "Shut up."

Jan retreated to the back of the shed in injured silence, and began sorting through the apple racks to find one less rotten than most. Pavel's unseeing gaze followed him automatically, his mind wrestling with the problem of warming Willie.

"Not one," Jan complained. "You'd think there'd be one."

Pavel blinked. "What? One what?"

"Half decent apple." Jan held out a handful for inspection. "See. Mouldy. They got fuzzy spots." He picked up a bucket and started dumping the rack. "Reckon we should have put 'em in straw like Grandpa did. These things are no good for nothing. Pig food, that's all they are now."

Jan was a man of few words, and even fewer of those intelligent, until it came to the subject of food. He brightened up a bit there, rising to a level only a little short of moronic.

"Hold it!"

Jan dropped the bucket on his foot and yelped. "What you do that for?"

Pavel slapped him on the shoulder. "The rack. That's it. You little beauty."

"I am?"

"Yea - well - that's what you call figurative, too." Pavel kicked Milo's foot. "Give me a hand to drag that rack into the middle."

"Whaffor?" Milo was comfortable and filling up nicely with beer.

"We ain't got a bath, right?"

"Right."

"So we steam him. Same difference."

"Steam him?"

Pavel frowned. "You hear an echo in here? Yes, you berk. Like Vassily does."

"Vassily? He don't steam people. He makes furniture and things."

"That's right, dummy. And what does he do to the wood?"

Milo's face lit with understanding. "He steams it and it goes all bendy."

Pavel shook his head. "Hit you hard enough with an idea and it does eventually sink in. Thank God one of us has brains."

Milo heaved himself up. "Which one's that, Jan?"

*   *   *

Uncle Willie looked quite regal, lying in state with steam rising from a row of saucepans under the rack. Pavel, who had a bit of imagination, plus having almost made it through junior school, was reminded of a picture he'd seen of a Viking chief on his funeral pyre. In fact, he thought, Uncle Willie looked about as good as he'd ever done, even alive, which wasn't very good.

He was supervising the steaming, giving the old man an experimental poke now and then, while Milo and Jan kept up a steady bucket line of hot water from the kitchen stove.

It was nearly two o'clock when he pronounced Uncle Willie "done", and they relieved him of his pants and jacket, to reveal a body that looked like a cross between a stick insect and a chimpanzee.

"Good God!" Milo breathed in awe at the skinny, hairy form. "You think Aunt Anna knew he looked like that?"

Pavel sucked a breath through his teeth. "They didn't have no kids, did they."

Milo giggled. "I'm not bleeding surprised. Imagine what they'd have looked like. I mean to say, she wasn't exactly an oil painting either, was she."

"More like a black buzzard," Pavel agreed, shuddering. "Don't bear thinking about." He produced a roll of unidentifiable clothing, strongly redolent of the farm yard. "Come on, let's get him in his old gear."

An hour later, Uncle Willie having reassumed the appearance they were all familiar with, that of a badly tied sack of potatoes, the nephews stood back to survey their handiwork.

Pavel yawned massively. "Not bad. Not at all bad. At least he looks more or less normal again."

"What we gunna do with him?" Milo asked. "Leave him here?"

Pavel shook his head. "Can't do that. He'd freeze up again, wouldn't he. Remember, he's gotta look normal on the train tomorrow."

"What's that?" Jan came alive again.

"What's what?"

"Normal."

Pavel sighed. He was tired. "Normal's what you're not, mate. You're subnormal. There's a difference."

"So what's normal for Uncle Willie?" Milo asked.

"Good question. I never did know. But what I mean is we can't wheel him onto the train looking like a bleeding statue."

"He's supposed to be stiff: you said so."

"Stiff drunk, not stiff dead. We gotta keep him floppy so he can sit down." He yawned again. "Help me get him inside. He can spend the night in the rocker by the stove."

"He'll like that," said Jan.

* * *

With Uncle Willie safely deposited in his favourite place, Jan gave the rocking chair a little push. It creaked back and forth on worn runners, its monstrous waving shadow dancing on the wall in the fire light.

"Quite like old times," Jan observed, happily.

"For Christ's sake, go to bed." Pavel's patience was wearing thin.

Jan grinned, patted Willie on the shoulder and shuffled dreamily off, calling out. "G'night, Pavel. G'night, Milo – G'night Uncle Willie."

Milo shook his head. "Makes you wonder, don't it."

Pavel raised his eyes to the ceiling. "Makes me wonder why I thought of this."

"You want to change your mind - go in the hearse?"

"Get real, Milo. We ain't got the money, and anyway, Uncle Willie's going to get his last train ride. I made me mind up."

* * *

Pavel went to the station next morning to get tickets, a wise precaution as the station master, who acted as porter and clerk, wasn't always around when the train came in. It wasn't really his fault, as the schedule was erratic to say the least. In fact, the train had been known to turn up on the wrong day on occasion. Nobody minded though. They weren't in a hurry.

Jan spent his day talking to Uncle Willie, telling him what fun it was going to be. Uncle Willie didn't answer: but then he'd never talked much when he was alive, so Jan didn't seem to notice the difference.

Milo went down to the store, bought a bottle of cheap plum brandy, drank it along with a dozen beers, and had to go back for another one. By the time Pavel decided it was time to leave, just in case the train was on schedule, he couldn't decide who was more trouble: Milo or Uncle Willie. On balance, he decided Milo was. At least Willie didn't go wandering all over the place, hiccoughing and singing. And as if to prove him wrong, at that moment he did as Jan had him on a two wheel baggage dolly and was running the old boy up and down the platform in style. Pavel shook his head and yelled out.

"Take it easy, you twit."

Jan grinned and slewed to a stop, beaming like the Cheshire Cat. He bent to say something to his passenger, who remained impassive. The scene gave Pavel the uncomfy feeling that his loony cousin was getting worse, and he didn't want his uncle falling all over and getting messed up. He sighed. But it did give atmosphere to the picture he wanted to create, of a bunch of merrymakers somewhat the worse for wear.

Milo's voice came plaintively from the darkness behind. Govina station didn't run to unnecessary lighting, when it had any at all, and he'd fallen into a weed choked flower bed. Pavel sighed again, and went to help, finding him lying on his back alternately giggling and trying to sing. The result was unmusical and not pretty.

"Whersatrain?" Milo blinked owlishly.

"Late, thank God."

"S'nothing to do with him."

Pavel yanked him to his feet. "Bleeding good thing it isn't. Might be time to sober you up, mate." He felt in Milo's jacket, producing the remains of a half bottle of brandy. "You got any more of this?"

Milo laid an unsteady finger along the side of his nose, and collapsed again. Pavel went to the fire hydrant, filled a bucket and threw cold water over him. The result was explosive. It also worked. Milo shot to his feet as if he'd suddenly found himself lying on a bed of hot coals, his language memorable as iced water dripped from head and shoulders into his pants.

Pavel laughed. "You look like you pissed yourself."

Milo took a swing at him, missing comfortably. "You'll piss yourself if I catch you," he shouted.

Four hours later, and three hours late, the train emerged from a drifting snow cloud like some antediluvian monster, hissing and wheezing asthmatically, and clanked to a shuddering stop with a tortured squeal of worn brakes. Pavel brushed snow off his shoulders and got up, slapping Milo on the back. Milo winced. The brandy had worn off, leaving him with an incipient hangover that threatened to be of monumental proportions.

"Come on, you two. Let's find a good spot."

"Bags a window seat," Jan announced, brightly.

"Uncle Willie gets the window. We got to keep him propped up, remember. And we got to keep him out of the way."

"But . . ." Jan protested.

Pavel gave him a push. "Inside, dopey."

It was difficult, very difficult.

The trouble with being early for trains on winter evenings, is that dead uncles lashed to luggage two wheelers, even if they've been lovingly steamed, tend to want to revert to rigor mortis, it's their natural state after all.

Willie was stiffening up again and the carriage step was icy, but the nephews' earlier antics had cleared a kind of safe zone into which none of the other waiting passengers cared to encroach. They got a compartment to themselves.

Milo sat miserably and blank eyed in a corner by the door. Jan sat eager and bright eyed at the other end of the same bench. Pavel sat in the middle opposite them, one arm outstretched, his hand on Uncle Willie's shoulder in a proprietary and friendly way. And Uncle Willie had the corner opposite Jan, face to the engine so he could see where he was going, legs crossed artistically, dirty hat pulled low over his face.

The compartment was dim, partly because the windows had about ten years dirt crusted on them, but mainly because Pavel had removed the two bulbs from the ceiling lights. And it stank like cheap bar on Sunday morning.

The train did nothing, and continued to do nothing except hiss and belch steam for the better part of an hour. This was partly for no reason at all, and partly because the driver was eating dinner and playing draughts with the station master.

Finally a whistle blew. The carriage jerked as if it had been hit by a runaway, there was god awful rattle of couplings and the lone, dim lamp on the platform slid past like a dingy ghost light. Pavel let out the breath he thought he'd been holding the whole time in a long, reptilian sigh.

"And you thought it couldn't be done," he said to Milo, jabbing his forefinger at the window. "Look at that. We're bleeding off, ain't we." He turned to Willie and patted his shoulder. "Enjoy it, old fella, it's your last one."

Milo belched and winced. "I could do with a beer." He looked across longingly to the bottle sticking out of Willie's pocket. Pavel intercepted the look and shook his head. "Don't even bleeding think it, mate. That's Willie's cover. You can bleeding wait till we get there."

"There'll be restaurant car," Milo said hopefully, and started to get up.

"Sit down you great wally. What d'you think this is, the bleeding Orient Express?" Pavel laughed. "This, mate, is local 501 from Kresslo to our nation's capital, via Govina and a lot of other little shit pots. What you see is what you bleeding get."

Jan, who had been listening with his usual puzzled, vacant expression, said. "I'm hungry." Then he leant forward and tapped Uncle Willie's knee. "You hungry, Uncle Willie?"

Pavel sighed. "You should have thought of that, Jan, and no, he's not. He's never going to be hungry again, is he? Use your loaf, boy."

Jan's forehead creased with the effort of thinking. "When we going to eat then?"

All his life it seemed to Pavel he'd been looking after Jan. But then he had, in one way or another.

It had been a different day, he thought, and as his mind drifted quietly, lulled by the slow clacking beat of the wheels, and the heavy, foetid warmth of the carriage, his eyes closed and his head slumped on Uncle Willie's shoulder.

* * *

"Tickets!"

The compartment door slid open with a bang and Pavel sat up with a jerk. His head twitched automatically to the sounds like a puppet on a string. A lifetime of totalitarian tyranny had conditioned him to the voice of authority like a Pavlovian dog; then he relaxed. Stuff 'em. Wasn't bleeding like that anymore, was it.

"What yer want?" He allowed himself the luxury of a truculent note: it felt good.

"Tickets. You got 'em?" The inspector's look gave the impression he doubted it.

Pavel stretched, slid a hand into his pocket and produced the four bits of pasteboard. He held them to the dim light from the corridor. "These what you want?"

The uniform grunted, reached across, and took them for minute and unnecessary scrutiny. Finally he gave them back.

"Who's the single?"

"What's it to you, mate?"

Outraged minor officialdom is a sight which manages to be both pathetic and awe inspiring. The uniform heightened and widened magically.

"Cos no drinking's allowed on the train."

It was a lovely bit of reasoning. When in doubt, or when the argument's lost before it's started, quote the book.

"Who's drinking?"

Pavel looked round the carriage suspiciously until his eyes rested on Milo.

"You been drinking?"

Milo opened his mouth fish-like, and closed it. Pavel shook his head.

"Course you ain't."

He peered at Jan, shrugged, and was about to declare mystification when light shone from his eyes and he snapped his finger. He beckoned to the uniform.

"C'mere."

Official eyes narrowed and moved a few inches. Pavel jerked a thumb over his shoulder.

"The old man," he whispered. "Been to a laying out. Going to a funeral tomorrow. Someone very close." His face twisted in a, I-know-it's-wrong-but-what-can-you-do look. "Been a bit much for the poor old . . ."

The uniform moved back, a flicker of understanding flitting over the suety face like a subliminal message. He sniffed.

"You're responsible. Any trouble and . . ." It was his turn to jerk a thumb, towards the corridor. A stern nod backed up the threat. "All of you."

"I need a drink." Milo's declaration emerged huskily but with definite authority from the seat opposite. He reached across the compartment, hand outstretched like a mummy's claw for the bottle sticking from Uncle Willie's pocket. Pavel hadn't the heart to stop him, and anyway, it didn't matter; in another few hours they'd be in the Capital.

He looked out of the dirty window. Ghostly trees slowly marched past. Only a couple of hundred kilometres, but at that speed, and three hours late at the start: they'd be lucky to get in by mid-day, if then.

He sat forward quickly as a whole new raft of problems presented themselves. Getting Willie from his house to the railway station in Govina had been a snap, but making it from the Grand Central Station to the family plot in what was once a little farming hamlet, but had long since found itself at the edge of a dreary suburb, was going to be a matter of tricky logistics. Eccentric behaviour in Govina, such as wheeling dead men about on luggage trolleys, didn't attract much attention, so long as they had clothes on, but big town people were different. They noticed things like that, took a poor view of corpses being displayed in public, and the cops just weren't friendly and understanding.

Pavel gave up. Thinking was giving him a headache, and something'd turn up. He wrenched the bottle from Milo's grasp with a bit of difficulty, as he had a kind of death grip on it, and tilted it back. Plum brandy slid down his throat like liquid fire.

He swallowed twice, wiped his mouth and slumped into his seat.

The train wheezed and farted and clanked through the night. The moon played hide and seek behind a patchy cover of clouds, and from time to time let its cold rays play on the miserable black and white winter world outside. Pavel lost count, not that it mattered, of the stops it made. Four was it, or five? Each time it seemed the journey had come to a premature end when after a bit of shouting and a toot from the whistle, silence descended. But each time there had been an unexpected jerk that nearly broke his neck and made Uncle Willie wobble disconcertingly, and the train had dragged itself arthritically out in the night again.

It was past mid-day when they arrived. The place was dead. Pavel was puzzled till a church bell rang and he remembered it was Sunday. It coaxed a smile from him. Maybe it wasn't going to be too bad after all.

Pavel had a headache and a mouth like a parrot's arse when they finally decanted themselves at Central Station in the Capital. The building was a piece of inspired communist era bad taste and utter lack of imagination, grafted onto what had been a rather nice example of late Habsburg era architecture. The result looked like the mating of a Borzoi hound and a Mastiff.

Milo stood on the platform blinking owlishly, wiping his hand across his mouth as he tried to home his booze radar in on the nearest bar or liquor store. At that time on a Sunday he was shit out of luck. Jan just looked even more owlish than his normal self.

They had uncle Willie sat between them on a luggage trolley, and it wouldn't have taken a Sherlock Holmes to figure out the old man had gone past the dead drunk stage to being straight up dead. Pavel was getting just a tad anxious.

"What we gunna do?" Milo came out of his booze-induced fog long enough to take a short-lived interest in their surroundings. And without waiting for an answer, said. "I need a drink." The observation was pretty much par for his course, but didn't add much to solving the problem.

"We gotta get to the cemetery," Pavel said.

"How far's that?" Milo's brain was peeking through the alcoholic haze.

Pavel had managed to acquire a town map. He stabbed a dirty finger nail on a green coloured patch. Milo peered. "How far?"

Pavel laid his equally dirty thumb against the scale and measured it off. "Five and a bit thumbs." His lips moved and he frowned. Mental arithmetic was not his forté. "About five kilometres."

"Taxi?" Milo said hopefully.

"No one'd take us. And if they did they'd drive straight to the cop shop."

"Why? We ain't done nothing."

Pavel sighed. Uncle Willie's last train ride was turning into a complicated exercise. He sighed again. "You get dropped off at a cop shop with a stiff and they'll make something up."

"But five kilometres!"

"Just think of it as a morning walk in the woods – with a bar at the end." Pavel knew how to get Milo motivated.

Jan decided to join the party with a pithy observation. "Uncle Willie's getting cold."

A railway freight operative came up. In the old days he'd have been called a porter. He stood looking at them, scratching his unshaven chin. "That's my trolley."

"What d'you want it for?" Pavel was reluctant to give up their only means of transport without a struggle. He wasn't prepared for a deadpan funny man. "About half an hour."

Pavel considered the information. "I've got a couple of crowns if you'll look the other way for half an hour." He jerked a thumb at Uncle Willie. "Poor old bugger's sick. Got to get him to the hospital."

"Call an ambulance then."

"Would it do any good?"

The porter shook his head. "Get there faster walking."

Pavel nodded. "See why I want your trolley then?"

The porter scratched his stubble again. "Still got to have it for half an hour." He squinted at Pavel. "Two crowns?" Pavel nodded. "Make it five and you can borrow it when I get back."

"In half an hour we'll probably have to take him straight to the cemetery."

The porter shrugged. "Take it or leave it. Best I can do." He held out his hand. "Five crowns."

Pavel gave him an old fashioned look. "You gotta be joking. C.O.D. mate."

The struggle of wills was hardly more than a mild disagreement not worth arguing about. The porter spat on his hand and stuck it out. Pavel spat on his, and they shook. Hygienic it wasn't, but it was better than a high powered lawyer's contract. Pavel told Milo and Jan to get Willie on his feet. He looked about and saw a stack of cardboard boxes. He pointed. "Take the poor old bugger over there."

The porter retrieved his trolley and trundled away. Fifty meters down the platform he stopped and turned. "Five crowns, right?"

Pavel stuck a thumb in the air. "And half an hour."

The last passenger had gone. The train pulled out to wherever it was that trains went, and Pavel slumped beside Milo and Jan. He looked at the boxes with disinterest, and then his interest jumped like a volt meter struck by lightning.

Very carefully and surreptitiously he pried open as box to his right, slid his hand inside, felt the familiar shape, and like a magician producing a rabbit from a hat, held out a bottle of plum brandy. He unscrewed the cap and had barely time to take a couple of good-sized belts when a hand like a mechanical grab closed over his.

"Where d'you get that?" Milo's eyes had the hunger of a pack of wolves circling a lone peasant in the pine forest.

Pavel let go. "Been saving it, ain't I?"

Half a litre of 40 proof alcohol later Milo came up for air with a long shuddering sigh. The smile on his face was beatific. He was ready for anything.

"We gotta get to the cemetery," said Pavel. It was a masterly statement of the obvious, but then he wasn't really talking to the others, more sort of trolling the problem through his mind and hoping to hook an answer. He slid his hand surreptitiously into the carton again and eased another bottle into his pocket for insurance.

"That fella coming back with the trolley?"

Pavel glanced at Milo. "If he wants his five crowns."

"You got five crowns?"

"We shook on it mate." Pavel's face was stern, as if it explained everything.

"Yea, but have you got it?"

"Course I go it."

"Show me." Doubting Thomas couldn't have put more feeling into the words. Pavel dug into this pocket. He pulled out a leather purse with a brass clasp, a length of string, a couple of rusty bolts and a few bits of fluff. He snapped open the purse and digging inside produced a collection of coins. He counted them.

"Three, three fifty, four, four twenty-five." And just as Milo was starting to look worried, Pavel stuck two fingers in his breast pocket and with a flourish pulled out a twenty crown note.

"Have I ever let you down?"

Milo snorted. "Lots of times."

There was the silence that precedes a storm, or a bloody good argument, when the silence was broken by the rattling of the luggage trolley as the ported returned from whatever mysterious business he'd been about, to claim his reward.

He brought the trolley to a stop and held out his hand. Pavel counted four-fifty, and then, seeing the man's brow turn dark, quit fooling a produced a half crown piece.

"How long you want it for?"

"How long can we have it?"

"Back here by morning, sunup, sharp."

Pavel nodded. "Then that's how long we want it."

The porter stared hard. "We shook on it."

Pavel tried to look offended but failed. "A gentleman's word is his bond. Sunup it shall be."

As railway trolleys go it didn't, at least not very well. One wheel was wonky and another had a mind of its own, which made steering a touch problematical and caused a lot of swearing and a couple of bruised knuckles until Pavel more or less got the hang of it and managed to pre-empt its worst lurches.

Uncle Willie was another problem. From bored stiff, he'd gone wet spaghetti limp. If they'd had a bit of rope they could have tied him down. But they didn't have any rope and Milo wasn't about to give up the piece holding his pants up at a point where common decency demanded they stay, despite the promise of another bottle of pain stripper. For a few hundred metres Jan sat holding Willie, but then the road tilted uphill and the surface deteriorated into frozen ruts and they both slid off. Pavel dropped the handle and swore comprehensively.

Jan watched blankly from his position on top of Uncle Willie, and Milo stared opened mouthed in admiration. He'd always known Pavel was a pretty educated smart sort of bloke. After all, he'd finished primary school, almost. But listening to the stream of inventive invective that came from him was a moment he was going to treasure. Finally Pavel tailed off. Milo took a short belt of brandy and wiped his mouth with the back of his hand.

"What now?"

Pavel's look would have frozen Lot's wife a sight quicker than it says in the Bible, but Milo was impervious, having a skin that would have been the envy of most rhinos, a biological and mental transformation of many years of alcoholic intake that had deadened any sense of shame. He continued to look blandly on as he awaited an answer. Pavel heaved an enormous sigh and raised his eyes to where he vaguely thought Heaven might be.

"Put him back on the frigging trolley, and this time, keep him there."

Milo and Jan grabbed either end of a very uncooperative corpse, which made loading Uncle Willie about as difficult as stuffing another python into a sack, for as no sooner had they got his feet on than his head lolled off. It was an exercise in frustration until Pavel grabbed his pants seat and heaved.

Uncle Willie stayed in the middle of the trolley, still and unsmiling, oblivious forever to the turmoil of which he was the centre. Pavel solved the problem of keeping him put by ordering Milo and Jan to walk along each side holding him, while he pushed. And in that somewhat undignified manner they crested the hill and started on the downward run to the cemetery.

And all was going well, indeed swimmingly. Pavel managed to raise a faint hope in his breast that they were actually going to get there, Milo had time for a couple of belts of brandy, and Jan was his usual beatific self with little idea of what was going on.

And then gravity took over.

Which was a bugger.

Pavel felt it first because he was the prime mover, captain and pilot of the craft. At first it was no more than a slight decrease in the amount of push required, then the required push lessened to zero, and with a cold feeling in his gut it flashed across his mind that any second things were going to get badly out of hand.

He applied the brakes. He dug his heels in, frantic for a grip, but the unyielding frozen snow was singularly uncooperative as far as traction went. He let out a yell.

"It's going! Hold the frigging thing!"

Milo's pleasant fog took too long to penetrate. Jan turned as he started trotting alongside the trolley like a presidential secret service agent. "Yer what?"

Gravity had the trolley in its grip. Pavel gave it his best, but his boots were unequal to the task. They shot out from under him and, as he landed painfully on his backside and let go of the handle he gave a despairing shout.

"It's going. Fer Christ's sake hold it!"

The fog got penetrated. The secret agent got the drift, mainly because he found himself running, which he hadn't been aware of doing a few seconds earlier.

Pavel sat in the road, staring in open mouthed disbelief as he watched chaos descend into the inevitable. Helpless, hopeless, balked by gravity just as they'd reached the last fence and were about to gallop to the finishing line, he watched.

Milo gave up. He wasn't built for speed, and careered away to trip on the verge and shoot head first into a heap of dirty snow. Jan valiantly clung to Uncle Willie and the trolley, his stride lengthening until it looked as if he was wearing seven league boots. And then his feet forgot which one was supposed to go first, and in a magnificent welter of arms and legs he somersaulted in a manner reminiscent of a racing car hitting the barrier, bounced a half dozen times and vanished through a snow-covered hedge.

Uncle Willie, sole survivor of gravity's victory up to that point, lay supine and forever oblivious as the trolley, miraculously and contrarily steering a more or less the straight course it had until then obstinately refused to even consider, rattled bumpily down the rutted slope.

The outcome was inevitable unless a higher power saw fit to intervene, as at the bottom of the hill the road took a sharp right hand bend where it passed the entrance to the cemetery and began to skirt the enclosing wall.

The higher power was at that moment either engrossed in more important things, or happened to be looking the other way. Pavel remained seated as the scene unwound through his eyes in what seemed like slow motion.

The distance between the trolley and the bend diminished. It was not a quite gravity's distance times seconds squared, but the end result was the same: the trolley put its foot on the loud pedal.

Pavel could stand it no longer. He closed his eyes just as the trolley hit the wall with a splintering smash that sent a cloud of roosting rooks squawking into the air in angry protest. Unable to ignore the consequences, he opened his eyes in time to see the limp and flailing figure of Uncle Willie clear the wall with the contemptuous ease of an Olympic high jumper, a scattering of shattered planks flying into the air, and one wheel negotiating the corner, to vanish God alone knew where.

He waited - there was nothing else he could do – until the debris subsided, the rooks returned to their trees, and silence descended. He took a deep breath that was more of a shuddering sigh, and slowly got to his feet. His priorities were plain: rescue Milo, find Jan, locate Uncle Willie and hide the evidence of the smashed trolley. After that, well, he had no bleeding idea.

Milo had gone to sleep. Half a bottle of cheap firewater and a comfortable snow bank, dirty or not, had done the trick. Pavel was tempted to leave him there until realized the silly bugger would probably freeze to death. It took a bit of doing and a lot of bad language of the more personal nature before Milo was on his feet, swaying like a pine in a stiff wind and looking owlishly at nothing in particular. Then intelligence emerged from the even deeper fog.

"Where's the trolley?" There was a pause because Pavel couldn't think up a suitable answer fast enough. Milo went on. "Where's Uncle Willie?" He looked around, shifting his feet to keep from falling. He was on a roll. "And where's bleeding Jan?"

The third part of the series was answered when a yeti-like apparition burst through the hedge on the far side, tripped over fallen branch and stumbled onto the road. The apparition stood, brushing snow from every crevice and surface until Jan appeared. Milo nodded sagely and looked back at Pavel.

Pavel pointed to the bottom of the hill. "Uncle Willie got there before us," he said by way of explanation.

"Got where?"

"The cemetery."

"What cemetery?"

Pavel sighed. "The one we're bleeding going to bury him in."

Milo brightened. It was coming back. "How'd he get there without us?"

"The trolley took off, down the hill. I, we, couldn't stop it."

Milo looked down the hill. "Where is it?"

"It isn't, not anymore."

Before pursuing what looked like being confusing, Milo reached into his pocket, and like a conjuror extracted the miraculously intact bottle. He took a couple of heroic swallows and wiped his mouth. "What d'you mean, not anymore?"

Pavel pointed. "It was going like a bleeding runaway pig and it hit that wall." He made an explosive motion with his arms. "Bang. No more trolley. There's bits everywhere."

Another silence from Milo as he digested the news. "Uncle Willie in pieces too?"

"No yer berk. Uncle Willie took off like a jet plane, right over the wall. Like I said, he got there before us."

Jan had joined them by that point in the question and answer routine. Milo started to laugh. First he pointed at Jan who still looked like a slightly tidied up yeti, and he laughed even harder. Jan tried to look offended, failed, and started to laugh as well. Pavel didn't think it was funny, not for a second or two anyway, and then he joined in.

In the end they were leaning against each other like three legs of a tripod, hiccupping and snorting, tears running down their faces until finally Milo's legs gave up the struggle and they collapsed in a messy knot.

Finally Pavel untangled himself and lay on his back, arms spread-eagled, gasping while Milo and Jan giggled helplessly.

"We got to get down there," he said.

Milo belched explosively. "He ain't going nowhere."

Jan shrieked a laugh that set the crows of again. Then he sat up, suddenly serious. "He can't, can he, he ain't got the trolley."

That did it. Pavel got to his feet, dragged Milo upright and held out a hand to Jan. "Come on you lot."

Milo took a slug of rotgut. "Where?"

Pavel closed his eyes and his lips moved. "Uncle Willie's in the cemetery. We've got to bury him."

The logic of the statement appeared unassailable, even to Jan. Milo, a touch more practical asked how they were going to do that.
Pavel patted him on the shoulder. "Pick and shovel, mate. We dig a bleeding hole and we put him in it, then we fill the hole back in. That's why they call it burying."

They went single file down the hill, Pavel in the lead, Milo following, and Jan slopping along behind as he usually did. It was like old times until they reached the cemetery gate and Pavel stopped and the others shunted into him with surprised grunts.

"What?" Milo peered over Pavel's shoulder.

"Cemeteries have people in them."

"So what. They're dead."

Pavel resisted the urge to smack him over the head. "Watchmen, grave diggers."

A sprinkle of snow began. It was not encouraging weather. Pavel opened the gate and peered cautiously inside at the uninspiring vista of tombstones, big and small, fancy and plain and just tasteless florid monuments. He pointed to a shed.

"Pick and shovel. Get them."

Milo balked at being ordered to do anything. "We don't have a key."

"Break in."

"What about the watchmen?"

Pavel sighed. It was a day for sighing." He waved in the general direction of everywhere. "You see any footprints?"

"Where's Uncle Willie?" Jan got to the nub of things, the focal point.

With considerable feeling Pavel said, "Shit." He looked at the point where the trolley had hit the wall. Two trousered legs were sticking out of a snow bank. He pointed. "There. Go get him."

Jan shuffled off, feet dragging through the virgin snow. Milo balked. Pavel raised a warning fist. His patience was running out fast and he was starting to wish they'd just buried Willie in the back garden alongside Aunt Anna. Milo grunted and followed Jan.

By the time they got down a couple of feet it the afternoon light was fading, the snow thickening, and what had seemed a good idea and a bit of fun was turning into a bloody hard chore. Milo wasn't cut out for hard work, or work of any kind that didn't involve a bottle, and after a couple of ineffectual attempts with the pick, he refused the fence and sat on a tombstone, and Pave's threats went over his head. Jan however kept at it like an automaton until they broke through the frozen layer and started making progress.

Darkness came down like a wet, snow speckled blanket. The top of Jan's head was still just visible when Pavel called a halt.

"That'll do." He held out his hand and gave Jan a boost out of the hole.

"What now?" Milo thoughts returned from wherever they'd been.

"We bury him, yer berk."

Milo jerked his chin at the slightly snow covered Uncle Willie. "Just like that?"

Pavel saw his point. "We need a shroud."

"A what?"

"A cloth. We gotta wrap him up in something."

"We ain't got nothing." Milo's logic was inescapable.

Pavel thought. "The shed. You see anything in the shed Jan?"

"What kind of thing?"

Pavel resisted the urge to go down on his knees and pray to an unhelpful providence. He felt the powers hadn't been taking his project seriously. "A sheet, sacking, whatever."

"There's a tarpaulin."

Pavel smacked him on the shoulder. "You're a good boy Jan." He stared at Milo. "A bloody sight better than that useless bugger."

Jan grinned uncertainly. Pavel shooed him off. "Go. Get it."

Jan loped away. Pavel called after him. "See if there's a flashlight." If Jan had been a dog heed have wagged his tail.

And so it came to pass that Uncle Willie was wrapped in a tarpaulin jacket redolent of grass clippings and gasoline, and laid to rest in the dark of the evening in what would be, for a while at any rate, an unmarked grave.

But, like all best laid plans it didn't run smoothly. Not that Pavel had come to expect anything else. He should have known better. A snowflake settled on his nose. He brushed it away impatiently and looked up from inside the grave. Milo's silhouetted head leaned over the edge. Pavel held out a weary hand.

"Give us boost," he said. Milo pulled him out like a landed fish. He looked back down into the grave where Jan was saying goodbye to Uncle Willie in a natural and conversational way. Pavel shook his head. Life had its burdens, but then, he'd done what he set out to do and given Uncle Willie his last train ride, and by this time next day they'd be back home.

"Here! You! What the hell you doing?"

Milo turned groggily in search of the angry voice. Pavel was standing beside him. Jan was in the grave. Uncle Willie was dead, so it didn't make sense.

It made perfect sense to Pavel. He dropped like a poacher nicked by a game keeper and dragged at Milo's coat. "Get down yer great berk." Milo tripped and fell, so the outcome was satisfactory.

A burly figure in a shapeless coat and woolly hat lurched out of the gloom. Pavel had sussed him right away as a watchman. He hissed at Milo to shut up and keep still. The figure stopped, uncertain of its next move. Logic said that people in graveyards at that time in winter were probably up to no good. Logic also said that he should pretend he hadn't seen anything and retire to the warmth of his shed where a stove and a bottle provided his comforts. Besides, he was paid to watch, not act, and certainly not get mixed up with grave robbers.

But curiosity got the better. He took a few tentative steps forward, narrowly missing standing on Milo's hand, and peered over the edge of the opening.

It was unfortunate. If he'd just gone his way, minded his own business as it were, he'd have been alright. But then he'd never have had a story to tell in the pub either. However, as he looked into the open grave, it was at that moment that Jan finished communing with Uncle Willie, tucked the flashlight into the front of his jacket, and looked up.

The watchman saw a ghastly apparition, a disembodied face illuminated by an infernal glow. And then the face spoke. "Get me out of here."

The watchman was normally an unimaginative man, not much given to fancies and solid enough between the ears to lack the basic sense that instils fear of the unknown and paranormal. But Jan's appearance was too much.

The watchman let out a yell that could have been heard a kilometre away. His eyes widened impossibly, his jaw dropped and his mouth opened like a stranded guppy. He dropped his lantern and stick, and took off as if all the devils in hell were on his heels. Pavel scrambled to his feet to watch the departing man and reckoned if anyone had had a stopwatch on the bloke he'd have been Olympic material. He made the first bend in the road in under ten seconds, easy, and later Pavel swore there were burn marks on the grass under the snow.

It was touch and go after that. Milo wanted to get the hell out, but Pavel insisted the job be finished out of respect to Uncle Willie: and anyway he didn't reckon the watchman was coming back any time soon. So they filled in the grave, or rather Pavel and Jan did while Milo sulked and sucked on what was left of his bottle. And then it was done. Jan gave the mound of earth a gentle pat with his shovel to smooth out a lump, sniffed, wiped his nose with his sleeve, and it was done.

As they trudged through the darkness, the city lights a beacon guiding them into port, Milo asked what they were going to tell the porter about his trolley.

"He won't be there, will he," Pavel said. "We said we'd bring it back sun up. You see any sun?"

The passed the first street light before conversation resumed. It was Milo again who wanted to know where he could get more brandy, and when the next train home was.

Pavel knew the answer to the first but wasn't telling, not yet anyway. As to the second, well, the job was done and he didn't really care. Instead he put a brotherly arm around Jan's shoulders.

"You did good there," he said. "Fair scared the pants of that fella. I'll bet he pissed himself."

He started laughing. Milo joined in because he thought it was funny, and Jan joined in because whenever Pavel found something funny, he did too.

My Grandparents
by Elizabeth Banfalvi

My grandparents came from Hungary in the 1920s. First my grandfather, John, came and then my grandmother, Anna, and their four children came after. My mother, Anne, was the oldest at 8 years old, then my namesake, Elizabeth, Margaret and John all varying ages. They settled in Beauharnois, Quebec beside the St. Lawrence River where my mother learned to swim. There is a large dam there in the river. I don't know what my grandfather did, but because my grandmother was such a good cook, they opened up a bordering house and rented rooms for fellow Hungarians coming to Canada at that time. I remember being told that men would pay to sleep on the floor to have her cooking. Soon 2 more children were added, Mary and Frank. My uncle is still termed the baby of the family to this day.

One day, my grandmother baked some apple pies and put them on the window sill in the kitchen to cool. Unfortunately she didn't realize some of the men were outside and smelled it. It didn't have time to cool on the window sill before they disappeared. She was angry but nobody confessed to eating the pies. My mother had to quit school at 15 to work cooking and cleaning the house while her other siblings remained in school. She wanted to become a nurse but that wouldn't come to be because she was needed to work helping her mother.

Eventually they moved to Brantford, Ontario and bought a tobacco farm. Elizabeth stayed behind in Montreal because she had met her future husband and eventually they married. All the children worked on the farm in the fields and in the harvesting of the tobacco throughout the year. Eventually life took over and my mother married and had 2 children. Margaret met her husband from Timmins, married and moved there. John married a local woman. Mary met a soldier from New Jersey visiting friends, married and moved there. Frank married a woman who came out of Hungary. Between all of them, they had 19 children except for Elizabeth.

I remember my grandparents. They were hard working people but you never left hungry from their table. They always had people coming and going.

My grandmother also organized the cooking at weddings. What a feat and feast it was! There weren't any caterers then. The women of the Hungarian community would gather together and plan the wedding feast and to estimate when the first child would arrive. They cooked for weeks with pastries and all sorts of goodies being prepared.

It was a 3 day affair then. Friday night was the pre-wedding party. Saturday was the full day with the church ceremony and then lunch and dinner. Then Sunday, all the friends and family would gather together to celebrate. I remember their farm with the large front lawn and how everyone would be mingling and talking on Sunday. Food and wine flowed on every day. The children were there and running and having fun among the adults.

Saturday night was the best. The children went to the wedding along with the adults and they stayed into the night. There was feasting but then there was the dancing. The band would play the different music but mostly Hungarian and the bridal dance would be later in the evening. People would line up to dance with the bride. The rouse of it was that they were selling the bride to the largest bidder. You would come up, throw some money in a large bowl, and have a shot of whiskey that my grandfather poured. The person would dance a few seconds with the bride and then my grandfather would yell at everyone that that person didn't pay enough so it was on to the next. On and on it went until only the groom was left. The groom would throw his whole wallet in and that would be enough to buy the bride. He would dance with her, pick her up and with the bowl in her lap, he would carry her out of the hall.

After that was the best. Everyone was pretty well tipsy and the traditional czardas would start. All the older people would join in and the hall was full of people dancing. Then my grandmother would come out of the kitchen at one end of the hall and she would shout for my grandfather. He was at the other end of the hall and he would answer her and make a loud whistle to call her. Everyone made a path for them through the middle of the dance floor; they would go towards each other, her chanting loudly and him whistling just as loud. They met in the middle and he would take her and dance spinning her around and around again both had one arm up and their other hands on each other's waist. It didn't matter if they were tired or anything, because they would just dance for the joy of it. Everyone would clap loudly when they were done and there were slaps on their backs all round.

This is what I remember most about my grandparents. I would stand quietly watching them and laughing and smiling the whole time. I could always find her in the kitchen cooking and baking and he was handing out drinks for everyone and they were always the centre of attention.

My children only met my grandmother but they felt close to her. She took care of my children when I went into the hospital to have my next one. She was always there and my children knew her. My two sons slept in a bunk bed with my youngest on top. The night I got the phone call that my grandmother died was the only night my youngest fell out of bed at around the time she died.

Reaching for the Stars

There's So Much Winter
by Veronica Lerner

there's so much winter
inside me
that the frozen rooftops
are my only cover
at nightime

there's so much grey
blanketing the hospital's white
that the cursed bodies
cast long shadows on the snowbanks
beyond the windows

there's so much frost
underneath my moving feet
that their praying is no longer audible

there's so much winter
covering the planet
that I seek refuge
into the words
yet-to-be-written

Operation:*Dreamgirl*

By Henry Shel

February 27, 2012

Sometimes I even amaze myself! Lol!

Either I'm REALLY falling for this Jinger chic OR I AM REALLY GETTING AWESOME AT THIS POETRY STUFF! Lol!

Let me explain.

I was talking to her earlier this evening (by talking I mean, we were having another one of our "it's 3 hours after leaving each other at work, and we are still knee deep in an all day text message conversation"). At some point in response to me calling her Princess she replied...

> :) Ur sweet. But u don't
> hav 2 keep calling me
> Princess

Feeling not too happy about it, I got a sudden urge to mess with her.
So I replied...

> But u are a Princess...
> as in a "Royal" PAIN in
> my ass! Lol!

Of course she didn't take kindly to that.
So she replied...

> Lol! What ev!
> ...why keep talking
> 2 me if I'm such a pain?

And it was right then and there, that I had a rare moment of pure genius & inspiration that was going to blow her mind!

Spontaneously I replied...

> Ur, not only amazing, but ur caring and pretty,
> Encouraging, playful, cute and witty
>
> I find u 2 be as smart as u are charming
> N all my defenses, u have a knack of disarming
>
> When ur around I'm compelled to focus on u.
> The world stops spinning, and everyone disappears too
>
> What I'm trying to say is...ur my Kryptonite.
> And I would give anything to be ur Superman - if only for 1 night!

DAAAMMN!!
How's THAT for romance? *(and they say chivalry is dead!* – HA!! (Lol!)

Well that was pretty damn romantic...if I do say so myself! Lol!

Now I'm not gonna try and say that miss "Tough as nails, always holds her cards close to her vest" Jinger, started swooning over me in response to my prolific display of romance and talent. BUT I'm 100% sure that it touched her.

She replied...

> ☺ SOO SWEET!
> Why'd u have 2 do that?!
> U know u already pull on
> my heart strings! ☺

HOLD ON...STOP THE PRESSES!!

"pull on her heart strings?" - Did I read correctly?

Hell YEAH! I knew it! She DOES have feelings for me more than just a friend!
(And *I'm* not going crazy...it's not just all in my own head.)

Word Fest, Celebrating Ideas

Yes! I finally got a confession of affection from Jinger, and I owe it all to my secret super human powers over poetry and prose! LOL!

Look out world, cause here I come.

Fathers hide your daughters!
...Bad boys hold on to your girls!
There's a NEW HERO in town! Nothing can stop me now! Today it's Jinger Girl...tomorrow...ALL the other beautiful women of THE WORLD!

MUHAHAHAHAHA!!!

(LoL!)

Ok. truthfully, I don't know if I'll ever be able to do anything quite as impressive as that again for Jinger, but I do know one thing for sure...

> If THAT didn't impress her...I don't know what in the world will!!

****

March 7, 2012

Speaking of impressing a girl...

Last night I had the opportunity of a lifetime and I BLEW IT!!

I guess that's what I get for talking all that smack about being so great, and awesome the last time I wrote something in here.

UGHHH!!! I should have known better than to be such a show off!

How does that old proverb go....pride comes before a fall...or something like that? Well, however it goes, I certainly set myself up to experience it the HARD way.

Chuh!!

I'll never forget last night...or more importantly...forgive myself for the ridiculously colossal fail that I allowed it to become, for as long as I live.

There is absolutely no excuse for the way I fumbled such a PERFECT opportunity to REALLY IMPRESS Jinger, on such an EPIC scale that I'm 150% SURE it would have catapulted my status with her right up to the same position as her man AND **cemented** my place in her heart FOREVER.

*SIGH...

Okay, let me explain...

Yesterday we had one of our mandatory quarterly store meetings in which everyone that works there is expected to attend. Now Fruit Computers being such a uniquely non-typical retail store & company, these meetings tend to be far from just your run of the mill "sit quietly listening to managers talk sales results for 3 hours" snore fest. No. On the contrary our meetings are quite varied, lively and even literally entertaining at times. Yesterday was no exception. In addition to the pretty awesome spread of food and refreshment provided, and a few "Hollywood" caliber icebreaker videos, our super cool managers decided they would also do something fun by having a few of us employees do a live Hip-Hop performance at the end of the meeting.

They conceived the idea only 2 days before the meeting, and it was supposed to be an excitement inducing "Company Spirit" type of thing featuring an original Fruit Computers themed song. So with barely 48 hours' notice to write and perform it, they approached my little bro, a couple other peeps, and of course, yours truly – Joe Flow!

GREAT...RIGHT UP MY ALLEY!! I thought to myself when they asked me to do it and I quickly told them yes.

I mean, I been recording and performing hip-hop since I was a teen and if there is only ONE thing in this world I'm 150% sure I can do WELL...it's RAP!!

Never mind the fact that my weekend was already jam packed and I would have next to NO TIME to write anything at all. It didn't matter. I've been writing songs in my head for YEARS and so, as far as I was concerned, I could literally write these rhymes in my sleep if I had to.

Heck...rhyming isn't something I just picked up and learned to do one day...it's just in my DNA!

And I'm not just talking writing songs and dropping pre-written stuff in the studio. Nope...I'm talking straight up old fashioned, live off the top of my head "b-rabbit" (a.k.a. Eminem) in 8 Mile, busting freestyle at the drop of a hat...type of rap.

So NO Problem...I got this!

MEANWHILE...BACK ON EARTH.

So I'm chilling in my room the night before the meeting, just casually thinking about what kinda rhymes to drop when it suddenly hits me...JINGER IS GONNA BE THERE, and she has NO *idea* I'm going to be performing, or that your boy here has a little rock star in him!

This could be good!

Like a wise man once said...YOU'RE BOUND TO GET NOTICED BY A GIRL (or 2) WHEN YOU'RE ON STAGE ROCKING A MIC! Lol!
Or more to the point...

Jinger *is bound to see me in a WHOLE other light, after seeing me rock the mic!*

The thought alone had me grinning like a kid in a candy store.

So of course, that's when my crazy child like imagination started to run wild...

Oh damn! If I'm really smart I can turn this whole thing into a **GRAND gesture** *that will totally knock her socks off! Give Jinger a shout out in my rhyme...and make it part of my last or best punch line. YEEAAH! That will impress her...and show her how I really feel about us. Heck...I can kill 2 birds with one stone...rock the mic, and* **rock Jinger's world** *all at once. He! he! he!*

Needless to say, I was now feeling quite pleased with myself.

I was inspired, and with thoughts of seeing Jinger unwittingly swooning over me, my creative juices really started flowing...

Preparing to start my trademark process of writing rhymes in my head, I sat up in my bed and turned on my reading light. As I did, the first thing that caught my eye was my Avengers' Movie poster on the wall above my computer.

Instant Inspiration!

Oh Snap...if I could do a rhyme about that...that would be WICKED!!

And so I did.

Not instantly of course. But after about 1 hour, 3 different instrumental tracks, and at least 5 or 6 re-writes, I eventually came up with this:

When the store's so busy that it drives you mental
My team saves the day like "Avengers Assemble!"

Selling mad products, flying out the door,
Fast as lightning striking from the hammer of Thor!

For sure, even when it's on Christmas Eve
We stock the floor with super human strength and speed,

And aim to please, never shooting no blanks

My sales team on the job, is like money in the bank,

Like Tony Stark, with a price gun in my hand,
I blow up the spot like a Black Iron Man

AND…my inspiration in case you didn't know,
Is my girl Pepper Pots: a.k.a. Jinger Rowe!

- the end -

NOT BAD RIGHT?!

Yeah, that's what I thought too! And so with no time to actually practice it, and even less energy to bother recording a rough copy to listen to, I went back to bed feeling pleased as punch with myself.

Tomorrow is going to be Epic!

FLASH FORWARD – 7 pm Sunday evening (the store meeting).

As busy as my weekend was, the only time I was able to spend practicing my epic rhyme of a lifetime, was quietly to myself on my journey from home to work.

Needless to say, I REALLY could have used some more time.

Full disclosure though, I did get to work early enough to do a live run through/practice with the rest of the guys in the back. And considering I didn't have the relaxed flow of it down pat yet, my overall execution was at least technically on point. I mean, I didn't miss a beat or a word. Most importantly of all, I hit my Jinger punch line right on the money!

The rest of the guys were blown away!

The whole practice stopped on a dime, while they all started giving me props and the track continued playing aimlessly in the background…

Word Fest, Celebrating Ideas

"WHAATT!"

"OHHH Snap!"

"WICKED My Yooot!"

It wasn't just that my metaphoric comparison of me as a Black Iron Man and the red headed Jinger, as Pepperpots was so clever. No, in my mind, it was also because it was the first time most of them probably clued in to *just how **deep*** this well-known work "friendship" between Jinger and I was.

Needless to say, I was pleased with myself.

If their reactions are any indication...then when we do this for real at the meeting I'm gonna have Jinger melting like silly putty in the palm of my hands. DAMN! I can't wait. Let's do this...I'm READY. I thought to myself.

So I left the practice room feeling good about everything except for one small tiny detail.

...REALLY, I **WASN'T** READY.

In my heart of hearts I knew it. But I was so eager to impress Jinger (and if I was lucky...potentially win her over too) that I didn't have time to give in to the tell tail warning signs that had me sweating like a river for the entire meeting.

I was an uncharacteristically nervous wreck the entire time. The only moment of peace I had was about 20 minutes before we were going to perform, when Jinger randomly texted me from across the room...

> Hey friend :)
> U can stop sleeping...
> snore fest is almost done. Lol!

I smiled. Partly at both the much needed warm greeting from my special friend, but mostly at the knowledge that Jinger had no idea what awesomeness was about to go down!

I smiled happily.

The next 20 minutes were a blur, and the next thing I knew my little bro was up at the front, with mic in hand, and the instrumental to M.O.P's "Ante Up" banging in the back, as he introduced the next rapper up to bat!

"Now it's time to pass the mic, off to my bigger bro"
"So put your hands up and make some noise for Joe Flow"

Then with as much b-boy swag as I could muster, I snuck out of the crowd and strutted up to the front getting hype to drop my verse while thinking how awesome it sounded in practice.

If I can just concentrate for the next 90 seconds of my life...just 12 measly bars of music...my friendship with Jinger will never be the same. I thought silently.

And so after a quick 2 bar intro, where I hyped up the crowd and got everyone (including Jinger) up on their feet, I opened my mouth and began to rhyme…

"When the store's so busy that it drives you mental"
"My team saves the day like "Avengers Assemble!"

"Selling mad products, flying out the door"
"Fast as lightning striking from the hammer of Thor!"

And that's when the crowd went wild! :

OHHHH!!! OHHHH!!! (Camera FLASH!) OHHHH!!! (Camera FLASH!) OHHHH!!! OHHHH!!! (Camera FLASH!)

And that's when for some CRAZY reason, for the first time in my ENTIRE life, I had an on stage brain freeze!

"For sure...uhh…"

(brain freeze…***brain freeze?***…oh crap! What the hell is going on!?

Don't panic Joe...keep it together...)

And then I continued with a spontaneous remix of the next line:

"...we're like...you can't believe,"
"doing so much more... with super human ease"

(HOLY CRAP! What the Hell am I saying...that's not the f$%#ing lyrics!

WHAT IS GOING ON With ME!??

Okay, okay, don't panic Joe...at least you kept the same rhyme sound as the original lyrics...now just get back on track, with the next line...)

And so, thanks to a lifetime of freestyle on the block, I managed to continue...all the while trying desperately to manipulate my flow back to the ever so crucial original "grand gesture" lyrics I had written...

"And aim to please...and never ask for thanks"
"Standing strong...like the Hulk...or a tank"

*Oh shit that's wrong **again!**...UGHHHH!* F%$# me!!

And now, I really begin to panic!

Holy crap, HOLY CRAP!! Tell me this isn't really happening! Only 4 bars left. I'm almost done...I HAVE TO GIVE JINGER HER SHOUT OUT!! This is my only chance. She's right there IN THE FRONT ROW!!! Please, please, please for the love of GOD and all that is Holy in Heaven and Earth, DON'T LET ME BLOW THIS CHANCE!!

In hindsight, it would have been SO easy to salvage the magic of the moment, and end my rhyme with an impromptu shout out line to Jinger. I mean seriously...as a seasoned freestyle rapper, I couldn't ask for an easier final word to rhyme with than her last name: "ROWE". But for the life of me, the closer I got to the end of my verse, is the more I panicked. And the more I panicked, is the more I just completely went blank. What I should have done, was simply abandon any notion of delivering my original super hero themed lyrics, and just relaxed and had fun dropping some filler freestyle rhymes for the last 3 bars that had nothing to do with The Avengers, BUT would at least finish up nicely with me giving props to Jinger.

Cause let's face it…in the end, all that other stuff wouldn't matter anyways. The most important thing that would have made the moment Epic, was simply my clever, PUBLIC declaration of affection for Jinger (and our not so secret, special friendship).

Simply put, ALL I HAD TO DO WAS SAY HER NAME! and the rest would have been history!

There's no doubt in my mind Jinger would literally have been glowing with excitement and admiration for me, while the rest of our staff would have erupted into a roaring frenzy of adulation and awe that would have made their first outburst seem like a cat's meow in comparison. But nope, silly me…just couldn't let my original intent go.

So with 2 bars left, I fizzled out with a feeble…

> "And that's all folks…I could rock some more"
> "But…time to hear from other peeps in the store."

annnd walk off stage…

BOOOOOOOOOOOOOOOOOOOOO!!!!

Is all I heard *in **MY** head* as I walked off the stage.

In reality, my crowd of coworkers loved it, and were actually cheering like I had just discovered the cure for cancer!

Which was ironic…because inside…
I was feeling ***SICK*** with personal disgust!!

SO LAME!

Life had pitched me an opportunity equivalent to a slow ball right down the middle and over the plate...and it makes me WEEP to think that I actually found a way to execute a pitiful "Swing...and a miss!"

*Sigh...

So in the end the one thing that should have made March 7th unforgettably Epic...just ended up being an EPIC FAIL!!

The Transporting Device
by Joseph A. Monachino
With Caroline Azar

Frank leaves a message with the authorities, shifting his voice, much colder and lower in register: *"I am a prominent businessman. I will make this message short so that you cannot trace it. I have left two million dollars in a locker at the Dulles airport in DC. You will get the key by courier in an envelope with a note indicating the locker number. I will watch the news tomorrow to see if the Terrorist Group has received their monies. And they better have released the passengers from Flight 363... or else.... Thank you."*

Thirteen months previous, Science Professor Frank Lyon was in his final stage of glory, having completed his grand and majestic invention. He had spent several years on creating a portable camera device that was the only one of its kind. It was a Transporting tool. He called it "Brigid". "Brigid", a machine, or more like a clone-cam, stores images in the memory of a chip that transfers you to wherever you desire to go, as long as the data is an image of a landscape or locale stored inside the device. "Brigid" helps you travel, without cost, passports, security, long lines and countless other pains. Call it a marriage of technology and sainthood, as St. Brigid was one of the noted Patron Saints of Travel. Frank presses his thumb on the electronic pad of the device, and the image transmigrates into a same time, life-sized experience, in a place other than where you began.

The first time, he succeeded in making this experimental dream come true; he could not speak for weeks. The elation was simply overwhelming. It was beyond Science Fiction, because it was happening in the dreariness of the here and now. Like the walking dead, Frank had functioned with mediocre purpose. His heart was ailing from having lost his dearly departed wife Brigid to Breast Cancer. Working on the invention, had a hand in healing Frank forward.

Having been a shy and awkward boy, Frank was fortunate in being accepted to M.I.T in the wake of computer technological advancements. But what made school even more exciting, was a lovely Irish exchange student who swore a mean streak, winning theoretical arguments with her advisors. Brigid had translucent skin; a strong maternal body like a Celtic warrior, with a walk that let the world know she was comfortably aware of her fine qualities. She never understood why beautiful American women insulted their looks, never finding solace with how the Creator had made them. They had a good eight years together.

After Brigid's death, months went by when Frank could not keep food down, rarely woke up on time to teach class, could not look people in the eye, or even react to what they were saying: he simply was not present.

One night, in a dream, a dream that felt like a nanosecond, Brigid visited Frank and reminded him of the importance of forging ahead for their son Jimmy, who at the time of her death was only 2 months old. "Oh Lover, get off yer arse... Frank, get the kid a Nanny...a female hand is important...and make sure she's a foreigner...everything foreign improves the American way. Don't you think it right, Frankie?"

Through the right references and channels, Frank had fortune in the form of a sweet boisterous Pilipino Nanny named Imelda Fernandez, who loved and cared for little Jimmy like he was her own. Most importantly, his guilt now alleviated, allowed him to focus on another inspiration, from another dream, another visitation from Brigid.

It was this dream, which was the turning point for Frank, who was certain that this was an exact and real conversation with the love of his life. "Frankie, get over it, get over me.. get back to work...I want you to think of all the crazy things we used to laugh about Frankie...D'ya remember Dolly the Sheep? Ach, that stupid Doctor must have been some nutty lapsed Catholic... I mean, the nerve! The nerve of 'im playing God was beyond rational comprehension. D'ya remember Frankie? Frankie m'love? And we used to laugh and laugh and imagine how you and I would one day inspire the world with a better cloning device, a tool that might clone vistas and the beautiful wonders of the world, rather than sheep and people...or *Sheeple* as we used to call 'em..."

In half-sleep, Frank, for the first time in a long while, was wearing the largest grin. A grin inspired by her dreamy smile, her ingenuity, peppered with their shared oddball humour. All of this was a nod to their great life together, where Husband and Wife were not only the best of friends and lovers but also a collegial team sharing a shrewd view of Science, inspired by their twin dismay of the modern world.

The dream was a wake-up call, reminding Frank of the potential abuse that would exist if human beings were to be duplicated. His Catholic upbringing and value for human life were still with him and sobered him from deep grief. "Cloning landscapes and inanimate objects might be a worthy project", he pondered. The technology he had at his disposal was not yet advanced enough to allow duplication of any kind. He now had his work cut out for him.

After hours of playing with wire filaments and travelogue imagery captured from a collection of the most updated and distinct Photo-journalism, Frank settled on the fact that the one locale he had the most images from, with the most angles and heights was Times Square in New York City. The prime objective was to build the device cleanly getting him standing in front of the famed statue of George M. Cohan, right in the centre of the hub.

The prime tool, or rather *Brigid* was thus far a black box – one by one by one cubic feet. The side of the box is concaved-a shaped glass semi-dome. This box is the portal meant to negotiate all the elements in play to making this fantastical travel happen. The last piece of this machine would be a platform or landing pad made of gold and zinc combined (he melted his and Brigid's wedding bands). Now, this landing pad receives the imprint of your thumb, where its valleys and ridges act as the transmission and the human fats and oils from the skin is the gasoline thus transporting the individual in question who will travel to the desired locale.

Unobtrusive, wooden and collapsible, the box seemed to nevertheless develop a mild but annoying presence that Frank developed great intimacy with. He would brew his coffee and begin his day chatting with the dusty box, staring at it for hours, sharing impressions of the world he believed he lived in, details about little Jimmy's abilities in improving his baby crawl. Like Mesmer, Frank would play a mind game with the box, forcing his will to find the gap that would see this experiment to fruition. He sang a song to it, his and Brigid's wedding song, "Sweethearts Together" from The Rolling Stones LP "Voodoo Lounge". It was then that he referred to the box as "Brigid". It was common practice for him to now imagine a musical Irish voice from the box consult him while he was working. "What coloured filaments and cables and in what configuration, order and frequency might create the strongest light source, Frankie? And which physical equation is gonna move you to a foreign dimension of an "elsewhere"? Think! Think!"

He had recorded 467 experiments since Brigid's dreamy visitation and progress was starting to show at the 427th exercise. These were increments of mild successes, which had Frank jumping with joy, even grabbing Nanny Imelda and twirling her in their bright red-tiled IKEA Kitchen, taking her away from preparing the baby's strained carrots. With the odd high, came many a low. Like the day his body transported for 12 minutes, yet he had only made it to the basement bathroom. Still, it was a form of progress. H.G Wells would be proud.

There was still one piece missing in this equation and it was driving Frank nuts. Depression and some procrastination set in, mostly in the form of renting out piles of Science Fiction movies, to see what might inspire him. He would not change his clothes for days. When his eyes became watery and tired from the late night viewing, he would find himself reading to little Jimmy at 6 am. But it was not Dr. Seuss.

Frank read the boy passages written by Isaac Asimov and H.G. Wells. Of course, the sweet Toddler did not understand, however was smiling with joy, sensing his Father's playful exuberance.

One Christmas, noticing his son playing with a Toy Ray gun, the thought came to Frank that he was living in the past with the spirit of Brigid. As well, he existed in a future dominated by the concept of this Transporting device that would conceivably function and change the human experience of Vacation Travel. The problem he realized, while looking at his boy, was with all this past and all this future, that he was not living in the present. It was at this moment, he decided to give up the whole struggle and simply be pleased that Jimmy, a blessed and biological remnant of both himself and Brigid would be enough in his life. Moreover, it should be enough! To simply love, cherish and raise a lovely angel as such, Frank decided at this moment to put the invention to sleep. To let it go. He needed to watch his son grow and be there and enjoy the details of the now, like how the boy's ginger hair resembled his Mother's colouring and how his smile was evolving to becoming hers.

During this bittersweet moment, little Jimmy was exhausting the plastic trigger of his new Ray gun, wearing out what was a simple mechanism. A metal piece dropped. The trigger was now stuck and the toddler cried in frustration. Frank picked up the mechanism and noticed it was simply a magnet, and that he should immediately repair it to bring a smile back on little Jimmy's face. It was impossible to fix the piece back into place, as the magnet kept attaching itself to other things like TV remotes, nail clippers and paper. Paper! It then dawned on Frank that if the image rested in the semi-dome was a developed black and white silver print of the landscape... along with magnets staggered from the thumbprint pad to filaments back to the silver image again, there might be complete impact and success! Moreover, this might be the relenting force field in facilitating the human body to be sent to another environment. He should have known of this! It was definitely an a-ha moment. Merry Christmas, Frank!

Soon enough, his body had made it as far as the front yard, 20 miles outside of Toledo, Ohio and Albany, NY. Each time he equipped himself with maps, cash and transit cards in making his way back home, to his lab, his son and his job. All he had to improve upon was the strength of the magnet, filament and silver presence of his Kodak developing paper.

On New Years' Eve, Frank had a hunch to book Imelda for a week to sit with little Jimmy. Wouldn't it be amazing if he could ship himself from his musty science lab in Readfield, Maine all the way to Times' Square in NYC? What a way to celebrate the passing of a new year! What a way to mark progress! This positive ray of hope was quite the contrast from the recent tragedy that befell the great city, known as 911. And this held some meaning for Frank. It was 11:50 pm and having cleaned his lab, stealing a sip of champagne, with a wing and a prayer... in an instant, the life-size image of the subway stairs were right in front of him. He folded up "Brigid" and put it in his knapsack. He did it! By the aid of his revolutionary invention, he had broken through the barrier of the image and found himself by the "1" Train, in the Times' Square station.

It was New Year's Eve, about to become 2002. The air was tense because of the tragic events that had taken place only 3 months earlier.

Frank Lyon was slapped with an eclectic spectacle of scintillating sight, scent, sound and people. Raucous yelling partnered with glaring spectrum of neon dancing around thousands of partying revelers. This was the cradle of capitalism: The billboard giants that are Coca-Cola, Toyota and TDK loom over the aggressive aroma of the hot dog smoke arguing with the stench of exhaust fumes. This made Frank both hungry and teary. Horns honking, sirens from emergency vehicles blaring, happy-go-lucky whistling with streamers tooting to signify that this year was dying, welcoming the birth of another.

Walking by the Hard Rock Café, where Frank was perusing a portrait of a dazed and confused Led Zeppelin, he overheard two older people engaged in conversation. One of them said, "Nothing is going to happen, because we all got faith." This signified the anxiety that people had about living in the wake of 9/11 and the fear of it being repeated. Nearby, Frank then witnessed a man holding a stack of balloons. In the spirit of giving, he handed a balloon to those who stretched their arms out to get one. 'Too bad that doesn't continue for the rest of the year', thought Frank.

Confetti of tourists with cameras worn around their necks clashed against the haggard homeless, who illegally solicited spare change, avoiding the army of security swarming every inch...

And the ball was about to drop as the humongous crowd yelled, "...3,2,1...Happy New Year!" Two-thousand and two was now upon us. Frank felt this was going to be a year of great significance.

He had 4 days before making it back home to Maine. So seizing the moment ASAP was the significant act in question.

He took "Brigid" out of his knapsack and inserted a picture of his hotel, from the pamphlet. In an instant, *Shazam* ...he was there.

"That's 3 dollars saved and also earned!" beamed the happiest Scientist of 2002.

On his bed, with a bag of BBQ Lays chips and full-on red Coca Cola Classic, like an anxious teen, he booted up his computer and "googled" the "new" 7 Wonders of the World. This was something he wanted to check off his "places to visit before I die" list. "Might as well, explore it now, while "Brigid" is in the zenith of her strong and willing function as the ultimate Transporting device- Mwah! He kissed the wood all around her.

For a moment, he wished of she: the Brigid in the flesh. He wished an image of the two of them as a pair of globe-trotting Aladdins wandering, buying time with the dream of shared memory. Like the memory of love they had pledged to one another. He wiped his tear quickly as to focus and escape New York, before check-out time. After all, he didn't want to be expensed the extra day.

And so... The List was an interesting one. It read: On January 1, 2000 an Organization announced a "new" set of the Seven Wonders of the World based on on-line voting from around the world.

1) Christ Redeemer, Brazil—Large Statue
2) The Great Wall, China
3) Chichen Itza, Mexico—Mayan City
4) Machu Picchu, Peru
5) Petra Jordan—Ancient City
6) The Roman Colosseum, Italy
7) The Taj Mahal, India

The third and fifth wonders were not priorities. But the others were. He thought to himself, 'I am going to visit these five places with the aid of "BRIGID". But why stop there? There are five cities he wanted to visit also. They are: Tokyo, Japan; Paris, France; London, England; Rio de Janeiro, Brazil; and Moscow, Russia.

Frank knew that time was on his side. He could visit these places extensively over several years, one hour at a time. How long did he have? About 17 years. He wanted to complete this excursion before his 3 year old son's 20th birthday.

He was to explore 3 main aspects of these destinations, namely the scenery, the food, and the weather. Frank saw endless possibilities. His invention was something he could now use to fulfill his main passion: Travelling instantly to exotic destinations.

Professor Lyon pondered which of the five of the Seven Wonders of the World he would start with. Would it be Christ redeemer in Brazil? The Great Wall of China? Machu Picchu, Peru? The Roman Coliseum in Rome? Or the Taj Mahal in India? Frank considered these destinations and concluded that he would visit them in the order that he listed them. This was the time to set out on his journey.

Yes, his dream came true. "Brigid" gave him the opportunity to visit these cities without the hassles of airport security, long flights, and passports. Frank knew that his time was limited to six hours on New Year's Day morning. That meant that he would visit only 3 of the 5 cities, namely Tokyo, Paris, and

London. He could now visit exotic locales simply by placing a thumb on a pad!

The first stop was Tokyo. He checked his watch. Tokyo already rung in the New Year and as much as Frank loved the experience, he always preferred it when the crowds dispersed. A New Year's Day brunch item much sought after was the sumptuous eating of *Dashi,* which was fish steak, in an outdoor restaurant. As that experience felt optimum enough for a satiated Frank, he was ready to say *Sayonara* to Tokyo.

The characters in this story are purely fictitious. Any similarity between actual characters and incidents is purely coincidental.

Thrills and Chills

Curtain
by Rashmi Pluscec

Every night the same dream hit
that same gruesome, sickening dream
always the same phantasms, ever the same terror
Each morning he would gasp back to life
drenched in sweat, scared beyond consolation
till it was time for the pattern to start all over again

      fall asleep. dream. wake up screaming.

As darkness approached
it slowly crept in to embrace him
bringing along faceless shapes in obscure pursuit
Piercing the deathly silence, an eerie groan
amid hazy outlines, a clink of bone, a thud of flesh
around a core of horror, a hint of blood, a smell of rot

      fall asleep. dream. wake up screaming.

Then came that night when there were no more dreams
even as he watched, those hazy outlines took shape
Lopped heads bouncing, loose eyeballs dancing
broken legs dragging, maimed arms flapping
An ominous wisp of pungent air and smoke
a dull trail of damp skin and bowels

      fall asleep. dream. WAKE UP screaming...

Suddenly in that last lucid moment, realization smashed through
his eyes *were* wide open, his mind *was* fully awake.
The curtain between dream and reality
had finally come crashing down.
The minions of hell
had finally caught up with him.

Murder Unedited
by G. Ian Stout

Chapter One

Michael hated being disturbed during a creative moment and looked with distaste at the phone before abandoning his keyboard to answer.

"Hello," he growled, not knowing who was at the other end.

"Hello Michael darling. Hello, hello, hello my darling Michael. Have you heard the news? I hope not because I want to be the one to tell you. Oh God I'm so happy to tell you. You'll never believe it. You'll never, ever believe it. Our 'piss poor publisher' is dead, deader than a doorknob." There was no mistaking the joy in the high-pitched voice of the caller.

"That's 'doornail' Rosanne, 'dead as a doornail.' My God, have you never read Henry the sixth or Dickens. It's doornail. Now stop fooling around. You're just being silly and I'm very busy. There's no way in hell I could have such good fortune. I'll never outlive that dishonest little snot."

"Michael, I'm not kidding, this is no joke. He was found on his back in an alley behind one of the watering holes he spent his time supporting and he bore all the earmarks of a bona-fide one hundred percent dead person." Rosanne's almost hysterical glee washed over Michael like a tidal wave.

"He had no pulse, he wasn't breathing, and you just have to hear this, you won't believe it. He wasn't screwing some poor writer out of all his hard earned money. To top it off, when someone offered to buy him a drink, there was no response, can you imagine that, no response. There is no question about it my dear; Peter our piss poor publisher is well and truly dead."

"Are you sure about all this?" Michael was still skeptical.

"Of course I'm sure, you silly. It's on TV, the radio, and the front page of our local paper has that horrid picture taken of him at the last book-fest. You know the one, when he got drunk and insulted poor Margaret Atwood."

"Hang on then" a completely changed and delighted Michael hollered to his caller. "I've got a bottle of champagne just for something like this. It's been waiting for a momentous event and by God this certainly meets all the criteria." Setting the phone down he heaved himself out of his chair and shuffled off to fetch the bottle from the wine fridge in the pantry of his tiny Montreal apartment.

Returning with two glasses, he balanced the phone on his shoulder while undoing the wire and easing the cork out, all the while chattering cheerily into Rosanne's ear.

"Dear Rosanne, do tell me the wonderful details leaving nothing out and please don't tell me it was sudden. You know what I mean. Nothing like a crass quick gunshot to the head or a large blade thrust straight through his black heart. It's important the little bastard suffered." Michael was bouncing in his chair with joy. "By the way, I have two glasses here, one for you and one for me. I can't celebrate this stroke of good luck alone, you know. It just wouldn't do. Of course I'll have to drink yours for you but you can pretend, although you're not missing much. It is French but not a very good year" and he downed both flutes before setting them beside the phone for refilling, all the while humming a happy tune.

Michael Kalishnikoff, who loved champagne and horse racing in that order, claimed to be an Englishman sired by two well-bred members of pre-revolution Russian nobility. His parents were amongst those who had the good sense to escape the motherland shortly after the Reds moved the whole Romanov family to a place called Yekaterinburg. Michael's dad, not a stupid man, bribed with a handful of gold coins a ship's captain, and moved lock, stock and family from St. Petersburg to London. Tucked carefully into his wife Katrina's hair and stowed in bags hidden beneath her floor length dress were most of the family jewels, several kilos of gold coins, and a small fortune in British five pound notes.

Looking much like a sickly woman barely able to walk and leaning heavily on the arm of her husband, Michaels mother and the crafty man she was married to managed to sneak out enough of the family fortune to acquire a splendid home in Kensington. They also had enough left over to maintain a reasonably upper class life-style for the next four decades.

As the years passed additions to the brood completed the stable to twelve Kalishnikoffs, with Michael the last in 1932. He always claimed he was the best because his parents finally got it right after so much practice.

Those early times were a blur of laughter, boating, and croquet on the lawn with older siblings. Michael quickly learned being the youngest and the cutest afforded him a distinct advantage and the little mischief-maker was quite the favorite of his aging father. Long before the war broke out and he was shipped to a relative's home in Canada he had won the heart of all he encountered.

To this day, more than sixty years later, he still thought he was cute and actually, sitting there with a champagne bottle resting against his ample stomach and the phone nestled in his perfectly trimmed beard, he looked like an impish Santa Claus happily taking orders for toys.

As the warmth of the champagne spread through him, Michael peppered his caller with questions, eager for details.

"Rosanne, tell me my dear, what happened?"

"Well, I have the paper right here and the details are a little skimpy but it would seem someone killed him with, of all things, a fountain pen. Now if that's not poetic justice, nothing is. Can you possibly imagine a more fitting way to do in that little twerp? Oh God, life at times can be soooo good." Rosanne was beyond happy.

"A reporter on local TV said there was a lot of blood around the body so he must have lain there quite some time before going to the great remainder display table in the sky so yes, I'd think he may have suffered somewhat."

Rosanne Drew was a poet and like Michael, under contract to the victim, the infamous much unloved Peter 'the piss poor publisher' Jefferson, founder and president of Crafty Press, known to many industry insiders as Crappy Press. Peter Jefferson was a man who had managed over the past two decades to alienate, aggravate and irritate every person with whom he came into contact, as well as many who were spared that misfortune.

Rosanne was the author of several very good children's books. She was considered quite gifted by Toronto's literati, if that meant anything because none of them ever purchased books anyway but were useful if you could use their verbal pontificating on the back cover of your next effort. Besides writing skills she was renowned as a genius for having coined the descriptive title of 'Peter the piss poor publisher'.

This incredibly accurate description of Peter Jefferson was born after Crafty Press produced and distributed hundreds of Rosanne's second book to sellers across the land with her name misspelled in large letters across the front cover. Rosanne's first book had been a great success, selling more than three thousand copies nationwide and Peter wanted to trade on her ability. The trouble was he didn't check the galleys as close as he should have.

Dismayed, the author demanded something be done but Peter dismissed her complaint. He said no one would notice an extra 'S' in her first name and snarled that he wouldn't waste money recovering the damn thing. When she demanded he recall the book, he told her to drop dead.

Being under contract to Crafty Press 'for life' Peter bullied her into believing if she took any action her literary career would be over. One email from him claimed a two-bit poet like her would spend the rest of her days in court and she'd never publish another thing again, ever.

Rosanne backed down, defeated by his verbal abuse, retreating to her apartment to lick her wounds. No one heard from her for weeks.

When she finally emerged, having decided not to press the matter, Rosanne, with great dignity refused to discuss the matter. She would just tolerate the screwed-up cover but she would never forgive Peter. From that day on her publisher became 'Peter the piss poor publisher' usually spit out with a snarl. She also made sure everyone in the industry knew his new nickname and understood the reason for it.

"Do the authorities have any idea who did it?" Michael asked.

"The official line says it was a bungled robbery, possibly by someone who thought it an easy hit because the twit was so drunk. That cheap fake Rolex he wore was gone. His wallet was gone along with all his maxed out credit cards. There was no cash on him, although the cheap little bastard never did have any when he was out, so if they're right and it was robbery it was by the world's dumbest thief. He was a first class bungler not knowing his victim was such a penniless loser" she spat.

"Gracious me, you say our esteemed publisher was under the influence? You mean Peter had been touching the demon rum? I'm shocked, shocked. The police should check the bar to see who was paying" Michael laughed.

"Good idea. I'll suggest they find the payee when they call, as I'm sure they will." Both Rosanne and Michael had a good chuckle over this because Peter's love of booze, any booze was legend around the publishing world, especially when it was free and served by some young beauty with long legs.

Michael's mind was churning but he was pleased at this apparent change in his career. He too was under a 'for life' contract with Crafty Press and this news was possibly life changing.

"It's so good of you to call with this wonderful news. I feel like I just won the grand prize in a lottery. I assume you'll be looking for a new publisher, as indeed I will. Please do keep me up to date on your efforts and any further developments in this heartwarming saga."

"I've already sent out feelers as I'm sure all of us will and of course I'll keep you up to date. I knew you felt the same of him as I did but I never thought he was in your champagne category. You owe me, you know" and she laughed like she did years ago at a book launch in Toronto.

"I'll always owe you my dear. I owe you because a long time ago you decided I was to be a member of your small circle of close friends. For that, I'll always owe you."

"Damn, Michael, you sure haven't lost the ability to sweet talk me" Rosanne said before hanging up.

Chapter Two

Detective Will Deas used his shoulder to push the heavy door of Police Headquarters open so his short somewhat overweight frame could make its way through. He wearily nodded to a couple from drugs heading the other way because his arms were full of files and papers on the last case he worked. He had been up part of the night finishing off reports for his boss Collin Fraser, head of homicide, and the prosecutor and he was tired.

His old bones, having done the same thing for thirty-five years somehow knew only six more were left before retirement and six months each year soaking up Florida sun. But between this day and then the rumpled suit of Will Deas along with his weary bones and sore eyes would continue to be the best Hamilton had.

He became a cop after being laid off as a burner in the flat-plate rolling mill of Dominion Foundries and Steel in Hamilton. At the time his pretty wife was pregnant with their first child and due in less than six weeks. His apartment's rent of a hundred and fifty dollars was due in two weeks and his pogey, as unemployment insurance was called, was due when the government decided to send his first cheque. The young Will knew Dofasco was the best steel mill in the world to work but waiting for a call-back wasn't an option. There was no doubt he needed a job with a secure pay cheque right away. He started looking.

Will soon discovered his city was looking for new policemen. Recruits had to meet a preset standard in intelligence, physical fitness and have the ability to handle themselves in the gritty back alleys of a tough steel town. Will Deas, only a few years out of the Gorbals of Glasgow, knew how to survive on mean streets better than most and decided the city needed him.

He breezed through the initial tests, was accepted and entered their training program. Throwing himself into the schedule he did well and his instructors noted the young Scot as one to watch. Four months later, with his again pregnant wife proudly watching with their newborn son in her arms, Will Deas was sworn in with eleven other new policemen and his long march to detective began.

Assigned to a beat in the notorious north end of Hamilton, Will the rookie was soon walking down James Street beside a huge grizzled old street cop who towered over Will's five foot nine frame.

This partner, who at first scared the hell out of Will was one Constable First Class Patrick Ryan, nearing sixty and as Irish as Paddy's pig. Ryan knew more about human nature, policing, and the needs and desires of those he policed better than anyone the rookie ever met, before or since.

Will's next seven years pounding the streets beside his tough old partner was like a continuous university course in human nature and deviant behavior. As an added extra Will received a first-hand education in all the non-police problems citizens ran into every day. He understood the pain of a mother whose husband dropped dead of a heart attack, the hunger children faced when the breadwinner of the family was on strike, or the anguish of a girl whose fiancé was arrested for some minor criminal act. He saw, but never mentioned his partner dipping into his own pocket to slip a dollar or two into the hand of someone down on his luck, shooing them away when they tried to thank him. Will grew in many ways during those years with PC Ryan. He became wiser, more understanding and learned to tolerate the idiosyncrasies of the world around him.

During that time the brass were taking note of his work and when Patrick Ryan retired they moved Will to the investigators division. They knew what they were doing because Will Deas developed into the best damn detective on the Hamilton Police Force.

"Collin wants to see you" called the Desk Sergeant as Will came through the door. The Sergeant didn't bother raising his head or taking his eyes of his morning paper because he knew Will from a distance by the smell of Will's pipe. It wasn't just any pipe. It was an ancient toxic briar always stuffed with Gallahar's Irish Plug. Though tucked into a pocket of Will's jacket the acrid smell of the course black tobacco clung to him and announced his presence to anyone within twenty feet. Most considered the aroma of his pipe a great stink.

"Gotcha" Will called back and turned to his right.

Collin Fraser was Chief of Detectives and would someday be chief of the whole place. About six foot two with a handsome square face and a charming smile, he moved about the community making speeches at service clubs and schools. If he hadn't become a cop he would have made a great politician. Everyone believed he would be the next Chief and Will thought about that as he rapped on Collin's door before pushing it open.

"What's up?" he asked of the man behind the desk.

"The Dundas killing" Collin said, waving him toward a seat. "The one on the morning news, I'm sure you heard. Nothing much gets by you."

"You mean the drunk in the alley behind the bar? Sure, I heard. Sounds rather routine."

"Probably is" Collin said and set aside some papers to give Will his full attention. "It appears to be an old fashioned mugging that went sour but you know the Dundas crowd. All those Foo-Foo people hiding in their million dollar homes need a little hand holding. The mayor wants a show of the old 'There's nothing to worry about' and maybe a little of the 'It's an isolated incident' thrown in. I'm having a press conference in an hour to announce that we're assigning our best detective to the case and I'll tell them he's working on it as we speak. You're in charge and this should be wrapped up very quickly." Collin smiled at Will.

"I wish you had warned me. I would have put on a clean shirt and shined my shoes."

"Don't worry, I doubt anyone would notice. Clean shirt, shiny shoes, even a brush through your mop would make no difference. You'd still smell like an old outhouse." Both laughed.

"Do you need me at the announcement?"

"No, you're not up to speed yet so best you be scarce. I'll say you were assigned early this morning, which you were, and you're working hard studying the evidence we've collected.

"Go see Ford in forensics and get what he has then check with Davidson. He was chief uniform at the scene last night and did the file. He'll be happy to turn it over. When you collect it all, go home. I want you to stay away until you're up and running and able to do your own press conference, now on your way" and he waved Will out of the office.

Leaving with a fake groan Will headed for forensics. He smiled at the idea of spending the rest of the day lounging near his pool with his old cat Sherlock and a dram or two of his favorite amber liquid close at hand. It certainly beat working.

Crickets
By Evelyn

It started off quietly, as always. She yearned for sleep and thus convinced herself the soft patter was just rain. She could see it now, slipping between the small gaps in the screen to tap against the window in her kitchen. Yes rain, that's all. A voice came up from the abyss that was her sleep shrouded mind, a voice of reason, a rational voice to cut through the fog. "Why is it never in the same place?" The apartment was small, practically all one room save for her bedroom at the back, no wonder the noise carried. She felt her cat stir, getting up from his spot at her feet to investigate the noise. Exhaustion beat out her sense of curiosity, pulling her eyes shut as her cat slipped out the door and into the hallway.

Groggily she reached out to tap her alarm, slowly her vision came to her and what registered first was the time, the green numbers on its familiar face did not say seven but rather three. She could not fathom why her alarm would be going off already, confusion built as she again reached out to turn it off, yet it was not her clock making the shrill noise that woke her. The floor was cold against her feet, almost wet to the touch as she slipped out from underneath her sheets. Her skin stuck to it with perspiration and fear as she made her way towards the kitchen.

An eerie shadow was cast upon the room, melding the sparsely furnished space together, cut only by the red light coming from the clock above the television. Crumpled in her sink, barely visible, was her cat; ears flat against its head, fur bristling, and yowling with its eyes fixed on something beyond her. Through the shrieks, she heard something else, almost inaudible, a very faint tapping. The tapping was coming from the wall she shared with her neighbors, the very spot her cat seemed to be fixated on. As she approached the wall the tapping grew louder and was now accompanied by an odd rustling. She brushed the few loose strands of hair away from her face as she pressed her ear to the wall.

The room grew quiet, the cool plaster met her skin and gooseflesh blossomed along her neck. All she heard was the pounding of her heart and then a tap. A soft knocking reverberated along the wall, constant and paced evenly yet it grew in volume, reaching out in search of something. Exhausted and driven mad by the noise, she thrust the heel of her palm against the wall. The plaster gave way, enveloping her hand, as both cat and owner were deafened by the ringing. A prickling, almost sticky sensation, consumed her arm in the darkness and small black beetles began pouring from the hole. She stumbled backwards, ripping her arm from the rapidly growing gap, and failed to notice the glass table behind her. Slipping she broke the surface. Waves of the small glimmering shards rose up, fiercely biting into her skin, before exploding outwards onto the carpet.

Tangled up in the iron frame she frantically twisted for freedom as masses of the black bugs teemed from the still crumbling wall. In her daze, the wall came alive, the dark figures writhing over the surface to become one living thing, dripping down the wall and pooling on the carpet below. She could just make out the scraping noise over the shrill ringing of the bugs, it was coming from inside the wall. To her horror it was moving towards the hole. Her eyes followed its progression across the wall, as she pushed herself out of the dilapidated frame and across the shimmering carpet. Glass bits shredded her skin and the loose fibers of the rug caught on the rough edges, stretching the jagged cuts and peeling them back. Upon its approach the little figures scattered, abandoning their trail across the floor. They flew across the room forming a long dark tongue probing the air in search of an escape. Crickets, she realized, that's what they were.

A hand reached out into the swarm of crickets that now filled the room, the fingers snatching the small airborne bodies and crippling them between its seized joints. She watched the hand disappear not exactly sure of what she had seen. This time when the hand reappeared it stretched out wildly finding it hard to grasp the frantic insects. She watched a small crack creep down the already crumbling plaster as the wall beneath the hole buckled under the weight of the arm. "NO!" She cried out but her words were lost in the twister of screaming crickets.
The last of the plaster gave way spitting out what appeared to be a man. Covered in the insects he pulled himself from the

wreckage of the wall, the red light dancing between the shadows off the skin clinging to his skull. His joints sticking out sharply from under his skin, she watched as they twisted to push him up. His eyes unused to the light seemed to have no focus, there were crickets crawling out of the carnage inside his mouth, some still alive struggled between his teeth, wings clung to his lips and glistened with the saliva that was now seeping down his chin. His eyes found her, he studied her shape. To her it seemed like he wasn't exactly sure of what he was looking at. The light caught his eyes, they were hollow and cold, it was not uncertainty it was hunger in his eyes. His fingers twitched as he crawled forwards towards her, she could hear the broken glass grinding underneath his nails. She opened her mouth to scream but was gagged by the mass of frantic crickets.

Still

By Angela Ford

Chapter One

On a warm dark summer night Brianna stood, motionless, in the park where the murder had taken place. There wasn't a single visible star in that pitch-black sky above her. Brianna veered off the lighted pathway and waited in the still of the night. The darkened shadows of trees surrounded her. Not a single consideration of fear crossed her mind. In fact, she felt nothing since the death of her sister. A murder she had become obsessed with to solve. She held her breath as she heard the sound of nearby footsteps. *Was it him?*

At twenty-eight, Constable Brianna Wilson was part of the Special Victims Unit. She had been with the police force for over five years. Her Inspector told her she'd let her sister's death become personal. He advised her to take the time she needed to grieve her loss and let the homicide department do their job. She couldn't let it go. She was determined to find her sister's killer. She owed it to her sister. She owed it to their mother.

She hadn't had a date since the night her sister was killed. Brianna swore she'd never date again. She was angry at herself for going out that night when she should have stayed home with her sister like she had promised. If she had, Lisa wouldn't have gone out to meet a man she had only spoken to online. Brianna had talked to Lisa several times about internet predators and the dangers of chatting online with strangers. She dealt with these issues daily on her job. *Why did my sister take the risk of meeting him face-to-face?* So many questions raced through Brianna's mind as she waited.

Footsteps echoed in the dark. She knew it wasn't the sound of an animal. Sadly, she hoped it was him. Despite the darkness and how unsafe it was to be there, she waited with her Smith & Weston .40 caliber pistol in her hand. Her finger rested on the trigger. She knew protocol was to have backup. She had let it become personal. Homicide hadn't been able to track the so-called predator Brianna found on her sister's computer. Brianna lured him herself.

Brianna swallowed hard as the sound of footsteps became inches away from her. She'd been waiting twenty minutes or so. He was late. Her eyes had adjusted to the night's darkness enough to determine shadowed figures. She felt his presence so close she could smell whiskey from his breath. Slowly she moved one foot to balance her stance. Before she grounded her foot she felt a sharp point at her back and heard his rough voice whisper, "It's your turn". The coldness in his tone should have sent a shiver up her spine. It didn't. In one quick sudden movement, her elbow jabbed him and dug in between his ribs. Her reaction had stunned him long enough for her to turn and point her pistol at him. Brianna could see his shadowed position but not his face clearly.

"Brianna?" The tone in his voice was no longer cold, no longer confident. It startled her that he knew her name. She tried hard to focus on his face but the shadow before her turned away. Before she could say anything he ripped a branch off the tree and tossed it between them. Then he was gone. She could only hear footsteps moving faster.

"How do you know my name?" she yelled out but there was no reply.

"Shit!" She stumbled over the tree branch and fell. She was tangled in the branch. She freed herself and headed in the direction of his footsteps. By the time she made it to the lighted pathway, there was no sign of him.

Chapter Two

"Don't worry mom. I'll stay with her. Go and have a great time. You deserve it," Brianna tossed the last pile of clothes into her mother's suitcase. Audrey Wilson sighed, "You're right. I need the break. I haven't seen my sister in so long".

Brianna promised to move into her mom's house for the weekend. Not to babysit but to have a sisters weekend or so she had tried to explain it to her sister. Lisa was seventeen and didn't require a babysitter. Audrey hadn't left her youngest daughter in seventeen years. She'd had Lisa in her mid-forties after finally finding true love. Steve Wilson was that true love. He proposed the day she discovered she was pregnant with Lisa. Brittany was ten when her mother married Steve. She loved him as if he had always been her dad. Brianna never knew her dad. Her mother had only told her it was a one-night stand and she didn't know his name or how to get in touch with him. Steve gave the signed adoption papers to Audrey on the day of their wedding. He told her they would be a complete family. Unfortunately he was taken from her when Lisa was only two years old. A sudden heart attack had left Audrey devastated and lost. She threw herself into her career and became an Honorable Judge before she turned sixty. The only other part of her life that was important to her was being a mom to her daughters. Brittany was ten years senior to Lisa and was more like another mother. Lisa was well loved and protected. The three women were very close.

Brianna had only moved out in the past year. She bought a condo close to work but spent any free time with the women in her life. They were shocked when Brianna hacked into Lisa's computer and discovered a chat group in which she'd been chatting. Neither woman believed Lisa just went for a walk in the park that night. Brianna knew there had to be a reason. She brought this information to the homicide Constable she knew from the training academy. She also began to investigate the chat group on her own. Her line of work dealt with online predators. The man on the chat was good at hiding his IP address. Brianna discovered he must be using a proxy server to make indirect network connections to the Internet to hide the IP address.

After Lisa's funeral Brianna plunked herself down on Lisa's bed and cried. She held tightly onto the teddy bear that always lay on Lisa's bed. Brianna had given her that the day she was born. Audrey heard her daughter's cries and let her be for the time being. She was mourning herself and wasn't sure if she was strong enough to be strong for her daughter. Angrily, Brianna tossed the bear off the bed and then felt bad for doing so. She reached down to pick up the bear and felt something sticking out from underneath Lisa's bed. Brianna was curious and leaned over to grab it. It was Lisa's tabloid. Brianna had forgotten about the tabloid she'd given her for Christmas. She already searched her laptop and found nothing in there. She turned it on only to discover it was password protected. Brianna looked around the room and wondered what her sister would have used. She looked at the teddy bear and smiled. *That would be Lisa.*

Brianna was stunned with what she discovered. "Mom...Mom! Come here," Brianna shouted out as she read her sister's tabloid in horror. Audrey entered Lisa's room, "What's the matter?" Brianna looked up at her mother and motioned for her to sit on the bed. She waved the tabloid in one hand, "I found this under Lisa's bed. Mom, she's been on a chat line. I've warned her so many times. This is not like her. She was chatting with a man she didn't know. And the last entry is dated three nights ago. She went to meet him in the park." Brianna began to cry again, "Oh Mom, it's my fault. I shouldn't have stayed home with her". Her mother's eyes filled with tears. Not only from the recent findings but for her daughter and the guilt she was carrying.

"Oh sweetie, there's only one person to blame. That man who did this to our baby. If we didn't know about her chat room, we would never have been able to stop her. It would have been that night or another." Audrey Wilson held her daughter and cried with her. Brianna swore to her mother between gasps of air that she would find the man responsible.

Brianna's promise became an obsession which forced her Inspector to release her from her duties. It wasn't a suspension without pay but more of a leave for her to take the time to grieve her loss and let homicide do their job. She didn't listen. Homicide wasn't working fast enough for Brianna. She knew their workload and the little information they had to work with. But it was her sister and she was determined to solve this crime on her own. She even kept it from her mother. Brianna began to chat in the same group she'd found, hoping to flag his interest. A couple of weeks later it happened. She received a message from the same name that had appeared in her sister's chats. Brianna smiled. Now she was ready to lure him in.

Chapter Three

"What the hell happened to you?" Audrey opened the front door. Brianna stood before her with dirt and scratches on her face and hands. Brianna took a deep breath, "I was in the park".
"At this time of the night!" her mother sounded terrified and didn't wait for an answer. "It's dark and late. Do you remember what happened to your sister? I know you're a police officer and carry a weapon but what the heck were you thinking! I've already lost one daughter," Audrey furiously rambled on as Brianna entered the house and closed the door.

"Mom, I'm okay and yes I carry a weapon. I found him. Well at least I found him but he ran away. But the creepiest part is that he knew me. He called me by name," Brianna kept walking toward the kitchen as she explained what happened. She headed straight for the coffee pot. She knew her mother was a workaholic too and there was always a pot of coffee on in her house.

"You're not making sense Bri. Who are you talking about?" Audrey stood in the kitchen and looked totally confused.

"Lisa's killer," Brianna turned to her mother and took a sip of her coffee. Audrey plumped herself down in the chair at the kitchen table, "Are you sure? How did you find him? And how does he know you? Who is he?" One question was asked after another. She didn't give her daughter time to answer in between. Brianna joined her mom at the kitchen table and set her coffee cup down. She reached over and placed her hand on top of her mom's, "I've no idea who he is. It was dark and I only seen a shadowed figure for a few minutes before he ran. He had come up behind me when I felt a sharp point in my back. I smelt the whiskey off his breath when he leaned in to whisper in my ear *it's your turn*. But when I startled him with an elbow hit to the ribs, I turned and he said my name. Then he ran off like a coward".

Audrey gasped and raised her hand to her mouth. The fear in her eyes scared Brianna, "Are you okay, Mom?" Audrey shook her head 'no' and tears began to fill her eyes. Her hands were shaking and Brianna tried to comfort her, "Mom, talk to me." Audrey inhaled quickly and wiped the tears from her eyes, "I'm just worried you're in danger. We've just lost your sister. I don't want to lose you too. Promise me you won't go out on your own again. Promise me". Audrey pleaded with her daughter. Brianna nodded in agreement to reassure her mother. Something didn't sit well with her. She knew there was something her mother was not telling her.

Brianna's phone beeped a new message.

"Who would be calling you at this hour?" Audrey questioned her daughter.

Brianna looked at her phone and then at her mother, "It's Peter Collins. I messaged him on my way here. I need his help". She answered by the third ring, "Hi Pete. Sorry to bother you at this hour but I need your help." Brianna got up from the table and walked toward the family room to finish her conversation in private. She didn't want her mother to hear the happenings of her night all over again. It appeared to have shaken her up a bit.

Brianna told Pete what had happened in the park because of the information she'd found on Lisa's tablet. Pete had called her daily since her sister's death. Brianna hadn't returned his calls until now. Now, she needed him.

"What the hell were you thinking Bri? You know better than to go in without backup," his tone sounded both worried and upset. For a moment she thought it sounded like he really cared about her. It had been five years.

She confided she'd been put on a leave from work, "My Inspector thinks I've let my sister's murder get personal." Brianna laughed.

"This isn't funny Bri. I think he's right. Maybe some grieving time is what you need. Let the police deal with the murder," Peter's tone was authoritative yet caring.

"I am a cop. I need to find my sister's killer. Homicide isn't finding anything. I tracked the murderer down. Then I lost him. I need your help in tracking him again," Brianna's tone was dead serious and Peter figured he wasn't about to win this argument. "What can I do to help?"

"Your expertise, you're the computer genius. Help me track this hidden IP address because I know for sure he won't answer on the chat group again," Brianna pleaded for his help. There was only one thing on her mind and that was to find her sister's killer.

"Thanks for the coffee Mom. And the listening ear. Don't worry. I'm armed," Brianna's tone was nonchalant. She kissed her mom's cheek and grabbed her backpack.

"Why don't you stay here tonight? I'd feel better knowing you were safe under my roof," Audrey reached for her daughter's arm. Brianna paused for a moment.

"Sorry Mom. I'm meeting Pete in ten minutes." She kissed her mom's cheek once more. Before Audrey could say another word, Brianna was gone. Audrey got up and locked the front door and with shaken hands, reset the alarm. She placed a hand over her heart and prayed, "Please keep her safe".

Brianna walked with confidence down the dim lit sidewalk toward the Tim Hortons she'd met Pete that fateful night. Determined to find her sister's killer again. *Who the hell was the man in the park? He seemed too cocky at first to be an amateur. He must have killed before.* Her car was already parked at Tim Horton's before entering the park across the street earlier. She unlocked the passenger side and reached for her tablet before going in. She grabbed a table at the back corner and waited for Pete.

"Brianna"

She looked up into glimmering hazel eyes. The same eyes that had pleased her attention back in college. His blond curls had darkened a bit over five years. The curls were now trimmed. In college they were longer and messed up in a sexy way. He still had that look that would make any woman look twice. She smiled, "Pete".

Pete smiled back, "Are you sure you're okay? Sounds like you had a dangerous night. Did you see a doctor?" The concern in his voice touched her heart. He was still sweet. He'd been her best friend in college. Good-looking and sweet she remembered. Not like the idiot she thought she was in love with.

"I'm fine. Just a few scratches. Thanks for meeting me so late Pete. I need your help." She stood up and hugged him. It felt the same. His arms embraced her and gave her that same feeling of comfort after her boyfriend dumped her at their graduation party. She'd forgotten how great he always smelled. A mixture of his cologne and manly scent played with her senses. She released from the hug and wiped those thoughts from her mind. She had a killer to find. "Can I buy you a coffee?"

He smiled, "Allow me. French Vanilla, still?" Brianna nodded. She bit her lip as she watched him walk to the counter. *Stay focused Brianna. You have a killer to find.*

Pete returned with coffees in hand and joined her at the table. He opened his laptop.

"I found the man in a chat group on Lisa's tablet that she last spoke with. It appears he's used a hidden IP," Brianna informed him and took a sip of her coffee.

Pete worked for IBM as a Technical Analyst. He was a genius when it came to computers. He accepted his first job on the west coast after graduation. Brianna had been accepted into the police academy at the same time. Their one steamy night together had been the night before he left. They kept in touch for a little while but both were enthralled in their careers. The miles in between hadn't helped.

Pete copied the IP into his program and began to work his magic. If there was one person who could track this IP, Brianna believed it was Pete. She watched him work. His fingers flew across the keyboard. His eyes swayed back and forth. They were dreamy eyes. He was amazingly sexy. *Quit it Brianna. Not now. Stay focused.* She let him work and took another sip.

"Got it!" His sudden words made her jump. It had been so quiet for the past fifteen minutes. There wasn't another soul in the shop besides them and the staff. He looked up and smiled. He moved his laptop around for her to see his screen. Brianna grabbed her phone and typed in the address.

"I don't know if you'll find him there but this is the address where that last conversation took place," Pete confidently assured her.

"It's only a couple of blocks from here," Brianna put her phone in her pocket and reached out to touch his hand, "Thanks Pete. I knew you could find it."

"You're not going alone?"

"I'm on suspension or leave for grief…however you want to look at it. My inspector believes I've made it personal…"

"Then I'm going with you."

"You're not a cop. I can't let you."

"I'm not losing you again, Bri."

Chapter Four

"Inspector?" Audrey hated to call at this hour but she was worried about her daughter's safety and she couldn't get those words out of her mind.

"Yes, who is this?" a sleepy voice confirmed.

"It's Judge Wilson. Audrey. I believe Brianna is in danger. Can you come over?" Audrey got right to the point as always. She was a driven powerful woman who usually got what she wanted. She was well-respected.

Audrey paced the hallway between the kitchen and the front door. She chewed on her nails. An old habit she had in college. The doorbell startled her. She was a bundle of nerves ever since her daughter repeated the words 'it's your turn'. Audrey opened the door to Inspector Paul Matthews. Brianna's boss and a dear friend and colleague of Audrey's for many years now. They had worked on many cases over the years but there was only one that the two of them never discussed. Not for twenty-eight years now. Audrey knew Paul since her days in the Crown's office.

"What is it Audrey? You look like you've seen a ghost," Paul hugged his dear friend.

"Derek MacLean," Audrey only needed to say his name to grab Paul's attention.

"What about him? He's in prison. I thought you said this was about Brianna," Paul threw her a completely confused look.

"Are you certain? I think he's the man responsible for Lisa's death. And I think Brianna is in danger," Audrey poured him a coffee. He took a swig, "What?" Paul shook his head.

"Brianna lured Lisa's killer on that chat group…that one that Lisa was on the night she was killed. Bri met him at the park tonight. He came up behind her and she felt a sharp point in her back. Then he whispered in her ear 'it's your turn'."

Paul stopped midway to raising the coffee cup to his mouth. His jaw dropped. Audrey knew he remembered the MO of Derek MacLean. MacLean whispered those same words in Audrey's ear. Right before he raped her.

"I need to make a call," Paul set his cup down on the counter and pulled his phone off the hook that sat beside his holster. Audrey waited patiently while he made that call. She had to know if MacLean was still in prison. She listened to his side of the conversation in horror.

"What do you mean paroled after twenty-eight years? He was sentenced to two life terms consecutively not one," Paul brushed his hand across the stubble on his face.

"I knew it. He's out," Audrey reached into her pocket and pulled out an envelope. She handed it to Paul, "You need to read this. This will confirm he's suspects who Brianna is". Paul opened the envelope and began to read the hand-written scribble.

"Does Brianna know?"

"No. I've kept it secret her whole life. I almost told her after she told me what the man in the park said to her but I couldn't," tears formed in Audrey's eyes. She began to shake. Paul took her in his arms and promised, "I'll find the bastard". He released from their hug, "Where's Brianna?"

"She left over a half-hour ago. She went to meet her friend Pete who's a computer whiz. She figures he'll track that hidden IP address and locate Lisa's killer." Paul dialed Brianna's cell number.

"Inspector? Everything okay," Brianna answered after the first ring.

"Where are you?"

"Out with a friend. Why?"

"I know what you're doing. Where exactly are you? I know who the killer is. You're in danger." Paul was not only her boss but a close friend of the family. He and his wife were Brianna's godparents.

"Who?"

"I'll tell you in person once I get your location," Paul wasn't the man to argue with and Brianna never tried him. She gave him the address.

"Your mother and I will be there in ten minutes." Paul disconnected the call and turned to Audrey, "Are you strong enough for this?" She nodded. She would do anything for her daughter even if it meant she was putting her own life in danger. There was nothing in the world she wouldn't do to protect her daughter.

"My mother?" Brianna starred at the phone after the disconnection and turned to Pete, "Why the hell is he bringing my mother?"

Chapter Five

Brianna pulled her Smith & Weston from its holster. Pete looked horrified, "Thought you were supposed to wait for your Inspector?" Brittany kept her eyes focused across the street on the man she noticed, "Can't...there he is". She opened the car door and turned to Pete, "Stay here and tell him I went in".

"You're crazy Bri. It's not safe to go in by yourself. Don't be so damn stubborn," Pete pleaded with her. He was unsuccessful. She closed the door and walked across the street to an older home but still a decent neighborhood. She figured he was middle class even to afford renting the place if he didn't own it. She crept up the walkway and kept against the bushes near the front door as she scouted her surroundings. She took notice to dim lighting. He wasn't in the front room. She looked up and noticed a light turned on upstairs. She made her way to the front door. She turned the knob slowly and discovered it was unlocked. Slowly she opened it and entered with her gun drawn. She felt a presence behind her and turned quickly. Her gun pointed directly at Pete. He put his hands up and whispered, "You're not doing this alone". She motioned for him to leave and he shook his head. She wasn't about to argue with him and make her presence aware to the man upstairs. With one hand on her gun she stretched her arm back to keep Pete safely behind her and moved to the bottom of the staircase.

"Put your hands where I can see them," Brianna ordered the man who appeared at the top of the stairs.

"Come on Brianna. You can't shoot your old man now," he began to walk down the stairs. He appeared confident again in a creepy way.

"Stop where you are and put your hands where I can see them," she demanded.

"Listen sweetie, I'm sorry about tonight. I didn't expect to find you in the park. I was just looking for a little fun. I'd never hurt you, only your sister and your mother. You're my flesh and blood," he continued down one step at a time. Slowly, like he was taunting her. Startled by his words she wondered what the hell he meant. Then she heard her mother's voice.

"Come any closer to her Derek and I'll shoot you myself," Audrey Wilson's words shocked Brianna. Paul moved Audrey behind him and motioned for Pete to stay with her.

"Well if it isn't Officer Matthews. What a reunion we have here," MacLean's sarcasm and laughter filled the room.

"Back-off MacLean, I have no trouble pulling the trigger on a bastard like you," Paul's disgust for the man was easily read.

"What the hell is going on here? Mom?" Brianna yelled out to her mother without taking her eye of the man on the staircase. Her gun still pointed at him. Before Audrey could speak, Derek MacLean took the spotlight.

"Guess your mother hasn't told you. I knew your mother twenty-nine years ago. She kept us apart all these years. I'm your father." Brianna wasn't sure if she was more horrified with his words or the cold-blooded tone of his voice when he spoke.

"You raped me twenty-nine years ago. You don't deserve to be a part of her life. You deserve to be behind bars," Audrey's voice echoed in the dark. Her tone scarred Brianna. She was trying to piece all of this together.

"That's not what you wanted back then. Our night was special. It was the night we conceived our daughter. I was never arrested or convicted for what you accuse me of," Derek made it sound as though Brianna was made out of love not crime. She trusted her mother. She knew she couldn't be lying. She didn't know this man to trust him.

Paul spoke up before Derek MacLean could continue, "It sickens me to listen to this. We made the best choice. The charges against the young girl you killed were dropped only to a mistrial of missing evidence. We could have charged you with rape and sent you to a Canadian jail for a few years tops. The FBI wanted you for two murders in the States. They said they'd put you away for two consecutive life sentences. That was the best choice. Get you out of the country and behind bars for the rest of your life."

"Don't listen to them Brianna. They're only trying to keep us apart. I'm your Dad. Trust me," Derek's evil tone ripped through Brianna. Not in fear but in disgust. She knew her mother better than what he was saying.

"Any man can be a father. It takes a special man to be a Dad. You definitely don't fit that category," Brianna quickly answered him. He took a step. He was now mid-way down the staircase. It was still too dark to see his hands.

"I said stop where you are and put your hands where I can see them," Brianna commanded. He took another step. The partial light from upstairs only lit half the staircase. Brianna could now see his hand slowly rise. He was armed.

"Stop or I'll shoot," she yelled.

"You won't shoot me. I'm still your father," he took another step with his gun pointed at the front door. Brianna knew her mother was behind her. Her gut told her he was going to shoot her mother.

"Now, it's your turn," Brianna whispered as the sound of the bullet left her pistol and took him down. Paul reached over and took Brianna's weapon. He felt for a pulse on Derek and shook his head. Then reached for Derek's weapon and called the shooting in.

Brianna ran to her mom. Tears flowed upon her cheeks. Her mother's hug gave her comfort. "I'm sorry Brianna. I should have told you. I just wanted to protect you."

"I know Mom. I know," Brianna released from their hug and smiled. Her mother wiped away her tears. She then realized Pete was standing there, "Oh, Pete, I'm sorry to have dragged you into this".

"Told you earlier there's nothing that can keep us apart again," Pete smiled and then took her in his arms. It was exactly where she wanted to be.

For the Love of God
by Nicholas Boving

"*For the love of God Montresor.*" How those words had at first thrilled and exulted him. He had had his revenge. But of late they had begun to haunt him. And now, as he lay on his deathbed with eternity staring him down, he felt a need to unburden his soul: not for any spiritual reason, but to let it be known that his one great crime, so successful, could at last be solved.

* * *

And so Montresor sent his coachman with a message summoning me – there is no better word for it was indeed a summons – to his bedside. I was to cease whatever I was engaged in and attend him immediately before it was too late and he had gone to whatever place the dead must go.

* * *

The curtains were drawn, the air stale with that smell all sickrooms have, and the man, once so robust, seemed shrunken to half his size. The hand of death had clearly seized him and had no intention of relinquishing its grasp.

He beckoned me, coughing feebly as he attempted to raise himself on his pillows.

"You remember the case of Fortunato?" he asked, his voice as light and rustling as winter leaves swirling on dry ground. I nodded. Of course I remembered. It had been fifty or so years ago when I was quite young. The man in question, reputedly a braggart and womanizer, had mysteriously vanished. There was something of a hue and cry as to his possible whereabouts, but nothing satisfactory had ever been discovered and the general opinion was that he had absconded rather than face the sword or dagger of an irate husband.

"I have a confession," he said. Then he shook his head. "No, not a confession but rather an unburdening of my conscience. The damned thing has been a trial to me these last fifty years, and now my time has come I must at the very least tell someone. Not to obtain absolution, you understand, merely to clear up what has been a mystery."

I told him that what he needed was a priest rather than a doctor, as there was nothing I could do to halt the inevitable hand of time. His reaction was somewhat shocking. His face darkened and his fingers clawed at the coverlet.

"Lice, parasites all on the corpus of mankind. Idle and good for nothing but trite, meaningless, quasi-comforting words spewed forth as the minds issuing them focus on something of more immediate benefit to themselves."

He fell back, his chest heaving with effort and emotion. Then his mood changed and he managed a crooked smile. "The clinical mind of a doctor is what is required, and then perhaps the police."

"The police?" I could not imagine why a man going to meet his Maker would want the law involved, unless what his conscience held was some great crime. But my knowledge of Montresor did not include criminal enterprises. He was, while not particularly sociable - in fact he mostly went out of his way to avoid the company of his fellow man unless there was business involved – a respected member of the community whose opinions were on occasion asked for on local matters.

But little do we know those among whom we spend our lives, for they guard their secrets unless some occurrence brings them into the cruel light of day, where they stand, blinking and exposed.

There was a long pause in which the only sound was his harsh, laboured breathing and the mesmerizing tick of the clock on the mantel. Then he cleared his throat and I looked at him.

"I killed Fortunato." There was a small chuckle, a dry rustle like beetles wings rubbing. "And yet that is not correct. Some might call it murder, but I do not. Better the truth and say I avenged an insult." He frowned as if conjuring a memory. His lips moved and I had to bend to catch the words. "*Nemo me impune lacessit.*" Which I took to mean; "No one insults me with impunity." Then the small chuckle came again and the words, "Yes, for the love of God. Drunk he was, and wearing a fool's garb, for it was a masque, a carnival." He chuckled again. "A fool's garb for a fool. Striped pantaloons and a conical hat with a bell that tinkled as he walked. I lured him to the catacombs with a promise of more drink, a wine I wanted his opinion on, a cask of Amontillado. The fool fancied himself a connoisseur and followed like a schoolboy eager for his first whore."

"Why tell me now?"

A small frown creased his forehead and he looked towards the window where light peeked in through imperfectly drawn curtains.

"A transgression, a crime, entering a man's life, eats it up like a malignant growth, consumes it like a fever." He breathed deeply and with great effort. "I lost my peace and now I must unburden myself before death claims me."

After that his eyes closed and he seemed to sleep. I rose to leave them room, for the truth was I had no wish to be involved in the confessions of a murderer, no matter how long ago the deed had occurred. But as I reached the door and quietly turned the knob, he called out.
"I have not told you the where of it. You will have no chance of finding the unfortunate Fortunato without my directions."

I went reluctantly back to the bed and looked down at the ashen, lined face. He smiled again.

"Fortunato was indeed a most inept name for one who had little good fortune at his end." He pointed to a portfolio on the nightstand. "In there you will find my confession and a map of the catacombs that are linked to the wine cellars beneath this palazzo. The whereabouts of Forunato's tomb is marked with a red cross."

I opened the leather folder and, taking out a much used parchment, saw a map of considerable complexity with tunnels seemingly wandering without rhyme or reason, an unplanned maze in which it might be possible to become hopelessly mired without such a chart. At the end of one obscure side passage there was a red cross. There was no legend, simply the sign and a date that would have meant nothing to the casual observer.

Montresor reached out a claw to take the parchment from me. He peered at it myopically and with a bony forefinger stabbed the spot.

"There. There you will find Fortunato, or what can be left of him after these fifty years." He gave me back the map. "Take it and go to the police. *Inspettore di polizia* Salvatore is a good man. He will know what to do." Seeing the surprise or perhaps alarm on my face he added. "I do not think he will waste his time arresting me: I am already condemned and the Angel of Death is outside the door."

I must have seemed puzzled, for he explained. "I chained him to a stake in one of the niches, then walled him in." There was an unpleasant twinkle in his rheumy eyes. "I believe death by starvation is particularly lingering."

* * *

A cold wind from the mountains was playing spitefully through the streets as I left Montresor's palazzo. I pulled the collar of my coat more closely around my ears, tugged my hat brim down and walked the short kilometre to the *posto di polizia*. Inspector Salvatore was in his office but engaged, and I was left to cool my heels with some impatience until he emerged. He spread his hands in a gesture of apology.

"Doctor. Forgive me." He stood aside and waved me into his sanctum. I removed my hat and sat down. Salvatore retired to the other side of his desk, pushed forward a silver box and offered me a cigarette.

"And what may I do for you?" he asked.

I had rehearsed my lines while waiting, but when the moment came I found myself somewhat at a loss. The story seemed implausible at best and a waste of a busy man's time at worst. I shrugged and lit my cigarette.

"I have just come from Signor Montresor's bedside."

Salvatore showed concern. "He is unwell?"

"He is dying," I said."

"My God! I had no idea. How may I help?"

I brushed his words aside. "That is not the reason for my calling on you. He has made a confession."

Salvatore frowned. "The sanctity . . ."

"Not that kind," I said. "Montresor has little time for priests. It seemed he needed to unburden his conscience, not save his soul." I took a deep draught of tobacco smoke. It soothed my nerves. "Does the name Fortunato recall any memories?"

Salvatore frowned, and then his brow cleared and he snapped his fingers.

"My father, who was a policeman before I, spoke of it. The man disappeared suddenly."

"His body is in the catacombs beneath Montresor's palazzo."

If I had desired to make an impression I would have certainly succeeded. Salvatore stared, his mouth slightly open. He sat back.

"And you know this how?"

"Montresor has just told me. There is a map of the catacombs indicating where the body lies. Montresor said he was chained to a stake, walled in and allowed to die of starvation."

Long seconds passed. A heavy cart rumbled by in the street, and there was shouting as a suspect was brought in for questioning. Salvatore reached out for a cigarette, lit it and said.

"The map is where?"

I took it from my pocket and passed it to him.

He took it between finger and thumb as if it were infected with some disease and spread it on his desk. He studied it, then glanced at me questioningly.

"The cross marks the place, one assumes."

"So Montresor told me."

He took his watch from his pocket. "It is yet early. Is Montresor well enough to visit, to question?"

I shrugged. "It can do no more harm. Do you wish me to come?"

He stood, threw on his coat and took his stick from a stand. "But of course doctor. If we find this unfortunate Fortunato I shall require your expert medical opinion as to the cause of death."

Much as I would rather have returned to my work and laboratory, there was little choice, and after telling his desk sergeant he would be out until further notice, we set off for Montresor's palazzo.

The wind had dropped somewhat and a watery sun made an attempt to add sparkle to the waters of the bay around which the town was built. We walked in silence, each buried in his thoughts until the imposing entrance was reached. Salvatore rang the bell and moments later we were inside.

Montresor's condition seemed unchanged, though I think he was displeased to see the Inspector, perhaps thinking the giving of the map and his confession to me would be sufficient. Salvatore went to the bedside. He looked down sternly at the dying man, and there was little sympathy in his face.

"The doctor informs me that you have confessed to the murder of the man Fortunato."

"Have you come to arrest me?"

The Inspector ignored the question. "Why did you kill him?"

Montresor cleared his throat. He asked for water. Salvatore again ignored him. "I repeat. Why did you kill him?"

Montresor glanced across to me; a plea for compassion or help. Salvatore waved me back with an imperious flip of the hand. He waited impassively. Finally Montresor gave a minute shrug. "Years of insults became unbearable. I conceived a trap, lured him to the catacombs and, well, you know the rest."

"And for a few insults you take a man's life in such a terrible manner?"

A flash of spirit came into the old man's eyes. "I only wish to God it had been worse." He gave a sigh and waved the Inspector away. "Go. You have a written confession. You have the map. Find Fortunato's pathetic remains and let us have done with it."

"You think I shall not charge you?"

Montresor started to laugh but fell instead into a prolonged bout of coughing. I brushed Salvatore aside, took a bottle of laudanum from the night table, poured some into a tumbler and made the dying man drink. The coughing eased and he fell back exhausted. He shook his head.

"You are too late Inspector. The wings of death hover over me and the Angel has already pronounced sentence."

There seemed to be a short battle of wills, and then Salvatore shrugged, turned to me and pointed at the door.

"Let us go and see if there is any truth to this matter."

* * *

A heavy oak door opened onto the start of a long, winding staircase that eventually debouched onto the wine cellars beneath the palazzo. According to the map, the catacombs lay at the north end. Salvatore lit a bull's eye lantern. The lamp light scarcely penetrated to the other side of the cellars.

"Are you game for this?" he said.

"A fifty-year-old mystery may be solved, Inspector."

Salvatore took a couple of steps forward, peering into the darkness. "The better question might be does anyone any longer care?"

As if answering his own question he set off. I was forced to follow or be left in the dark unless I chose to turn back. However, curiosity got the better of me.

We passed racks and rock cut shelves laid with straw on which were row upon row of crusted wine bottles, some thick with the dust, attesting to the age of the vintages. Salvatore ignored them, concentrating instead on the map which he held so the light shone on it at all times.

The path through the catacombs appeared to continue downwards judging from the trickle of water that gathered from the constant dripping from the nitre covered roof. The dripping of water was a constant, making the ground beneath our feet muddy and soft, forcing us to splash through puddles. It seemed strange to me that the floor of a maze such as that should be of soft material and not of rock as were the walls and roof. But I put the explanation down to some minor geological phenomenon and thought no more of it. There were also many places where rocks and debris had fallen from the roof, which suggested that there might have been disturbances in the past.

Our passage through the tunnels was sufficiently eerie as there was no sound but the drip of water and wet splash of our boots, but it was made the more so by the massed ranks of bones and grinning skulls staring blindly from niches cut into the walls. I knew nothing of the history of the Montresors, but it must indeed have been a long one if all those remains belonged to members of the one family.

Finally Salvatore stopped. We had reached a low ceilinged chamber with but two exits. The air was moist and growing more and more foul, causing the lantern to flicker orange rather than with a healthy yellow gleam. He folded the map and thrust it into his coat pocket.

"There," he said. "The left entrance leads to Fortunato's supposed tomb."

Somehow I was loath to go further, as against all common sense I could not help feeling that perhaps a man who had died such a miserable and lonely death still remained in spirit, unable or unwilling to pass on to whatever reward awaited.

Salvatore being an unimaginative policeman used to facts and not fantasies had already ducked into the entrance and once again I was forced to follow or be left in darkness.

The low tunnel opened into a small rotunda. There were three niches. Two were unoccupied, while the third was blocked, its whole entrance being obscured by a pile of bones. Salvatore placed the lantern on a pile of rocks.

"There it is. The top of the wall is just visible beyond the bones."

And so saying he began to scrape the bones away until the pile collapsed, leaving the courses of masonry exposed. I peered forward. There was no doubt the brickwork had been as it was for many years to judge from the black mould of decay on the mortar and the trailing green slime of algae.

"How are we to break our way in?" I said.

Salvatore thought for a moment then, picking a rock the size of a large melon, he threw it with all his strength against the mortared bricks. There was a hollow ringing crash that echoed throughout the chamber, followed by a trickle of debris. He held the lantern high, and to my surprise the beam showed a considerable crack had formed.

A half dozen more violent blows by both of us sent a section of the upper part of the wall tumbling inwards. Salvatore kicked aside the last of the pile of bones and bare handed ripped the courses down until there was an opening large enough for a man to squeeze through.

Wary of bad air at my insistence, he thrust the lantern through the gap. The flame continued to burn and I judged it safe to go in. The inspector scrambled over the fallen bricks and disappeared. For a moment there was no sound, and then a loud and inventive curse. Salvatore's head emerged.

"Nothing," he said, spitting dust. "The damned man has sent us on a wild goose chase."

He climbed out and I took the lantern and pushed past him to see for myself. It was as he said. Instead of the expected skeleton attached to a stake by chains, there was nothing. I spent a moment or two scouring the niche, no more than the size of a jail cell, but found nothing. At that moment the flame of the lantern began flickering and there was no choice but to retrace our steps as quickly as possible as we both knew that without it we would never find our way back to daylight and safety.

As we emerged into the wine cellar the flame finally died, but it was a matter of a few seconds before we climbed the winding staircase and came out into the lower offices of the palazzo.

Salvatore dusted himself down, showing every sign of being annoyed, and I had to admit his annoyance seemed justified.

"The man has deliberately misled us," he said.

Indeed it seemed so, but I could not reconcile such mischief with a deathbed confession. Salvatore was forced to agree that it was illogical.

I protested. "And yet we have a signed confession of murder. We have a map."

"We have no corpse, doctor. Which begs the question: do we in fact have a crime?"

For a while we discussed the possibility of rats disposing of the corpse – but then what of the chains and wooden stake? Salvatore suggested the whole might have rotted away over fifty years, until I reminded him that as a doctor I found such an event unlikely in the extreme. And again, there was the matter of the chains. Despite everything it seemed that Montresor had indeed made a bogus confession. But to what possible end? The man I we had both known, although somewhat taciturn and unsociable, was definitely not given to foolish pranks.

The fact remained that Fortunato had gone missing. But then so had many others for reasons of their own, and not necessarily the result of foul play. But I had been at Montresor's bedside just a few hours before and had detected nothing but the truth from a man whose conscience was bothering him and who had a need to unburden himself.

The alternative was that the map was in error, but we discarded that theory as implausible. No doubt there had been many false maps regarding treasures, but why create one that served no purpose but to provide evidence of a grisly murder?

Salvatore wanted at that point to question Montresor further, but on being reminded of the man's feebleness and approaching end, he shrugged and said it could wait till the following morning.

As it turned out the following morning was too late, for Montresor died in the night, and once again I was called to his bedside by his coachman, but that time to attest to his death and provide a certificate.

I looked down on the ashen face one last time. Death had shrunk it even further so the skin sat tight against the skull, the lips slightly drawn back from the teeth. The shadow of a smile, perhaps? Had Montresor had the last laugh, sending us on a fool's errand? But to what purpose? I pulled the sheet over his face and nodded to the women who would prepare the corpse for burial.

As if left the palazzo something continued to bother me, something unanswered, perhaps unanswerable tugged at my thoughts. I knew in my heart that Montresor had indeed done as he had said. Fortunato had been chained and walled into that niche in that noisome catacomb, left to die a slow and painful death. And yet, both Salvatore and I, not fanciful men, could attest to any court of law that the body and the chains that held it were no longer there. Somehow, and there I knew it was by logical means as I utterly discarded fantastic or the supernatural, Fortunato's earthly remains were gone.

The impossible had occurred. As one whose life revolved around research of the natural sciences, there was no such thing as the impossible. God might perform miracles, but man did not.

On my way back to my house and laboratory, I attended a street accident between a carriage and an unfortunate porter. The man had a badly broken leg. I had him delivered to the nearby hospital and attended to the fracture, by which time the late afternoon had arrived and my dinner and a comforting fire took all my attention. As is said, sufficient unto the day is the evil thereof. Montresor and the mystery of Fortunato were driven from my mind in anticipation of creature comforts.

It seemed to me the investigation had literally arrived at a dead end. But Inspector Salvatore surprised me as he became stubborn. He refused to give up. He ordered a complete search of the house for secret panels and hidden rooms, but despite the best efforts of his men found nothing. I met him shortly afterwards as I was on my way to see a patient. We discussed the mystery briefly as I was in a hurry. His parting words echoed my thoughts.

"It is as if he had been spirited away. But that is nonsense: there must be a logical explanation."

After that I considered it had ceased to be his business. I had told the police, helped as much as I could and was glad to get back to my work.

*   *   *

Perhaps a little about myself may go some way to understanding my thought processes that eventually led to the solution of Fortunato's almost magical disappearance.

I qualified as a doctor of medicine at the university in Vienna, receiving my degree *cum laude* in the year 1882, and returned to my native Italy with the intention of setting up practice in my home town. I did indeed spend two years as a general practitioner, but to my disappointment found the work tedious and unrewarding, both emotionally and financially. The enthusiasm with which I had started off rapidly dwindled in the day to day business of attending to a succession of minor ailments, the occasional accident and one occasion an outbreak of typhoid which fortunately ended before it could expand to epidemic proportions. Other than that, I looked forward to very little and a long tedious future.

But life has a way of serendipitously altering our paths; and so it was in my case when I received a letter with the name and address of a firm of solicitors in San Francisco, informing me that a great uncle who had neither child nor wife, and whom I had seen but once as a boy, had made me sole heir to a fortune gathered in the goldfields during the great rush of 1849. I could scarcely believe my luck, and a few weeks after providing them with the necessary proofs of identity and particulars of my bank, a very large sum was credited to my account: a sum sufficient to allow me to abandon the drudgery of general practice and allow myself to indulge in a field of medicine which had increasingly been engaging my interest – namely that of herbal medicine.

For nearly three years I travelled the world amassing a considerable collection of valuable herbs and medicinal lore from shamans, wise men and women, and those other native peoples around the world for whom such things had for centuries been the natural way of life.

The final result being that I set up a considerable laboratory attached to my home for the intensive study, trial and development of medicines to replace the accepted ones among my profession, but which I had come to believe were either useless, harmful or downright dangerous. This became my life's work. It also unexpectedly provided me with a vital clue to the unexplained disappearance of Fortunato.

* * *

It was a month or so later towards the last week in December with the Christmas season fast approaching – not that I concerned myself overmuch with such things as I was a bachelor – that found me as usual in my laboratory pondering over a method to improve the distillation of the bark of the cinchona tree for the treatment of malaria which was a scourge in many parts of the world, decimating large numbers, when I was disturbed by the passing of a huge dray pulled by four great horses and carrying several great barrels of wine. Feeling the need for a break from my studies I went to the door to watch the magnificent creatures pass and to breathe some cold, clean air. The dray drivers saw me and waved a cheery greeting, to which I responded.

And then my attention was caught by the sound of rattling glass behind me and, fearing damage I turned back to prevent any breakage. On seeing that there was nothing but some tinkling of glass against glass I was about to resume my short break, when my eye was caught by a most unusual movement.

There was a lily, a fine and rare specimen I had collected a year before on a trip to the upper reaches of the Amazon River, which I had set up in a redundant fish tank, planted in a heavy collection of leaf matter, sand and clay, the whole being mixed with dark, viscous mud from a nearby river bank. Around the lily I had, in a moment of whimsy, placed a collection of small stones and a rat's skull which gave it a certain verisimilitude to its original surroundings.

As the heavy dray continued on its way up the cobbled street I saw the lily trembling, and then to my utter amazement the stones, the rat's skull and the lily began to sink into the mixture as if drawn down by some unseen hand. On examining it closely I found that the whole mixture of sand, clay and mud had liquefied, and was even then trembling, bringing a layer of water to the top.

For the rest of that day I confess my attention was taken completely away from the cinchona bark and concentrated on what had occurred in the tank. By assiduously recreating the conditions in the tank each time, and beating rhythmically against the bench with a hammer, I was able in two instances to cause the same phenomenon to reoccur. I made notes of what I had seen and done, and again finding time had passed unnoticed, closed the laboratory and returned to my house for an evening with my books and a good bottle of wine.

Several nights later – I think Christmas had passed and New Year fast approaching – I started from my sleep as a result of an extraordinarily vivid dream in which I had a clear picture of the catacombs beneath Montresor's palazzo. My dream took me deep into the catacombs, winding through the tortuous passages until I stood before the niche where Fortunato had been entombed. As I stood, contemplating the entrance, and being able this time to see the corpse of the unfortunate man, the ground began to shake, small stones fell from the roof, piles of bones rattled, and then, to my amazement Fortunato's body, chained to a heavy stake driven into the floor of the niche, slowly began to sink into the earth until it vanished. At which point the tremors ceased and the ground returned to normal, except there was no longer any sign of its recent inhabitant.

I sat back, resting on my pillows, watching the moonlight through my window, trying to understand what the meaning of the dream might be. And then it came to me with a suddenness that made me cry out in a Eureka moment. The lily in the laboratory and the strange occurrence in the dream were one and the same phenomenon.

* * *

The next morning after a hurried breakfast saw me once again on the street, hurrying to the offices of *Il Quotidiano,* the local paper that served the town and surrounding area. I had on occasion before used the services of the dusty rooms in which they maintained copies of all the back numbers, and the paper had been a fixture of the town's life for as long as living man could remember.

Once divested of my coat and hat I sat at a table with paper and pen to hand and daunting piles of yellowed papers that covered the ten years after the date on Montresor's map. There was nothing for it but to wade into the small mountains of newsprint like an explorer into an unknown swamp.

Even as I quickly scanned and turned each page my heart sank at the size of the task ahead. Twice during the morning the elderly custodian of the archives in his kindness brought me coffee, until eventually as the clocks struck the noon hour I had completed about one third of my self-appointed task and had achieved nothing but ink stained fingers and a persistent sneeze from the dust.

I was on the point of calling a halt and returning to my house for sustenance both solid and liquid, when a headline in bold print sprang out at me. "Earthquake! Tremors and aftershocks! Citizens panic!" The date was some eight years after that on the map. The article was a somewhat exaggerated account of what appeared to have been little more than a substantial tremor that caused minor damage and disturbed some coping on the town hall. But it was exactly what I had hoped for. I had found a clue to the puzzle. I thanked the custodian and made a donation to his retirement fund before returning home.

That evening I went for dinner at my club, something of a rarity as I generally preferred my own company and that of my books, not to mention my cook being superior. But I had a reason in that a member of some standing was an eminent engineer much concerned with bridges and viaducts and therefore their foundations.

Signor Moretti was a tall, erect man with close cropped hair and a white Van Dyke beard that leant him an air of authority and learning. I approached him and suggested we share a table as I had a matter of some importance and wished for his expert opinion. He graciously consented and after the first course which was an indifferent fish dish disguised by a tolerable sauce, I explained what had happened in my laboratory and asked if he had any experience of such a phenomenon, and whether it could indeed have been caused by the passing dray. His answer was immediate if somewhat long-winded, a fault that I have found common in most experts in any field, and no doubt I have on occasion been guilty of the same.

"It is called thixotropy," he said. I endeavoured to lessen the blankness of my mind with an air of expectancy. Moretti continued. It appeared that the term referred to the property of certain gels or fluids that are thick or indeed apparently solid under normal conditions, but flow or become thin and less viscous over time when shaken, agitated, or otherwise stressed. He was entirely certain, he said, that such was the case with my fish tank. I also inquired whether he had any knowledge of the earth tremors of '54. Again he launched into what can only be described as a lecture which I was forced to endure long after having obtained the information I required.

Dinner finally ended, but after that some eminent member felt the need to make a speech of the kind that dragged interminably and with little clear point. But at last I was able to make my excuses and escaped into the street. The lamp standards cast pools of light on the frost covered ground, and there were bunches of evergreens tied with red ribbons to mark the festive occasion.

I confess to feeling at peace, but it may have been the club's wine and the satisfaction of believing I had the answer to the mystery within reach. Whatever the cause I returned to my home in a mellow mood and in an unusual fit of generosity informed my servants they could have the following day to themselves as I should be out and did not expect to return till late.

* * *

Morning came clear and bright and I set out briskly to see Salvatore. And that time he received me immediately, offered cigarettes and insisted on serving coffee while I told him my suspicions and deductions.

When I had finished he peered at me from beneath his heavy eyebrows in such a manner as must have cast fear into his underlings, and then shrugged.

"Moretti says this is possible?"

I nodded. "My inquiries were general. I did not tell him of Fortunato or the catacombs."

He grunted. "That is as well." He leaned forward. "The man has been missing for fifty years. Montresor confessed, and yet we found nothing. Doctor, with the best will possible I find it difficult to justify the further expenditure of money and men. You say we must descend with at the least four strong policemen, together with sledge hammers and shovels?"

After a moment of acute disappointment I assured him that I would underwrite the entire enterprise and the police department would not be required to pay for even the men's meals: I would provide everything except the tools.

Salvatore considered for a moment, then reached across the desk and shook my hand. It was agreed we should meet at Montresor's palazzo in one hour. I thanked him again and hurried back to my home to collect the map, an additional lantern with a flask of spare oil and to fill a leather satchel with sausage and bread. The wine we would collect along the way from Montresor's extensive cellar.

* * *

The ancient palazzo already had an air of disuse even though it had been but a day or two since its owner died. The servants, after throwing dust covers over the furniture had been paid off by the solicitor who handled Montresor's affairs, and to my knowledge, although admittedly incomplete, there were no heirs. It appeared that with his passing the line for so long in that house as attested by the copious bones in the catacombs, would die out, and unless some claimant came forth the ancient building would be allowed to collapse through disrepair.

But that was of no interest to me: the catacombs were.

Salvatore and six burly policemen carrying picks and shovels were waiting as I hurried to the front entrance, and without further ado we went into the house and immediately descended the winding stair to the cellars. As we stopped for a moment before going further into the catacombs I noticed one of the policemen crossing himself, while another took a medallion from his tunic and kissed it. I felt a certain sympathy as I had also felt some trepidation on my previous visit to those noisome tunnels. This time however I was eager to get to the fatal niche and put my theory to the test.

How different it was when in the company of a group of large uniformed men, each well capable of tackling the meanest of criminals. The light from my bull's eye lantern cast a steady glow ahead, and the tramp and occasional squelch of boots was a comforting sound that spelled of purpose rather than my earlier anxiety. There was even a moment of jollity when one of the policemen pointed to an almost complete skeleton leering from a niche, saying that it reminded him of his cousin Bepe. During our decent I also collected some bottles of Medoc as I had a feeling the work might be arduous and thirsts great.

Gradually the air became foetid and the temperature increased. And then we arrived at the small rotunda and before us was the black hole of what Montresor had told us was Fortunato's tomb. I went forward and shone my lantern through the opening. It was the same as before. There was no sign that a man had ever been imprisoned there, let alone chained to a stake.

Salvatore peered over my shoulder. "No miraculous reappearance, doctor?"

I took his skepticism in good humour. "Have patience Inspector. Let us see if my theory is correct."

"And if not?"

I shrugged. "Then I am out of pocket for your men's wages and little else but my own time."

He slapped me on the shoulder and gave the order for his men to come forward. "They are yours to command doctor. Use them as you wish. They are good men and will obey cheerfully."

I went into the niche and called for two of the men to follow me and to bring sledge hammers. There was little enough room after they had come in, so I gave them their instructions and left to similarly deal with the men outside.

"Gentlemen, on my mark and as I call out, do you all strike the rock walls of the inside and outside of this small chamber at the same time."

Salvatore looked quizzical. I enlightened him. "I wish to recreate the conditions as they may have been during the earth tremor of '54. The striking of the hammers against the rock should set up considerable vibration."

The inspector held up the other lantern so that its light was spread throughout the rotunda. I took a deep breath and shouted. "Now."

Six sledge hammers struck the rock simultaneously causing a vibration as if a giant gong had been rung. I crouched down at the niche entrance to better see what happened inside, and called out again for the men to strike with their hammers. Nothing happened and I wondered if perhaps it was necessary that a certain rhythm was required to attain the necessary resonance.

I gave the instruction, and for a full five minutes the six men struck at each down stroke of my arm until the sweat shone from their foreheads.

I was on the point of calling for a halt when my lantern caught the glint of moisture on the floor of the niche, and as it happened one of the men inside shouted that his feet were sinking. Immediately I ordered them out of the small chamber, but the men outside continued with their work, a heavy synchronous beat at two second intervals.

"There," I shouted. "There it is. Look Salvatore, there is water rising." And indeed the whole of the floor in the niche was covered with a thin film that glinted in the lantern light.

I turned. The excitement must have shown on my face for Salvatore laughed, and I could tell he was amazed. I instructed the men to cease which they did willingly enough and all sat down on rocks to mop their streaming faces.

"So now we know that your theory works, that this phenomenon exists. What of it?"

I pointed to the ground under our feet and then to the niche. "Are we up to our ankles in mud? Do you fee yourself sinking?"

Salvatore frowned. "Are you suggesting it only occurs in that one place?"

I spread my hands in a gesture meant to indicate that I did not know. "There may be others, but there is definitely one where Fortunato was imprisoned."

"I assume you have a plan."

Salvatore was either playing with me, or else the inspector was somewhat lacking in intelligence.

"Why else do these fine fellows carry shovels? Of course there is a plan. I intend that they should dig until they either find evidence or fail."

Salvatore snapped his fingers. "Very well. Let us start."

But I restrained him. "An hour Inspector. There may still be quicksand conditions there." I took my satchel and produced the sausages and bread. "Let us eat and wait. After fifty years there can have been little change unless our hammering has sent Fortunato closer to hell."

When the hour had passed I went into the niche to test the ground. All seemed well. The water had disappeared leaving no more than a slight dampness and was firm under foot. I called upon two of the policemen to join me and gave them instructions to dig a hole in the centre where I judged Montresor would in all likelihood have driven the stake.

Again, it was hard work. The air in the confined space became increasingly foetid making regular changes of men absolutely necessary. I refilled both our lanterns and trimmed the wicks, and was beginning to consider the possibility that the evidence was so far down as to be beyond our reach, or that Montresor had indeed played a reprehensible prank, when the was a shout from inside the niche and the policemen stumbled out.

One of them gasped. "There is something there, Signor." He was covered in dirt, wiping it from his face, but there was a grin of excitement showing through.

I hastily took up a lantern and went into the niche. The hole was some five or six feet deep and as many in diameter, with the bottom a slurry of mud. But sticking up from the bottom to a height of some three or four inches was the top of a rotting wooden post. I called for a shovel and scrambled into the hole.

I confess I attacked like a demon, careless of my suit and white shirt. More than once I stopped, panting, to lean against the side. Salvatore tried to persuade me to let the policemen dig, but I was obstinate, feeling I was within reach of my goal and to be proved right.

And then my shovel struck something solid. I dropped to my knees in the filth to scrape away the wet sand with my hands. My fingers touch something smooth and round; and there it was, the domed top of what looked like a human skull. I called out to Salvatore, laughing in my triumph.

"He is here, Inspector. Fortunato is here. Montresor spoke the truth."

Salvatore reached down to grasp my hand and pull me from the hole. He held the lantern down as far as he could to examine the evidence, then stood up. He took my arm and led me from the niche.

"Will it be possible to dig further? The ground is wet and keeps refilling the hole."

I made a futile attempt to brush dirt from my clothes. "We must have evidence," I said. "The skull may belong to anyone."

"And yet we know it is Fortunato's."

I nodded, sure of what he said. "And yet it is strange that no one came forward those fifty years ago. Montresor said he invited Fortunato to the palazzo. There was a carnival. Fortunato wore motley and a fool's cap with a silver bell. He would have stood out, even in such a place."

Salvatore's answering look was that of a world wise policeman who was surprised by little. "People see little and speak less if there is the chance they will become involved."

"Then you will do nothing more?" I desperately wanted to exhume Fortunato's remains from his awful grave, but to do so would have required bailing, if not a hand pump – and to what real end. Salvatore shook his head. I went back into the niche, holding my lantern high for what I realized would be one last look. Salvatore was right, and already the hole was filling with water and the sides crumbling. I watched for a few moments, and then the skull was gone.

I was about to leave when the lantern light caught a glint of metal. I went to it and found, held fast in a small fissure, a small silver bell such as might have been on the top of a fool's cap.

Contributors

Cheryl Antao-Xavier is an author, editor and publisher. She has published **Dance of the Peacock,** 2008; **Bruised but Unbroken,** 2011; **Welcome to Maple Woods, 2014;** and an anti-bullying poem *RISE Up, Rise ABOVE!*
Website: *inourwords.ca/cherylantaoxavier.html*

Chitra Ayyar spent twenty years raising her family in Mumbai, India, which has seen repeated terrorist attacks. This story aims to highlight the tragedy that terrorists inflict on innocent, unsuspecting victims.

Bev Bachmann, a retired high school teacher, lives in Mississauga with her family. Her mystery novel *Christmas Touches* is available in print and e-book format at Amazon.com.

Elizabeth Banfalvi teaches workshops on meditation and stress. She is an author of a meditation book series and short stories and is published on Yahoo, Apple, Amazon and Balboa Press. Website: *www.elizabethbanfalvi.com*

Nicholas Boving is the author and publisher of the "Maxim Gunn" series of action - adventure books for readers of all ages. The second book in the series, "Maxim Gunn and the Demon Plan" was a finalist in the 1998 Crime Writers of Canada, Arthur Ellis Award.

Evelyn is currently studying English Literature at Wilfred Laurier University. This is her first publication and she is currently working on a collection of short horror stories.

Angela Ford is the best-selling author of three Romantic Suspense novels. She works in Finance with Peel District School Board, a member of the RWA and Mississauga Writers Group.
Website: *www.angelafordauthor.com*

Samna Ghani is a published author and works as a freelance Creative Writer. Her work has been featured on Yahoo, Capital Liberty News, Career Addict and several other online platforms.

John Henderson is a writer, motivational speaker, executive coach and Registered Couple & Sex Therapist. Life, poetry, short-stories, self-help articles, helping others and a sense of humor are his domain.

Veronica Lerner is a chemist and expert in gas analysis. She has published five books of prose and poetry; is part of five published anthologies; is an editor to "Observatorul"; and is a contributor on literary sites.

Joseph A. Monachino is married and his hobbies include writing, reading, and exercising. He graduated from Sheridan College certified in Sales & Marketing and presently works as a manufacturing plant assembler. Website:
www.transportingdevicestory.weebly.com

Maria Cecilia Nicu born in Bucharest-Romania, Canadian citizen (1980), Master in Literature & History, three published books, novel, short stories, poetry, Romanian Newspaper Observatorul columnist, collaborations (print/virtual) in Romania, France, Ireland, USA.

Rashmi Pluscec is the author of "Chaos" and a poet on anthologies "Threads", "Passages" and "Ballads". Rashmi's work has been featured on Dagda Publishing, Yahoo Contributor Network, CommuterLit and Amazon.
Website: *http://rashmipoetry.com/*

Jasmine Sawant is the Co-Founder, Artistic Co-Director, Actor, Writer and Manager for Sawitri Theater Group. Her most significant being The Kallus Next Door and a dance-theatre script titled One World Our World for SAMPRADAYA Dance Academy.
Website: *http://www.jasminesawant.com/*

Henry Shel is a Comic Fiction writer from Mississauga, with a passion for superheroes and romance. His novels ***OPERATION:Dreamgirl***, and ***Space, Love, Superheroes!*** are available through Heromantic
Publishing at ***www.lulu.com/henryshel***.

G. Ian Stout's first two novels can be found in public libraries, most quality bookstores and online seller's websites. His third, Murder Unedited, is due out in the fall of 2014.
Website: ***www.writerstout.com***

Copyright Acknowledgements

1. Making a Difference

Dealing with Stress....*Cheryl Antao-Xavier – Original work 2014 In 2013, I began a series of poems based on stress-busting tips*

Between Two Worlds....*Veronica Lerner – Original work 2013 translated by Sorin Finchelstein*

The Scruffy Boy.... *Elizabeth Banfalvi – Published Yahoo Voices December 2013*

Style and Essence....*Maria Cecilia Nicu – Published in France – 2010*

Laughing therapy....*Veronica Lerner – Original work 2012 translated by Sorin Finchelstein*

Sanctum Sanctorum....*Rashmi Pluscec – Copyright © 2014 Rashmi Pluscec*

My Wish Granted.... *Elizabeth Banfalvi – Published Yahoo Voices January 2014*

A Different Kind of Friendship ....*Veronica Lerner –Original work 2012 translated by Paul Tauberg*

2. The Challenge of Life

Drowning....*Maria Cecilia Nicu – Original work - 2012*

In Search of Normality....*Veronica Lerner – Original work 2013 translated by Sorin Finchelstein*

Haiku Inspired by Artwork....*Cheryl Antao-Xavier – Original work 2014 From a gradually expanding much-loved collection of my haiku, begun in 2008.*

Spotlight....*Rashmi Pluscec* – Copyright © 2014 Rashmi Pluscec

Fantaisie Impromptu....*Maria Cecilia Nicu* – Original work - 2005

The Table....*Elizabeth Banfalvi* – Published Yahoo Voices May 2013

Lessons from Nature....*Cheryl Antao-Xavier* – Original work 2014 From an in-progress collection 'Inspired by Nature'

Habit –Impetus or Burden? ....*Veronica Lerner* – Original work 2012 translated by Sorin Finchelstein

The Anatomy of Fear....*Maria Cecilia Nicu* – Original work - 2012

Second Chance....*Bev Bachmann* – Published in CommuterLit, March 18, 2014

Rebate.... *Maria Cecilia Nicu* – Original work - 2008

The Other One....*Elizabeth Banfalvi* – Published Yahoo Voices June 2013

3. In the Neighbourhood

Murder....*Rashmi Pluscec* – Copyright © 2014 Rashmi Pluscec

A Dark and Stormy Night.... *Nicholas Boving* – Copyright © Nicholas Boving

Church Lets Out.... *Bev Bachmann* – Excerpt from Christmas Touches 2014

My Neighbour....*Veronica Lerner* – Original work 2012

The Kallus Next Door.... *Jasmine Sawant* - Copyright © Jasmine Sawant, 2007

The Old Man....*Elizabeth Banfalvi – Original work 1958*

Salma....*Chitra Ayyar – Copyright* © *Chitra Ayyar 2007/8 excerpt Moments in Time*

4. Matters of the Heart

Rewind.... *Rashmi Pluscec – Copyright* © *2014 Rashmi Pluscec*

Putting Loving Sex Back Into Your Relationship!....*John Henderson – Copyright* ©*2010 John Henderson, Published on OAMFT web site*

Felt by the Heart....*Angela Ford – Copyright* © *Angela Ford 2014*

Turn Back The Clock....*Samna Ghani – Copyright* © *Samna Ghani 2014*

5. Loss and Hope

Mother's End....*John Henderson – Copyright* ©*2014 John Henderson*

When he is Gone.... *Elizabeth Banfalvi – Original work 1967*

Elegy for the Creative Soul....*Cheryl Antao-Xavier – Original work 2014 Seeing too many people mired in mundane employment, with no time and energy to free their 'creative soul.'*

Aniruddh Remembered.... *Jasmine Sawant – Original work January 13, 2014*

Do not scold me ....*Veronica Lerner – Original work 2010 translated by Sorin Finchelstein*

The Phone Call....*Elizabeth Banfalvi – Published Yahoo Voices June 2013*

Let Him Go.... *Jasmine Sawant – Original work February 3, 2014*

Ruins.... *Rashmi Pluscec – Copyright © 2014 Rashmi Pluscec*

6. Creating Success

Today.... *John Henderson – Copyright ©2014 John Henderson*

The Role Model.... *Bev Bachmann – Original work 2014*

A Woman's Way.... *Elizabeth Banfalvi – Published Yahoo Voices August 2013*

Golden Age Sonnet....*Veronica Lerner – Original work 2010 translated by Radu Stefanescu*

Where is YOUR ATTITUDE AT? .... *John Henderson – Copyright © March 2011John Henderson*

Failure leads to Success.... *Elizabeth Banfalvi – Published Yahoo Voices October 2013*

7. Discerning Thoughts and Beliefs

Epitaph....*Rashmi Pluscec – Published "Dagda Publishing" Copyright © 2013 Rashmi Pluscec*

CBC gossip....*Veronica Lerner – Original work 2013 translated by Sorin Finchelstein*

Cowboy.... *Maria Cecilia Nicu – Original work - 2013*

What is it but just a Game ....*Joseph A. Monachino – Copyright © 2014 Joseph A. Monachino*

With – or Without – Entitlements ....*Veronica Lerner – Original work 2013 translated by Sorin Finchelstein*

A Photograph.... *Elizabeth Banfalvi – Published Yahoo Voices October 2013*

Aha....*Maria Cecilia Nicu*

8. Family, Friends, Lovers

Historia....*Maria Cecilia Nicu – Original work - 2010*

The Fruity Pen....*Elizabeth Banfalvi – Published Yahoo Voices May 2013*

Soul Mates....*Rashmi Pluscec – Copyright © 2014 Rashmi Pluscec*

Willie's Last Ride.... *Nicholas Boving – Copyright © Nicholas Boving*

My Grandparents....*Elizabeth Banfalvi – Published Yahoo Voices June 2013*

9. Reaching for the Stars

There's So Much Winter ....*Veronica Lerner – Original work 2013 translated by Sorin Finchelstein*

Operation: *Dreamgirl ....Sheldon Henry – Excerpt from the novel OPERATION: DREAMGIRL – The Reluctant Diary Of A Lovesick Average Joe!*)

The Transporting Device....*Joseph A. Monachino – Copyright © 2013 Joseph A. Monachino*

10. Thrills and Chills

Curtain.... *Rashmi Pluscec – Published "Dagda Publishing" Copyright © 2013 Rashmi Pluscec*

Murder Unedited.... *G. Ian Stout – Copyright © G. Ian Stout*

Crickets.... *Evelyn – Copyright © Evelyn 2012*

Still....*Angela Ford – Copyright © Angela Ford 2014*

For the Love of God.... *Nicholas Boving – Copyright © Nicholas Boving*